# SUKUMA LAW
# AND CUSTOM

# SUKUMA LAW
# AND CUSTOM

BY

## HANS CORY
GOVERNMENT SOCIOLOGIST
TANGANYIKA

WITH A FOREWORD

BY

## J. P. MOFFETT
LOCAL COURTS ADVISER TO THE
GOVERNMENT OF TANGANYIKA

**NEGRO UNIVERSITIES PRESS**
WESTPORT, CONNECTICUT

Originally published in 1953
by Oxford University Press, London,
for the International African Institute

Reprinted in 1970 by
Negro Universities Press
A Division of Greenwood Press, Inc.
Westport, Connecticut

Library of Congress Catalogue Card Number 70-106831

SBN 8371-3453-6

Printed in the United States of America

*To*

## R. de Z. HALL

MEMBER FOR LOCAL GOVERNMENT
TANGANYIKA

*who initiated this book*

# FOREWORD

THE author has suggested that in this foreword I should say something about the local court system in Tanganyika: how the courts are constituted, how they have developed out of the indigenous pre-European judicial institutions, the law they administer and, generally, show the practical application of the results of his researches, so as to enable those unacquainted with local conditions to obtain a fuller picture of the actual operation of the customary law in the courts.

As regards their past, it is common knowledge that the courts are no new thing introduced by the European, like the use of the plough or the bicycle, but are an outcome of those local arrangements which everywhere obtained for the settlement of disputes. Mr. Cory has shown, in the part of his introductory chapter which describes the judicial organizations of the Sukuma, that an essential function of both chief and village headman was to administer justice and has given an account of how their 'courts' operated. This account is indeed typical of the pre-European 'courts' in many of the Bantu tribes in Tanganyika and illustrates the more striking aspects of customary law in operation—the use of compensation rather than punishment to right wrongs, the importance of the elders in assisting the court-holder to give judgement, the informality of the procedure. To this may be added that great pains were taken to get both the parties to accept the decision taken and that the 'court' relied almost entirely on the force of public opinion to ensure that its judgements were carried out.

There is no doubt that these 'courts' administered substantial justice by local standards, that they were popular, and that the people had confidence and trust in them. It was for these reasons that the decision was taken to give formal recognition to them and to establish them as 'Native Courts'. The first courts were set up in the year 1919 and their operation was later controlled by the Courts Ordinance, 1920, and by the Native Courts Proclamation, 1925.

Now the establishment of native courts, wherein African court-holders dispensed local customary law, was an innovation in Tanganyika. The Germans had not set up such courts. Nor is this surprising when the history of the recognition of customary law in the colonies generally is considered. During the centuries in which colonies were being established by various powers all over the world it was taken for granted that the colonizing power took its own law with it wherever it went and that only in exceptional circumstances would recognition be given to any local law. Such circumstances would be, for example, where it was already in a highly developed form and had been reduced to writing. But even when formal recognition had been given to it this law

was administered in the courts of the colonial power, by its officials, and
not in indigenous courts. Thus in most of the early British colonies the
Common Law was administered in British courts by British magistrates.
In some, at a later date, local law was administered in British courts, but
again by British magistrates. Only of comparatively recent years has
local law been administered in local courts by local functionaries.

When this third and last step was taken in Tanganyika and full effect
given to it by the enactment of the Native Courts Ordinance of 1929
(when Sir Donald Cameron was Governor), a decision of the greatest
importance to the future of the courts was also taken—it was decided
that they should be completely separated from, and free from the control of, the High Court. In this respect the system of native courts in
Tanganyika was unique. In all other dependencies there was some link,
however tenuous, with the High Court. But it was thought that at the
stage of development then reached by most of the courts their growth
and further development would best be supervised by the District Commissioners, under the over-all control of the Provincial Commissioners.
The Provincial Commissioner was thus empowered, subject to the approval of the Governor, to establish within his province such native
courts as he thought fit. The courts had jurisdiction over all Africans
within their area and they were authorized to administer the local native
law and custom. They were also empowered to hear cases for breaches
of orders and rules made under the Native Authority Ordinance, i.e.
orders concerning such matters as the sale of intoxicating liquors, gam-
bling, forestry, veterinary and agricultural practices, the reporting of
locusts, and many other matters of importance in the daily life of the
people. In addition, some were given a very limited jurisdiction under
certain of the territorial Ordinances, e.g. the Arms and Ammunition
Ordinance. The overriding consideration was that the courts should be
established as nearly as possible on local 'constitutional' lines, that is,
that they should be merely a formalized version of the indigenous judicial
institutions, following their own procedures and administering their own
customary laws unhampered by alien ideas. The only restriction was
that their laws and procedure should not be repugnant to justice or
morality nor inconsistent with the provisions of any law in force in the
territory.

Their powers were at first limited to two classes, 'A' and 'B'. Class 'A'
courts could hear civil cases where the value of the subject-matter did
not exceed Shs.600/- and in criminal cases could impose a sentence up
to six months' imprisonment with hard labour, a fine not exceeding
Shs.200/-, or corporal punishment of eight strokes. In class 'B' courts
the limits were Shs.200/- in civil cases; in criminal cases, one months'
I.H.L., fine of Shs.50/- and six strokes. Later, 'I' class courts were
established with powers intermediate between 'A' and 'B'. The fees
charged in civil cases were uniform throughout the territory and were

5 per cent. of the value, with a minimum fee of Sh.1/-, and Shs.2/-
where the value could not be assessed.

The District Commissioner was entrusted with the close supervision
of the courts and was responsible to the Provincial Commissioner for
their efficient functioning. He was given powers to revise any case in
such way as he thought fit, so as to ensure that justice was done, and
appeals lay to him.

There are now about 600 local courts (formerly known as native
courts) in Tanganyika, and they hear about 100,000 cases a year, the
numbers of civil and of criminal cases being about equal. The bulk of
the civil work of the courts (and a considerable amount of the criminal
work also) is concerned with cases arising out of customary law, especially cases touching marriage and divorce. The local law is, of course,
well known and equitably applied, but without an authoritative statement of it there can be no certainty that mistakes of interpretation or of
application will not be made from time to time—indeed, it is almost
inevitable that a court consisting, as it usually does at present, of a chief,
two or three elders, and a clerk, should err from time to time in the
settlement of a difficult case to which no written law applies. This is one
reason why the recording of customary law is so essential—to enable the
courts to refer to a generally approved or an 'authorized version' of the
law, sanctioned by chiefs and people. Without a written record there can
be no certainty in the law, nor is it wise to bring about changes in the
law (the necessity for which arises with increasing frequency) without
that sure knowledge of it, and of its underlying principles, which only
written records can give.

But if one looks for such written records in Africa the available
material is meagre indeed. And Tanganyika is no exception in this
respect. Apart from chapters in such works as the Culwicks' *Ubena of
the Rivers* (the Bena tribe), Brown and Hutt's *Anthropology in Action*
(the Hehe tribe), and papers on the Nyakyusa by the Wilsons and
R. de Z. Hall, we are indebted almost entirely to Hans Cory for our
knowledge of tribal law and custom in Tanganyika. His *Customary Law
of the Haya Tribe*, written in collaboration with Mrs. Hartnoll and published by the International African Institute in 1945, was a striking
example of the results to be obtained from a combination of the methods
of anthropological investigation and the analysis of cases tried in the
native courts. But it was stated, in an otherwise appreciative assessment
of the value of the methods used,[1] that it was open to one grave objection.

The record produced in this way is inevitably a picture of customary law at
one particular point in its evolution. It will be difficult to judge whether the law
at any one time in its growth has reached a stage when record would be desirable.
Indeed, to reduce a customary law to writing at any one time without taking into

[1] 'Methods of Recording Native Customary Law.' A note by the African Studies
Branch of the Colonial Office in the *Journal of African Administration*, vol. i, no. 3,
July 1949.

consideration the trends of development over a long period may be dangerous. To meet this difficulty it may be necessary for native law to go through a process of clarification or formulation before recording is attempted. Time is needed for public opinion and the courts to adjust their attitude, on confused points, to the needs of modern conditions.

It will be apparent from Mr. Cory's description of the way the present book has been compiled,[1] and from the frequent recurrence of the statement 'this rule was agreed by the Chiefs and their people in 1949', that the same criticism can hardly be levelled at it, and that the 'process of clarification' has resulted in a remarkable degree of agreement. The people and their leaders have been consulted throughout, and their consent to the adoption of those many 'rules' which are in the nature of a compromise is a really striking tribute to the success of the methods used—and to the insight, understanding, and patience of the investigator. Only those who have themselves tried to formulate statements of the law similar to those set out in this book will appreciate the difficulty of the task. The elders in any primitive community, who are usually those best acquainted with the local law, do not, of course, think of it as a series of rules, nor can they so expound it. They are as oblivious of the principles underlying their system of law as they are of the rules of syntax which govern the language they speak so grammatically. Presented with a set of facts, a claim or an accusation, they can say what the judgement should be if the facts are proved, but they will be hard put to it to explain to the satisfaction of an alien inquirer the reasons for their judgement. It is for him to extract the principle from the mass of cases which exemplify its operation. This is no mean task, and it is not made any easier by the fact that those who have been born and bred in a completely non-scientific, non-critical atmosphere take so much for granted and assume so readily that what is obvious or elementary to them must be equally so to others; so that it is only by testing a supposed 'rule' in all its possible settings, in every permutation and combination, that the investigator can be sure that he has set it down correctly. The rules in this book have been subjected to such testing in two ways: firstly, by comparison with decided cases heard in the courts, and secondly, by being translated into the vernacular and referred to the people for their comments. The rules have triumphantly survived both tests and it is a striking tribute to the care taken in the preparation of the text that not one rule has had to have other than minor verbal alterations made to it.

The author mentions that the method he employed—consultation in the first place with a carefully selected group of some twenty-eight elders, from all parts of Sukumaland—recommended itself because of the degree of authority which would attach to the work of such a distinguished body. But he omits to mention the consummate skill and tact which

[1] See pp. xiii, xiv, xv.

must have been required to keep such a number of comparative strangers together over a long period and to obtain their ready co-operation and support. The method in less skilful and sympathetic hands might well have produced a statement of the law unacceptable to chiefs and people, and the very greatest patience and understanding must have been needed to obtain the degree of compromise and uniformity in local variations which was eventually achieved.

The Swahili version of the 'rules', without the explanatory notes, is being published separately as a handbook for use in the courts. Any alterations to them which may be required in the future will be discussed by the Sukuma Council and no changes will be made without its full approval. The means therefore exist both to bring about amendments to the law as these become necessary and to ensure that such amendments have the same validity and authority as the rules they replace.

As it is here set down, the law and custom of the Sukuma is a vindication of the faith of those who for many years have been urging the need for the recording of customary law. One of the principles of the Rule of Law, fundamental to the British way of life and an indispensable part of any system of British administration, is that the law should be certain. It is more likely to be certain in the form herein recorded than if left to be enunciated *ad hoc* by different courts of widely varying ability and knowledge.

Nor does it follow that this recording will have the effect—so often gloomily foreseen by those who oppose any recording of customary law—of codifying or ossifying the law. One cannot read this book without the conviction that the attitude towards compromise, and the readiness of both chiefs and people to adopt a variation in a rule because it has proved to be the best in local conditions, will ensure the gradual development of the law along the right lines. The law as it is today has been recorded, but not crystallized; in the method of its recording there has been clearly revealed the way of development and advance.

Finally, it is perhaps not too much to say that this record is a signal contribution to the enunciation of a definitive statement of those principles of Bantu customary law which are believed to underly the numerous tribal variations which research is bringing to light. Some day it may be possible to set out these broad principles, and to appreciate the operation of the local variations in the light of our deeper knowledge, but it is only by the intensive and comparative study of such records as this that any degree of certainty in the result can be attained.

J. P. MOFFETT

# PREFACE

*Terms of Reference*

MY terms of reference, the results of which are presented in this book, were:

1. That the Customary Law of the Sukuma tribe should be recorded.

2. That the differences in Law which have grown up in the various local federations and lower courts should be discussed and, if possible, eliminated and a unification of the Customary Law effected.

## Methods employed

It was clear from the beginning that a special method would be necessary because of the extent of the work and the number of variations which had to be dealt with.

These variations had developed within the tribe primarily because of its size. In times when communications between the populated areas were poor, when permanent inter-tribal warfare existed, when wild animals endangered the life of the traveller, and superstitious fear was dominant, exchanges of cultural achievements were not common. Therefore, partly owing to the influence of neighbours in the boundary chiefdoms and partly through the action of autocratic rulers, laws underwent local changes. Many recent examples can be found where a chief has decided upon a beneficial change of anachronistic laws for his own area; such changes have seldom been accepted by others, even if their advantages were clear, because jealousy has been greater than insight.

The methods which I have employed in former recordings of Customary Law have here been developed to a degree not needed on previous occasions. I have found that the truth is more readily arrived at if a question is put to an assembly of experienced men who are free to discuss and argue until they all agree on the answer. This method seemed to be preferable to sitting *in camera* with two or three men, questioning them, and later repeating the same procedure with others for confirmation. With a small number of men, one member may dominate the rest and, even if he has great knowledge, one man alone is not infallible. At the same time a man of this type makes the others lazy thinkers and arguers. The research worker himself may also get tired of repeating the same questions over and over again and of recording similar answers. I am aware that the task of directing, keeping interested, or even just keeping together, a big assembly of informants needs more experience than does the usual method. But as soon as the necessary technique is acquired and the consent of administrative officers secured, the progress of the research is quicker and the validity of the results is incomparably greater. This method recommended itself also for another and even more important reason. Practical results in a work such as this depend on its popularity and on the conviction of the whole tribe that the recording of the law and the changes made in the rules have been agreed by a considerable number of men who can be trusted to do the right thing.

The actual work began in April 1948, but it was preceded by intensive preliminary studies extending, with many interruptions, over a period of about ten years. Mwanza, the seat of the Provincial Administration, was chosen as headquarters for the research work. The first step was to call together a meeting of well-informed men representing the chiefdoms of the Sukuma Federation. Fifty elders arrived and, as might be expected, they were not all of equal knowledge and intelligence. After a few days of test conversations it became clear which of them were capable of the task and which were not. The failures were returned, sometimes with a request for a replacement. It was not difficult to pick out those chiefdoms in which the laws were identical in every detail and thus to reduce the number of members of the assembly to twenty-eight. After some initial hesitation on the part of all concerned, a growing enthusiasm captured the assembly, an enthusiasm kept alive by their own recognition of the value of this work for the whole tribe. I would like to take this opportunity of thanking the hundreds of Africans—chiefs, headmen, and clerks, and especially the permanent and temporary members of my assembly—for their co-operation, their patience, and their willingness to endure many discomforts due to their prolonged absence from home. There were no clocks in the various places where we had our daily meetings and the debates of the delegates, often heated by reason of their real desire to find out the truth and perhaps, in some cases, because of an inherent obstinacy which refused to see the good points in other people's versions of the law, were only brought to an end by the cooling evening breeze. These first meetings lasted for six weeks, during which were recorded the rules given in the chapters on Bridewealth, Marriage, Inheritance, and Children.

After an interval of one month, during which the notes were transcribed and typed and the variations separately recorded, a meeting of eight suitable chiefs, delegated by the full council of the Federation, took place in Mwanza. The meeting lasted a fortnight and the chiefs were assisted by court clerks and a group of court assessors, to whom I added for my own assistance a few of the most experienced participants in the previous meeting. This assembly discussed the possibility of unifying the recorded divergencies. It achieved, again only after very intensive and learned discussions, a unanimous acceptance of compromises in all outstanding questions. These compromises were then laid before the full council of chiefs and their *bagunani* (councillors) in Malya for their final approval.

This procedure was repeated three times during 1948 and the beginning of 1949 for the recording and unification of the rules on Divorce, Guardianship, Land Tenure, Cattle, and Sale. In order to be absolutely sure that the record was correct a Swahili translation was prepared, copies of which were sent to all local federations with the request that they be circulated in the chiefdoms for criticism, amendments, and corrections. I visited each of the local federations in turn, after they had had their Swahili copies for a time, to make sure that the contents were understood and found correct. These visits took a considerable time, as the chiefs and their people, who were all very interested in the issues, took great pains in all cases to clear up discrepancies. Sometimes, naturally enough, a lack of sense of proportion was shown and minor differences in customary procedure were taken more seriously than important differences in points of law.

The expenses of the meetings, including travelling expenses and board and lodging for the participants in the meetings in Mwanza, were defrayed by the Native Treasury of the Sukuma Federation. The practical purpose of the work was explained to the chiefs and their people at the beginning. They were informed that the result of their labour, namely a common customary law for all Sukuma, would be available for every court in Swahili. For this reason the payment of expenses for the African collaborators by the Native Treasury was considered to be justified.

### Unification of the Sukuma Customary Law[1]

The idea of the unification of Sukuma Customary Law is not a new one. As early as 1932 the chief of Ng'wagala, during a meeting of all the Sukuma chiefs in Mwanza, mentioned in his speech from the chair the necessity for a unification of the native law. The same point was placed on the agenda of the Kwimba Local Federation. At a second general meeting of chiefs held in 1933 the secretary of the assembly wrote in the minutes: 'The stress of the whole meeting was on the consolidation of the tribal law and custom of the Basukuma.' These general meetings were not continued and no further mention of this matter can be found.

---

[1] The chiefdoms west of Smith Sound comprising the administrative district of Geita have been included in the Federal Council of Sukumaland (Appendix I). This Mweli Federation (mweli in Sukuma means west) is inhabited by the Zinza, who are ethnically nearer to the Haya than to the Sukuma, and by the Sumbwa who are nearer to the Nyamwezi than to the Sukuma and the majority of whom live in chiefdoms which belong to the Western Province (provincial headquarters Tabora). As there is little basic difference between Sumbwa and Nyamwezi and Nyamwezi and Sukuma, there is also no fundamental difference between Sumbwa and Sukuma. The case of the Zinza is different. They do not belong to the Sukuma–Nyamwezi language group; they were included in the Sukuma Federation because in all the chiefdoms of the Mweli local federation the Sukuma element, immigrating in a steady flow, is already a majority. All these chiefdoms were, before the recent immigration of the Sukuma, very underpopulated—some of them still are—and they are being opened up as a rehabilitation area to be developed by the immigrants. The Zinza, Sumbwa, and Longo, the original inhabitants of these chiefdoms, follow rules of customary law so different from those of the Sukuma that a unification of the two codes must be considered impossible.

With regard to the present work of unification, one general guiding rule was accepted as being of fundamental importance and was observed, with very few exceptions, throughout: to find a compromise, where differences in law existed, by adopting the rule which appeared to be the best one, wherever that might be in use. It was not considered equitable to decide any question by counting the areas which followed certain rules and accepting the rules of the majority. Existing variations of a rule were judged on their merits and the acceptance of a certain version was agreed upon by all, irrespective of the number of areas which had previously followed this version. A good example of this procedure is the acceptance of rules 529 and 530 in regard to the sale of improved houses. These rules have been followed in the Usega chiefdoms for a long time, especially in the chiefdom of Masanza II (about 800 taxpayers). When the chief of this small chiefdom explained how his court handled this question all the other representatives at once showed great interest and finally adopted the Masanza procedure.

The strict observance of the above rule prevented the introduction of innovations, in accordance with Professor Malinowski's advice: 'If anything has been proved by recent anthropological research and colonial practice it is the truth that you cannot with impunity undo or subvert an old system of traditions, of morals or laws and replace it by a ready-made new morality and sense of right.'[1]

Wherever rules which formerly differed have been unified the original forms of the rules in the different areas are given. This is considered advisable for the following reason. It is to be expected that some of the courts and assessors may, in ignorance or by design, apply the original rules in a judgement. They might, if interrogated (for instance, in case of the routine inspection of court books), argue that they had applied the rules of their country and could prove their statements by producing similar judgements in previous law suits. The possibility of being able to see at a glance what the old rule was and how it has been altered should make the answer easy.

## The purpose of the book

This book is intended to be used in Native Courts and in European Appeal Courts in civil cases; and its purpose has determined its character and arrangement. The material is presented in short paragraphs which are connected logically with each other, but each of which can stand by itself if it should be necessary to quote it in a judgement. It was considered important to preserve the logical connexion of paragraphs even if this sometimes entailed repetition. Such repetitions are indicated by cross references.

The index is extensive and for the above reason duplications in it have not been avoided. The glossary gives the numbers of the para-

[1] 'Practical Anthropology', *Africa*, vol. ii, no. 1, 1929, p. 28.

graphs in which each vernacular word occurs, so that a magistrate who
hears it mentioned in court may readily find the relevant paragraph.
The frequently quoted vernacular words and phrases are intended to
facilitate mutual understanding between judge and parties.

The purpose of the notes included after many of the rules and of the
introductions to the chapters is to assist magistrates by giving them some
idea of the background and of the social institutions relevant to points
of law. As might be expected, it·was not always easy to decide whether
certain customs should be included in the text of the law or appended
as notes. This difficulty was experienced in particular in the compilation
of the chapter on Marriage. The method has been adopted of including
in the text customs which in certain circumstances might be of direct
importance in the hearing of a court case. Many of the notes simply give
the literal commentary on laws supplied by the men who worked with
me. Thus the notes are in fact the result of field work. Sociological
theories appear rarely, and only when the opportunity occurs for quot-
ing paragraphs of the law text in substantiation of theoretical statements.

I am indebted to Mr. Julius Lewin, Senior Lecturer in Native Law
and Administration at the University of the Witwatersrand, Johannes-
burg, for his advice, chiefly in regard to the arrangement of chapters;
to Mr. R. de Z. Hall, Member for Local Government, Tanganyika, for
his great interest and help during the recording of the law and the compilation of the book; to Mr. J. P. Moffett, Local Courts Adviser to the
Government of Tanganyika, who has read through the whole of the
manuscript and helped me greatly with criticism and suggestions—he
also undertook, despite much other work, to write the foreword to the
book; to Dr. W. J. Maynard of Nkolondoto for his help in correcting
the glossary. I would also express my gratitude to the Tanganyika
Government for a generous grant towards the costs of publication, to
the International African Institute for undertaking the actual work of
publication as well as contributing to the expenses, and to the Institute's
secretary for her labours in preparing the manuscript for press and
reading the proofs. Finally, I wish to record my special thanks to Mrs.
E. B. Dobson for much painstaking work in the correction and preparation of the manuscript.

# CONTENTS

PART I

# INTRODUCTORY: LAND AND PEOPLE

*Land*

SUKUMALAND proper is situated to the south of Lake Victoria and comprises the four administrative districts of Mwanza, Kwimba, Maswa, and Shinyanga. To this must be added the country to the west of Smith Sound which comprises the administrative district of Geita. The whole area is a part of the cultivation steppe, the largest homogeneous inhabited area in Tanganyika Territory.

Sukumaland covers an area of about 19,000 square miles and is to a great extent uniform in its topography, altitude, geological structure, and rainfall. The general altitude is 3,800 to 4,000 feet above sea-level; the average rainfall over the whole area is about 30 inches a year, the heaviest rainfall occurring in the vicinity of Lake Victoria. Normally water is available in sufficient quantities for household and stock consumption without undue toil, but for stock the situation may become precarious in years of drought. This danger is being increasingly met by the construction of artificial reservoirs. There are very few permanent watercourses.

The country consists of wide, undulating plains, interrupted here and there by low ridges and mountain ranges of no great height. Characteristic of many parts of the country are the granite outcrops, which introduce some variation into the otherwise flat cultivation steppe. 'The term cultivation steppe comprises that form of dense land occupation by natives practising a combination of both agricultural and pastoral exploitation of the soil which leads to an almost complete eradication of the original vegetation cover, replacing the latter by a checkered pattern of cultivated fields and low-grass steppe.'[1]

*Origin and history*

Sukuma proper is inhabited by roughly 1,000,000 people. They belong to the Central Eastern Bantu and comprise, with the Nyamwezi and related tribes, a group very closely related in language and customs. It is, moreover, so strong numerically that it has successfully maintained its culture against the influences of different tribes living on its perimeter, such as the Taturu (Hamitic) in the north-east, and the Masai (Nilo-Hamitic) in the south-east. On the southern border, between Sukuma and Nyamwezi, the Nyamwezi influence is marked, but the two groups

---

[1] C. Gillman, *Water Consultant's Report No. 6*, 1940.

are so closely connected that this cannot be described as alien influence. Part of the present Shinyanga district was originally included in the Nyamwezi (Tabora) administrative area, but no difficulty of any kind arose when the chiefdoms concerned were incorporated in the Sukuma district of Shinyanga.

Strictly speaking there is no tribal name for the Sukuma people. The word 'Sukuma' means 'north' in the Nyamwezi and Sukuma languages and originated probably when the pioneer travellers passing through Nyamwezi were informed about the country to the north—Sukuma; the name then came to be applied to the whole area and its inhabitants. They themselves adopted the clan names of their ruling dynasties as their specific tribal names, so that a man from Ng'wagala (BD),[1] if asked the name of his tribe, would probably answer 'Binza' if he thought that the questioner knew the country, otherwise he would call himself a Sukuma in acknowledgement of the increasingly frequent use of this name.

There is no tradition extant about the original inhabitants of the area. According to the Sukuma themselves, before the arrival of the Hamitic families the country was overgrown with bush, dense in some places and sparse in others. An old explorer wrote that the Sukuma drive their cattle into the *forest* during the dry season. The country was everywhere sparsely populated. The scattered human colonies consisted of a hundred odd people under the leadership of a *ntemi*, a name which only later became the title of a chief. *Kutema* means to cut down trees in the bush, indicating that the *batemi* of this time were pioneers who opened up the country and retained the leadership of their followers, who were mostly members of their own families. The various settlements had little communication with each other and no conception of tribal unity. The *batemi* never thought of extending the areas under their influence except for the purpose of enlarging the hunting grounds. The people were not only hunters, however; even at that time they tilled their fields and drove their cattle to pasture. But hunting was an important activity, necessary to protect the fields in the bush against marauding game, to provide additional meat for the pot, and later to obtain ivory for trading.

When the Hamitic people from the north began a southward movement, several families penetrated to Sukuma via the west and south coast of Lake Victoria (Bukoba and Zinza). C. G. Seligman writes, in *Races of Africa*, about the lacustrine tribes round the shores of Lake Victoria and Lake Albert, among whom the Sukuma are included: 'It seems that all these tribes have a Hamitic (presumably Galla) element brought in by the Bahima. . . .' These Hamitic families established authority over sections of the indigenous population. It is remarkable that the customs and language of these peaceful conquerors have been wholly absorbed into those of their Bantu subjects, and only tradition

[1] For abbreviations denoting groups of chiefdoms see Appendix I, pp. 170-1.

remains to tell of the invasion and the establishment of ruling dynasties in this wide area. The most important among the immigrating families were the Binza, Kwimba, Siha, Golo, and Sega. There are many conflicting accounts of their early history, their adventurous travels and their conquest of Sukumaland. Almost every Sukuma chiefdom has its own tradition which tends to exaggerate the importance of the first arrivals and to compete with chiefdoms ruled by other branches of the same family. Generally, it can be stated that the leading members of these families were not military conquerors and they were obviously accepted as leaders by common consent, since no major fights between them and the people they found living in the country are recounted. It seems that at the time of their arrival the country was becoming sufficiently densely populated to make a common leadership for groups of isolated settlements desirable. These immigrants met this latent demand in many ways. They were ideal judges, for they belonged to none of the local clans; they were the best arbitrators in the distribution of the spoils of the chase and of clan warfare. They may also have impressed the indigenous population with their superior mental and physical qualities.

The history of the Sukuma and their alien rulers has on the whole been peaceful; internecine wars occurred here and there, but they were brief and not very bloody. Mirambo,[1] a Nyamwezi chief, who died in 1884, was at one period determined on the conquest of Sukumaland, but never succeeded in getting farther than the borders of Urima (NF). His wars with the Sukuma left no mark on their social organization because his raids were of short duration, though their losses in men, cattle, and grain were considerable. In Sukuma proper there was little menace from alien invaders, so that there evolved a type of scattered settlement with farmland surrounding each homestead. In the south, where Masai raids occurred, the people lived in close settlements, on the Nyamwezi pattern, for defence purposes. The Sukuma were also spared the depredations of slave traders which occurred in other parts of the territory, although the Arabs penetrated the country for trading purposes long before the first European arrived.

Speke discovered Lake Victoria in 1858 during the Burton and Speke expedition. Many other famous explorers passed through Sukumaland. When the Germans finally took possession of Tanganyika (1886) the Sukuma did not make any attempt to rebel against them, as did other tribes, but settled down peacefully under their rule. Catholic and Protestant Missions were established early in this part of the country, but the Sukuma have not embraced Christianity to any great extent.

## Agriculture

The Sukuma are an agricultural people but, like many other Eastern Bantu living in areas free from tsetse fly, enthusiastic cattle breeders as

---

[1] See 'Mirambo', by R. J. Harvey, in *Tanganyika Notes and Records*, July 1950.

well. Their methods of agriculture are extensive rather than intensive, population pressure being met by emigration to sparsely populated areas. The peasant has always had a good name as a cultivator of the soil.

The native cultivator and his family are mainly dependent on the work of their hoes for food and money. At certain seasons of the year they will work very hard indeed in order to obtain little more than a subsistence, when with careful planning and forethought they could obtain much greater returns. There is, however, such a wealth of sound knowledge and power of good judgment of agricultural matters held by the average native of the cultivation steppe, that if he was once given the lead, and his extreme conservatism broken down, the possibilities of his development would be very considerable.[1]

In recent years efforts have been made to educate the Sukuma in improved agricultural methods, a process which is likely to receive a powerful impetus from the activities of an enterprise operating in the area led by the Sukumaland Development Organization in Malya. Soil erosion has, however, become a real menace to the fertility of the cultivation steppe. 'The human and cattle population is concentrated where water supplies are good and tsetse. flies absent, and this leads to exploitation of soil fertility, overgrazing and destruction of vegetative cover in these areas.'

The principal grain crops are sorghum and pennisetum. The latter is predominant in the north, and in all parts of the country it is the more important crop of the two. Sorghum is the crop grown for beer-making throughout the area. Maize is grown on a much smaller scale. Groundnuts and cotton are the two main economic crops; the former is decreasing rapidly in favour of the latter, but groundnuts are also consumed locally in some quantity. The cultivation of rice in north Sukuma is on the increase; it is looked upon as a commercial crop and is seldom used by the cultivators as a staple food. The subsidiary food crops are cassava, sweet potatoes, legumes such as bambarra, groundnuts, and various kinds of beans and peas. The Sukuma has not changed his diet under the impact of outside influences, except that he now perhaps eats rather more meat and drinks rather less. beer. This phenomenon is not the outcome of successful education, but is the result of the change over to money economy which gives him cash in his pocket for the buying of meat.

## Cattle

About 50 per cent. of the Sukuma are cattle-owners, and the number of cattle in the possession of individuals does not vary very greatly. This means that there are few owners of large herds. The number of cattle per homestead in the south is 22 and in central Sukuma 20; in the north it is 8 per homestead. Thus the average size of a herd, since only half

[1] N. V. Rounce, *The Agriculture of the Cultivation Steppe of the Lake, Western and Central Provinces*, from which the following information about crops planted in Sukumaland is also taken.

the population owns cattle at all, is 40 in the south and 16 in the north. (All these figures are, of course, approximate.)

The cattle are all of the shorthorn zebu type. The production of ghee and of cattle for beef industries in other parts of Tanganyika are on the increase at the present time. Goats and sheep are very numerous throughout the country and are popular for feasting purposes on all important ceremonial occasions. The Sukuma, like so many other Bantu, does not breed stock for quality, being primarily concerned to increase the number of beasts in his possession without regard to the economic management of his herd. It is very difficult to teach him even the most fundamental principles of animal husbandry.

## Special tribal characteristics

The Sukuma have certain widely known traits and characteristic institutions, which have probably developed because of the large area they occupy, their numerical strength, and the density of the population. Together with the closely related Nyamwezi they form a large proportion of any contingent of labourers to be found in the Territory. They have always been, and still are, very good workers.

They were employed on the trade routes as porters before the arrival of the Europeans, and afterwards on railway construction. On all these occasions they made contact with very many other tribes. When European agricultural enterprises were started they became the most valued labour force in the camps. Today groups of them are frequently found near the big estates, living on their own land and still working for the Europeans. Sometimes they have become . . . detribalized and supply the local markets with the produce of their fields. Everywhere some member or another of the Sukuma–Nyamwezi tribal group has preserved the manifold knowledge of his fathers and practises a little medicine here and a little magic there, or is popular as a diviner.[1]

For an indefinitely long period secret societies have thrived in the home areas. These societies are organized to the extent that any person who wishes to become a member must undergo an initiation, a hierarchy of members is acknowledged, certain rules of discipline are followed and the societies have specific purposes. Their activities are treated by the members with great secrecy. With a few exceptions, the activities of these societies are not overtly malignant; they take the place of the initiation schools found among other peoples, in which the young receive formal instruction in behaviour towards elders, social unity, and, to a certain extent, a moral code.

Especially popular are the societies of snake charmers[2] and porcupine hunters, but there are other societies devoted to more serious pursuits, the members of which are initiated into the rites of ancestor worship, and there are those whose membership consists exclusively of parents of twins. All these societies form strong and disciplined fraternities and

[1] H. Cory, 'The Ingredients of Magic Medicine', *Africa*, vol. xix, no. 1, 1949.
[2] See H. Cory, 'The Buyeye', *Africa*, vol. xvi, no. 3, 1946.

members are bound to help one another in field cultivation and in meeting such obligations as custom and law may impose on the individual.
Their local leaders are usually outstanding men, popular practitioners
and famous diviners who are frequently consulted by chiefs and village
headmen in the interests of the community. As well as following their
more serious pursuits, all these societies arrange frequent dance meetings in public; some of them also perform certain parts of the initiation
rites in public—mainly as propaganda for enrolling new members from
among the spectators.

Song and dance play a large part in the life of the Sukuma. All over
Sukumaland in the evenings when the moon is shining the young people
meet for dances. They are divided into two great groups of dance societies (*bagumba* and *bagika*) to one of which all the other smaller dance
societies belong, and competitive dances between the various societies
are extremely popular. On a day chosen for a competition two singers
and their respective followers meet; they form two groups which take
their stand at some distance from each other. Each group sings a song
prepared by the leader especially for the occasion. Sometimes both
groups sing and dance at the same time. The victor is the leader who is
able to draw the majority of the spectators over to his side. Many means
besides songs are used to arouse the interest of the spectators, such as
miming, acrobatics, and skilful deceptions, or the mock killing and re-
suscitation of a member of the group. The dancers of the societies of
snake charmers and porcupine hunters particularly excel in such tricks.
The words of the songs are intended to hold the opponent up to ridicule;
a singer may insult his adversary as much as he likes with impunity.

*Economic organization*

A man's social status is not determined by his material possessions;
even the possession of a large herd of cattle, the most highly valued of
all commodities, does not in itself make the owner a dignitary of the
community, nor are his words in council listened to with any particular
respect on account of his wealth. Naturally enough it is not unusual for
a clever man, respected among the community for his ability, to be a
large cattle-owner; but there are also rich cattle-owners who play no
part in public life.

The economic organization of the Sukuma today still follows very
simple lines. The individual prefers barter to sale in transactions in the
commodity nearest to his heart—cattle. Money seems to him a perish-
able commodity and he can live without it. The variety of economic
crops and the increasing number of market transactions in stock are
beginning to turn the Sukuma into a capitalist, but his heart is not in it.
It almost looks as though he dislikes becoming rich beyond a certain
limit, perhaps because he is afraid of the envy of men and spirits. As
the customary law shows, he has not yet adopted to any extent money

transactions, such as loans, mortgages, purchases on credit or by fixed instalments, which would require laws to regulate them. Sukumaland did not offer favourable conditions for European agricultural enterprises at a time when white settlers started to acquire land in other parts of the country. Therefore the European population of this area consists mainly of government officials, missionaries, and the employees of a few, but very important, diamond and gold-mines.

## Political organization

The various aspects of Sukuma social organization are fully represented in the recorded law and custom. Likewise religious conceptions, which conform to those held by the Bantu elsewhere, are implicit in the text. The law, however, contains very little which throws light on the political organization of the tribe, and for this reason a short description of the political structure may be useful as a background to certain chapters.

The political life in a chiefdom has always centred round the chief and still does so. The sources of the chief's authority were originally the belief in his magico-religious functions; his position as supreme judge of his people; his wealth, which was mainly derived from the annual tribute paid by each household; his leadership in war, which consisted rather in the preparation and conduct of a campaign by providing magic medicines than in actual leadership in battle, which was rare; and his administrative-executive powers. As befitted his semi-sacerdotal position, he was surrounded by his courtiers, the *banang'oma*, whose positions were hereditary and confined to a few families. Their most important function was the election of a new chief from among the sons of the sisters of the former chief. They performed this with the assistance of divination, using the intestines of a chicken. A chief elected in accordance with these rules of matrilineal succession might have spent years as a commoner among commoners, far from the atmosphere of the court, since his mother was probably married to a commoner and might be living anywhere within the chiefdom. For this reason elaborate enthronement ceremonies were evolved to give external and public significance to the inward change which was supposed to take place in the chosen person—chiefly his transformation from a commoner to a person with powers over the spirits of the country. Thus, there were two almost contradictory elements in the relationship between the people and their chief, a contradiction which found expression in times of distress. A chief might be held responsible for a disaster such as lack of rain, and would be deposed on the grounds that he must have lost the favour of the spirits and was therefore no longer in possession of his magical powers. In such cases, though the individual chief was changed, the ruling dynasty remained.

The *banang'oma* not only selected the new ruler, but they also in-

structed him in tribal history, and his duties towards his subjects; the
moral principles of his office and his responsibility for the prosperity and
health of his people, their children, and cattle. They remained his permanent councillors and courtiers throughout his reign and controlled
all his private and public affairs. They were the delegates of the chief
in the frequent negotiations with practitioners, diviners, and rain-makers
whose help he had to employ in the interests of his people; they acted
as assessors in his court; they assisted him in his magico-religious rites;
they went with him when he left his residence; they chose his wives for
him; they looked after him when he was ill; they were his informants
on everything that went on in the chiefdom. Since the arrival of the
Europeans these *banang'oma* have lost or are losing their influence in all
the fields of their former activities and their office of mediator between
the chief and his people has almost ceased to exist.

The actual administration of the country was in the hands of the
*banangwa*, the village headmen. Nearly all these men were originally
sons of chiefs who, under the rules of matrilineal succession, could not
succeed their fathers. A few of them were commoners who as pioneers
had opened up uninhabited land and become headmen when other
families had followed them into the new area. Many of the rights and
duties of the chief were delegated by him to these headmen. As relatives
of the chief they had their own magico-religious functions, held their
own courts, and were powerful men in their own areas. The headman
was responsible for the collection of the yearly tribute in kind payable
to the chief. (This payment was never rigorously enforced and in years of
bad harvest might be waived.) The headmen still make an important
contribution to the smooth running of the Native Authority machinery,
but they have lost much of their original independence. Nevertheless,
their influence in their own villages is still considerable.

The people themselves were organized in two groups or clubs—the
*ihane* and the *elika*, of which the *elika* was the more important. Its
members were mainly the younger generation, though graduation from
it did not necessarily depend on the attainment of a certain age or social
position. In each village this group had a leader, the *nsumba ntale*. The
duties of these leaders, and the extent of their influence, varied considerably in different places, and there are still wide differences. Their influence is greatest in central Sukuma (Maswa) where they are not only
the leaders of the organization for mutual help in field work—the chief
function of the *basumba batale* all over Sukumaland—but also the
administrators of land, a duty which in other parts has been taken over
by the headmen. This village organization maintains a certain discipline
which does not interfere with the private lives of its members but regu-
lates their public duties.

The members of the *ihane* are the *banamhara*, which means elderly
men, but here again the age-group idea is not strictly adhered to. Just

as in the *elika* there may be men of over thirty, though the majority are young men, so in the *ihane*, though the majority are older, there may be quite young men who have either been included because of some outstanding qualities or have been able to afford to pay immediately the various entrance fees, which generally take years to pay. These *banamhara* are the men to whom the name 'village elders' is given. They are the unofficial councillors of the headman in all the affairs of the village and, in fact, it would be difficult for any headman to execute work affecting the community without their moral support and co-operation. They are consulted as arbitrators by parties to disputes which for some reason they are reluctant to bring to court, and their decisions are usually accepted. The older members of the *ihane* are expert diviners and members of a certain rank are initiated into the art of soothsaying. They are also usually called as witnesses to allocations of land, bridewealth, or other customary payments, and there is no public or private ceremony within the village to which these elders are not invited and in which they do not have their specific functions.

## Judicial institutions

Three courts of law existed before the arrival of the Europeans:
1. The court of the *banamhara*; 2. The court of the *banangwa*; 3. The court of the *ntemi*.

These courts did not represent different stages of appeal; each had its defined limits and the decision of each was in practice final, since the *ntemi* was very reluctant to re-open a case which had already been decided by a *ng'wanangwa*.

## The court of the Ntemi (chief)

The *ntemi*'s court was *de facto* a criminal court; civil cases might be heard by the chief, not because of any particular importance attaching to a case, but if one or both parties were near kinsmen of the chief.

The court consisted of the *ntemi* as president and the *banang'oma* as assessors. The functions of the court were not divided as between judge, crown counsel, and counsel for the defence. One of the *banang'oma* opened the case by questioning the defendant or the witnesses, the other *banang'oma* assisting him. Sometimes the *ntemi* would interrupt and even an elder sitting among the listeners was allowed to put questions to witnesses or to give his opinion as to their reliability. Each party had to pay five goats or hoes before a case could be heard in the chief's court. Of these, five went to the chief and five to the assessors—usually *banang'oma*. The fee was high in order to prevent frivolous litigation. No fine was imposed on the guilty party, but he had to pay compensation or *njigu* to the wronged person. The chief received his share of this compensation; for instance, if *njigu* was paid he got one or two cows.

Very little formality was observed in court. Assessors, or even the chief, might leave the assembly for short periods without it being considered necessary to adjourn the proceedings. The code of law by which the case was decided was known to the assessors through the practice of many years, but even among the commoners there were everywhere a number of older people who knew the traditional laws. Precedents were admissible as arguments but were never considered decisive. The proceedings were short because the depositions of witnesses and the investigations of the *ng'wanangwa* were not always repeated in court, but were conveyed to the chief and his assessors briefly and privately by the *ng'wanangwa* before the case was tried. The *ng'wanangwa* of the village in which the crime was committed was always present and was heard if the case became involved and if the depositions of the witnesses were contradictory. When necessary the *ntemi* and his assessors retired for a council (*kisaka*) before the *ntemi* gave his judgement.

The court of the *ntemi* tried cases of murder, high treason, assault causing serious injury, witchcraft, and cattle theft.

## The court of the Ng'wanangwa (headman)

Many transgressions, such as cattle theft or assault, were not automatically brought before the chief. Some of the *banangwa* were prepared to hear cases which others would have been reluctant to judge in their courts; much depended on the closeness of the kinship between the chief and the headman, and in some cases also on the weak régime of a chief or the strong character of a *ng'wanangwa*.

Every *ng'wanangwa* had his court, the assessors of which were selected by him. These assessors attended the court regularly and, as they were very often also the councillors of the village headman in all matters, the constitution of the court presented no difficulties. The cases heard were mainly concerned with assault and wounds resulting from drunken brawls, civil suits arising from quarrels over boundaries, domestic quarrels and divorce, debts and complications resulting from certain traditional compensation payments.

As in the chief's court, a man bringing a case before the *ng'wanangwa* had to pay a fee called *lutwi*; this was generally paid in kind in such commodities as hoes, goats, or measures of *mtama*. It was distributed between the members of the court if it was a sufficiently large fee; if not, it was put aside until enough fees had been collected for, in the case of *mtama*, beer to be brewed. The amount of the payment depended not so much on the amount involved in the dispute as on the means of the plaintiff.

When an assault took place or a man was injured in a quarrel, the case was not heard immediately. The injured man was given a white bracelet to wear on his left wrist. If he died compensation was payable; if he recovered the bracelet was removed and the man who had caused the injury had to pay compensation. It was not customary to impose fines, payments being made in the form of compensation. Only in cases where malefactors repeatedly came before the court for the same transgressions did the ng'wanangwa and his elders impose a fine; this was divided between the members of the court or, if it was a cow or goat, slaughtered and eaten by them at a communal meal.

It sometimes happened that parties to a case refused to accept the judgement of the village headman and decided to bring their case before the chief's court. Such procedure was rare, however, and if the chief refused to hear the case nothing more could be done. There was no right of appeal.

## Modern Trends

It is clear that in the original Sukuma tribal structure there were many institutions which might be termed democratic in so far as they gave to groups of people powers which limited the authority of the chief. The latter was not formerly an absolute autocrat, though the extent of his authority varied according to the character of each individual chief. As in all royal dynasties, there were in the Sukuma ruling houses a certain number of mighty warriors or highly successful performers of magico-religious functions, many average men whose rule left no mark, and a number of cruel men, drunkards, and fools. Almost all these chiefs were able to follow their natural bents and very few of them resisted the traditional restrictions or tried to extend their prerogatives unduly. The Sukuma chief was a 'Democratic Feudal Leader' (H. S. Senior).

The traditional positions of all the members of the tribal structure— the banamhara, basumba batale, banang'oma, and the chief himself—have undergone considerable changes since the introduction of a European government. The tribal structure has been given a new direction; its equilibrium has been destroyed, not intentionally but by the very presence of foreigners who were powerful beyond imagination and inevitably propagated their own ideas. The rights and duties of the indigenous tribal dignitaries and corporate bodies lost much of their significance, and they could only continue as factors in public life in so far as they were authorized to do so by their new masters. Of all the conceptions underlying indigenous institutions one alone became immediately clear to the European new-comers—that of chief—not in Sukumaland alone but in general throughout the country. The foundations of his authority, however, had to undergo great changes. Of those traditional sources of power which I have mentioned, all but one have more or less lost their importance by a slow but continuous process of evolution. The administrative authority of the chief, which has been effectively supported by the Central Government, has gained strength to such an extent that it has not only become the main source of his power, but has steadily reduced the influence of those indigenous institutions which restricted his authority. The control of the chief's activities has fallen entirely into the hands of the Central Government. If the history of the last twenty years is studied, it will be found that there is hardly a case in which a chief has lost his position on account of the complaints of his people. Almost all the changes in chiefs have been made by the direct action of the Central Government when it found the transgressions of a chief sufficiently grave to warrant his dismissal.

Recently the policy of the Central Government has turned to the question of the reformation of the native administration in accordance with present needs by the introduction of popular representation.

## General

Sukumaland's general development must be considered in the context of the development of the whole of Tanganyika. It comprises one-eighteenth of the total area of the Territory but includes about one-seventh of the whole African population. In the absence of serious economic or political conflicts, it has provided favourable conditions for collaboration between different races. Therefore progress initiated in Sukumaland may well provide a pattern for the rest of the Territory.

# PART II

# THE LAW OF PERSONS

## CHAPTER I

## BRIDEWEALTH

### (*BUKWI* OR *MPANGO*)

### INTRODUCTION

THERE are several theories about the function of bridewealth: in Sukuma Customary Law its main function is to determine the status of children. If bridewealth is paid the children belong to the paternal family; if no bridewealth is paid, to the maternal family (269A, 275).[1] The payment of bridewealth is the condition *sine qua non* of a customary marriage and guarantees the legitimacy of the offspring, although the act of paying bridewealth does not legitimatize the marriage (146).

As long as bridewealth is not returned, the children borne by the wife belong to the paternal family, even if the husband is dead or absent for many years (607). If a father wishes to disinherit a son, he demands from the receiver of bridewealth the repayment of a customary portion of the bridewealth (628); whereupon this son becomes a member of the maternal family, having lost his membership of the paternal family.

If, in the event of a divorce, the husband demands the return of the whole bridewealth, he must renounce his rights to his children and must hand them over to the maternal family (244). If later he changes his mind and wishes to claim his children, he must repay an appropriate portion of the bridewealth to the maternal family (246).

These examples show that the purpose of bridewealth payment is to secure for the paternal family possession of the children of the marriage and that the consequence of receiving bridewealth is the abandonment by the receiver of all claims to the children. The procreation of children and the perpetuation of the family are very strong motive forces in the African mind. The whole family is involved in the payment of bridewealth and every member of it is ready to pay his share. The notion of such common responsibility is shown in many provisions of the law. For instance, cattle belonging to an absent relative can be taken by his next-of-kin to pay bridewealth and no complaint can be made later even if the absentee's permission was not obtained (360, 364). A gift of more than two head of cattle is not recognized as a gift after the donor's death except when the cattle were given to a relative to pay bridewealth (494).

---

[1] References in parentheses are to paragraphs of the text.

The eldest brother, as guardian of his minor siblings, is entitled to use the cattle of the estate for the payment of bridewealth and the siblings have no right to require from their brother at a later date an account or the repayment of cattle which he has used for this purpose (352A). Further, no man can ever be required to return cattle given to him by a relative to pay bridewealth (497).

The stress laid on the importance of the possession of children is the natural consequence of that aspect of the religious belief of the African commonly called 'ancestor worship'. The spirits of deceased relatives are very much alive and enjoy the attentions of the living as long as any remain to invoke their help, to pray to the ι, and to bring them sacrifices. If the family dies out the spirits also die a second time. The people most interested in the future child are its grandfather and father; they will be the immediate beneficiaries, after their death, of the son's and grandson's devotions. As the external sign of the close connexion of the generations, the son's second name is the name of his father, while his first name is very often that of his grandfather, particularly if the latter has died before the birth of his grandson. Quite logically the bridewealth is in most cases paid with the property of the grandfather and/or the father.

Material factors are also taken into consideration by the family. Every relative is interested in the continuous growth of the family because he knows from experience the advantage of a big family as a kind of 'Mutual Insurance Company'. This does not mean that any relative who helps in the payment of bridewealth can expect a direct return of his gift when a daughter of the union marries, because the cattle of bridewealth are not divided between the kinsmen (Note to 33); but it does mean that he can get help in many other ways from the family.

The Sukuma himself is aware of this material function of bridewealth; he says: '*Biswe tutibana ba baba biswe aliyo tulibana ba ng'ombe ya baba siswe.*' (We are not the children of our fathers; we are the children of our fathers' cattle.)

The stabilizing function of bridewealth often mentioned in this connexion is not in the foreground of the Sukuma people's mind. This is obvious from the fact that women who wish for a divorce do not concern themselves much with the consideration that their fathers or next-of-kin have to pay back the cattle of bridewealth. The fathers themselves do not interfere seriously because they always hope, usually with good reason. that the divorcee will remarry (69).

## PAYMENT OF BRIDEWEALTH
### General rules[1]

1. Bridewealth is cattle or other property handed over by a prospec-

[1] Rules regarding bridewealth paid in non-pagan marriages are not included here because such rules do not originate in the customary law of the tribe.

tive bridegroom (*nkwilima*) to the father or other male relative (3) of a girl whom he intends to marry.

2. The *nkwilima* himself is responsible for the payment of bridewealth although members of his family may aid him in the fulfilment of his obligations.

NOTE. In the majority of cases a man obtains the cattle for his first marriage wholly or partly from his father, brother, or maternal uncle. For a second wife assistance from relatives in the payment of bridewealth is rare. The nearest relatives feel a moral obligation to use cattle in their possession, especially inherited beasts, for the assistance of younger members of the family, who expect this help and approach their seniors without hesitation though with the conventional humility of applicants. It would be considered a fault and an indication of a mean disposition, if an uncle, even if he were not directly interested in the fortunes of his nephew (38), should refuse such help while having plenty of beasts in his kraal.

3 A. The person entitled to receive the bridewealth is the father of the bride or his legal heir, excluding the daughter in respect of whom bridewealth is paid.

B. If the father is not alive the legal heirs are: the eldest living full brother, or him failing, the eldest living half-brother, or him failing, the eldest living paternal uncle, or him failing, the nearest living paternal relative.

C. If a daughter is her father's heir, bridewealth paid for her is received by the relative who would be heir if there were no daughters (53, 79).

NOTE. The most common terms of relationship are:

### A. *Consanguineous kin*

| | | | |
|---|---|---|---|
| *baba* | my father | *mami* | mother's brother |
| *so* | your father | | (but the Swahili |
| *ise* | his father | | word *mjomba* is |
| *siswe* | our father | | used as well) |
| *simwe* | your father | *sengi* | father's sister |
| *sabo* | their father | *mayu* | mother's sister |
| *mayu* | my mother | *guku* | grandfather |
| *noko* | your mother | *mama* | grandmother |
| *nina* | his mother | *ng'wana wa baba* | father's brother's |
| *niniswe* | our mother | | son |
| *ninmwe* | your mother | *ng'wana wa mayo* | mother's sister's |
| *ninabo* | their mother | | son |
| *ng'wana* | child | *baba* | father's sister's son |
| *nkulu* | elder brother | *ng'wana wane* | mother's brother's |
| *baba* | father's brother | | son |

### B. *Affinal kin*

| | | | |
|---|---|---|---|
| *ngoshi* | husband | *nkwilima* | son-in-law |
| *nke* | wife | *ng'winga* | daughter-in-law |
| *baba buko* | father-in-law | *nkwela* | sister- or brother- |
| *mayu buko* | mother-in-law | | in-law |

*Amount of Bridewealth*

NOTE. There has been a tendency all over the country, but originating in the south, to increase the amount of bridewealth.

In 1916 an attempt was made to fix a limit of five head of cattle for commoners and ten for chiefs. In 1920 the order was repealed and it was decided that the amount should be agreed upon by the parties. A reason for the failure of this attempt at limitation was said to be that the Administration from 1916 to 1920 was not as well established as it is now. The necessity for limiting the amount of bridewealth has recently been generally agreed for the following reasons:

(*a*) Poor men cannot marry because they cannot afford to pay the high bridewealth. The consequence is an increase in concubinage (*butende*).

(*b*) In case of divorce and repayment of bridewealth the father or next-of-kin is very often not in a position to repay a high amount. The consequence is an increase in litigation.

(*c*) The price of cattle has increased during the last few years out of proportion to the prices of other commodities and to wages. There is therefore no reason for increasing the number of cattle to be paid.

Initially the limitation will be mainly operative in SS and KS, since in the other chiefdoms the ceiling of fifteen cattle has hardly been reached. Thus it may be hoped that limitation of bridewealth will now be successfully effected, partly with the help of the provisions indicated in para. 7, and partly because it will not involve changing a custom already widespread, but will merely prevent its introduction.

4. Rules restricting the amount of bridewealth were proposed by the chiefs of the Sukuma Federation and their people in 1949 (Appendix II), the amount of bridewealth payable being limited to the maximum amounts shown in the following schedule:

5. For all chiefdoms except those of ZM, SM.

A. If the bridewealth is payable in cattle, 15 beasts, of which not less than 3 shall be bulls.

B. If the bridewealth is payable in goats or sheep, 135 (on the basis that 1 cow is equivalent to 10 goats or sheep and 1 bull to 5 goats or sheep).

C. If the bridewealth is payable in cash, Shs.540/- (on the basis that 1 cow is equivalent to Shs.40/- and 1 bull is equivalent to Shs.20/-).

NOTE (see Note to 331). The money value of cattle recognized in the courts does not correspond to the market price because, in general, commodities and money are regarded as separate values which are only occasionally connected. The cattle-owner may sell a beast at auction for Shs.80/- or 100/- but the computation of bridewealth at 1,000 shillings is beyond his comprehension; on the other hand fifteen head of cattle is something which he sees every day. The increased cattle prices at auctions do not impress the cattle-holder deeply because he never contrives to assess the cash value of his herd; in his mind the value of the herd can only rise if the number of beasts increases. The rules still require payment of compensation in kind (302), but in practice this is not always easy. The older generation—at least those who are men of property and consequence—have their complaints about the situation. They must give their sons cattle for bridewealth and they must pay customary compensation in cattle, if the necessity arises, because it would be shameful for a respected man to pay bridewealth, &c., in money; but sometimes the bridewealth they receive for their daughters and, more often, the customary compensation, are paid in money. To refuse to accept money is not advisable because, in case of bridewealth, the refusal may lead to concubinage and, in case of compensation, may mean an interminable debt and finally a total loss. It is to be expected that in course of time the rate of exchange between cattle and money will adjust itself to market prices.

6. For ZM, SM.

A. If bridewealth is payable in cash: Shs.300/-, in addition, Shs.4/- and 1 castrated goat;

B. If bridewealth is paid in hoes: 300 hoes and in addition Shs.4/- and 1 castrated goat.

NOTE. In the chiefdoms situated near Mwanza town, payment in money is becoming more frequent. In Maswa and Bukwimba bridewealth is paid in cattle, goats, or sheep. In Shinyanga payments in cattle and in money occur. In the southern parts of the Mweli Federation payments in hoes and/or money are frequent.

Although on the market one hoe costs Shs.3/- to Shs.4/- the chiefs and elders of the SM chiefdoms insisted that in case of bridewealth one hoe should be equal to one shilling.

7. All courts will take cognizance of bridewealth only up to the maximum limits. Any payment made in excess of these limits will be deemed to have been a free gift on the part of the husband and to be irrecoverable at law.

8. In every case ceremonial beasts or gifts handed over at the conclusion of a marriage, and which can be claimed in the event of divorce, shall be included in the limits set out under items 5 and 6 above.

9. The above limits do not refer to the bridewealth payable or received by chiefs in respect of their wives or female relatives.

10. The maximum limit of bridewealth to be paid or received by a *ng'wanangwa*, *munang'oma*, a regent, a direct descendant of a chief or a deposed chief shall be increased by one-third of the amounts specified in 5 and 6 above.

Formerly the average amount of bridewealth varied much in the different local federations and even in their chiefdoms.

(*a*) In NF, UF the average number was 7 to 8 cattle and bridewealth of 10 to 12 cattle was considered high.

(*b*) In KF, BSN, BD the average number was about 10 to 12 cattle.

(*c*) In SS, KS the average number was over 20 cattle and payment of bridewealth of 35 to 40 cattle was known.

(*d*) In ZM the average number was 4 to 5 cattle.

(*e*) In SM the average amount was about 300 hoes or Shs.300/- but payments of larger amounts occurred.

NOTE. The amount of bridewealth varies, not only in different areas and among men of different social status as mentioned in 10, but also within the same area. The conditions of each marriage are the result of all the circumstances of the case. Some examples of such varying circumstances are:

1. *Personal*

A. *Father.* The father, aware of the unstable character of his daughter, may demand a small bridewealth because he is afraid that sooner or later he will have to return cattle in the event of divorce. In another case the father may feel that his daughter has already missed many chances and that he should facilitate negotiations.

B. *Bridegroom.* The circumstances of the bridegroom may be of importance. For example, the niece of an elderly pagan (her father being dead) was married for an unusually high bridewealth. The old man explained, 'Bride and bridegroom were both Christians and educated in the same mission. I was not afraid to ask for so many cattle, because I knew that the missionaries would not allow a divorce and I would therefore never have to return the bridewealth.'

C. *Bride.* Sometimes several men woo the same girl and may raise the amount of bridewealth by competing against each other. (It is not held that the girl (*nsungi*) must marry the man who makes the highest bid.) Generally, the appearance of the girl is of no great importance; the bridewealth does not vary on account of beauty or otherwise. The saying is: 'The face does not bear a child and the neck does not handle the hoe.' The existence of an illegitimate child does not influence the amount of bridewealth. The bridewealth for a widow or divorced woman who remarries is often smaller than that for a girl, but not always. If the woman has acquired a good reputation during her first marriage, a man may pay a high bridewealth for her, at least as much as is usually paid for an inexperienced young girl.

2. *Economic*

A. *Father.* A rich man may ask for a higher bridewealth because he is not afraid, as a poor man might be, of having to repay it in the event of a divorce. This point is of no great importance as it is not usual to think of divorce before the parties are even married.

B. *Bridegroom.* The father-in-law may agree to accept a small bridewealth from a poor suitor if he sees that his daughter loves the man, and if the suitor has succeeded in ingratiating himself with the old man.

The demands of the girl's father are, generally speaking, fair. Fathers who exaggerate their claims do not enjoy the approval of the public; and public opinion is still influential owing to the publicity of private life. If the daughter of a rich man falls in love with a poor man, the young couple will usually succeed in getting parental consent, although the bridewealth finally agreed upon may not be adequate to the status of the father-in-law and his family. The possibility of paying bridewealth in instalments may also ease the situation. The matter is differently handled when the family of the bridegroom is not poor. The girl's father will remain adamant and will finally declare that he refuses to accept any bridewealth because he does not want his daughter to marry the man. If the young couple wish they may live in concubinage. This attitude of the father is an effective weapon since the children of the union will then belong to him and not to their own father. Members of the bridegroom's family will probably help him to pay the bridewealth or a first instalment of it, particularly if the girl becomes pregnant (270). The institution of bridewealth has not up to now resulted in the division of common people into different classes. It is a democratic institution which does not preclude marriage between a poor man and the daughter of a rich man.

### Replacement of cattle paid as bridewealth

11. The son-in-law must replace any beast forming part of the bridewealth if this beast dies.

This obligation lasts up to and until the marriage is consummated or legalized in accordance with native custom (146).

NOTE. This rule was agreed by the chiefs of the Sukuma Federation and their people in 1949. Formerly different rules were applied in different chiefdoms:

(a) In BD the rules as stated in para. 11 were followed.
(b) In BSN the obligation lasted until a *ng'ombe ya lushu*[1] was paid, usually with the first instalment of bridewealth.
(c) In NF, SBS, SS, BS, KS, UF the obligation lasted until a *mbuli ya lushu* was paid (recently payments of Shs.4/- have been accepted instead), or until the birth of the first child.
(d) Nowhere could the father-in-law refuse to accept the *mbuli ya lushu* with the first instalment of the bridewealth.

12. If the father-in-law desires the replacement of a beast which has died, he must inform his son-in-law and ask him to come and take the carcass away. The father-in-law is under no obligation to inform his son-in-law when a beast of the bridewealth falls sick.

NOTE. Usually the father-in-law does not demand a replacement, but prefers to forego his right, and use the meat himself and keep the hide.

13. The cause of the beast's death is of no importance; whether it has died of a disease or a snake bite, by being struck by lightning or by falling into a hole, the son-in-law must replace it on demand. If, however, a beast is stolen or disappears without trace the son-in-law has no obligation to replace it.

14. If a beast of the bridewealth dies and the bridegroom is absent, any of his near relatives, females included, can act for him.

15. The son-in-law is obliged to replace a cow of the bridewealth which does not calve, although the animal may have calved in his own herd.

But if a heifer, which has been accepted by the father-in-law, fails to calve in due time, it does not have to be replaced.

16. A bull which does not cover cows must be replaced, but a bull calf which later fails to do so need not be replaced.

17. A cow which calves but gives no milk to the calf must be replaced.

18. A beast which shows habits detrimental to the herd, though these only reveal themselves in course of time, must be replaced.

### Customary payments other than bridewealth

19. During the negotiations concerned with the amount of bridewealth, other payments, some obligatory and some not necessarily so, are specifically mentioned.

NOTE. Considerable variations exist regarding payments of ceremonial beasts.

[1] See Glossary, pp. 177-186.

As these payments are customary ones no co-ordination of rules has been attempted. The provisions of para. 8 are probably the only possible solution for the present.

## 1. Ng'ombe ya Maji or Ng'ombe ya Itono

20. The *ng'ombe ya maji* is an obligatory payment in all chiefdoms, except those mentioned in para. 22*d*.

21. The payment consists of one bull or ox and is made with the first instalment of the bridewealth.

22. The custom regarding the use of the beast varies:

(*a*) NF, UF. The beast is slaughtered after the consummation of the marriage, therefore normally on the morning after the wedding, and is considered public proof that the parties are now married.

(*b*) SBS, KF, KS, KM. The beast is killed at a feast arranged several weeks after the marriage, when the two families meet. It is considered the official confirmation of the bond which now exists between the two families.

(*c*) BD, BS, SS. A *mbuli ya maji* (goat) instead of a *ng'ombe ya maji* (bull) is killed at any time after marriage, but only if the couple had no sexual intercourse prior to marriage.

(*d*) BSN, ZM, SM. Neither *ng'ombe* nor *mbuli ya maji* payments exist.

23. If bridewealth is paid in money, a sum of Shs.20/- specifically called *ng'ombe ya maji* is handed over in addition to the amount of the bridewealth.

24. The slaughter of the *ng'ombe ya maji* is nowhere obligatory and a father-in-law can keep the beast in his herd even in those areas where it is more usual to slaughter it.

NOTE. The slaughter of the *ng'ombe ya maji* is not legal proof of the consummation of marriage and therefore does not legalize the union.

For return of *ng'ombe ya maji* in case of divorce see 80A.

## 2. Mbuli ya Kilezu

25. The customary gift of one goat made by the son-in-law to the maternal grandfather of the wife. It is handed over to the wife's father who passes it on to the grandfather only if the latter demands it. Recently payments of Shs.2/- to Shs.5/- have been accepted instead.

The *mbuli ya kilezu* is a customary payment in all chiefdoms except BSN, SBS, KS, where one head of cattle is given instead of a goat.

NOTE. For return of *mbuli ya kilezu* in case of a divorce see 80B.

## 3. Ng'ombe ya Bugabu or Ng'ombe ya Butigu

26. The customary payment of one cow made by the son-in-law to his father-in-law in the event of his wishing to take his wife into the home-

stead of his own father before he has completed payment of the whole bridewealth. If the young couple wish to move into their own homestead, no *ng'ombe ya butigu* is payable.

NOTE. The significance of the payment of *ng'ombe ya butigu* and *ng'ombe ya kugila* is that with the entrance of the son's wife into his paternal home her work will benefit her husband's family.

For the return of *ng'ombe ya butigu* in case of divorce see 80c.

### 4. Ng'ombe ya Kugila

27. When a daughter-in-law arrives in the homestead of her husband's father, she customarily refuses to take food in the house and will eat with neighbours or will only eat food brought for her from her parents' house, until her father-in-law has given her a cow, the *ng'ombe ya kugila*. In some areas a goat is given instead of a cow. A little later the husband's sister or other female relative goes to the wife's father and reports on the well-being of his daughter. He gives this relative a bull which is sent to the husband's father.

NOTE. For rules regarding repayment of these beasts in case of divorce see 80D.

### 5. Mbuli ya Luswagilo or Mbuli ya Mumagulu ga Ng'ombe

28. The gift of a goat made by the bridegroom to the delegates of the bride's father when they come to fetch the cattle of bridewealth (112).

NOTE. For return of this gift in case of divorce see 80E.

### 6. Tumbati (tobacco)

29. Formerly a quantity of tobacco was given as a present by the son-in-law to his father-in-law; nowadays instead of tobacco the son-in-law makes a present of Shs.2/-.

NOTE. For return of this gift in case of divorce see 80F.

### Legal aspects of payment

30. The amount of bridewealth and the form of payment are entirely matters for agreement between the son-in-law and the father-in-law.

31. The father-in-law and the son-in-law are jointly responsible for ensuring that the payment of bridewealth is made before at least four witnesses, two from each party.

NOTE. In the chiefdoms of BD, BSN, and BS the *basumba batale* (leaders of village organization) are called as witnesses.

32. All laws relating to bridewealth or marriage are valid irrespective of the amount of bridewealth.

33. The cattle of the bridewealth become the exclusive property of the bride's father who cannot be held accountable for their use or disposal. Any offspring of these cattle become the property of the bride's father

and cannot be reckoned towards payment of any portion of the bride-wealth still outstanding.

NOTE. The receiver of the bridewealth has no obligation to share it with his kinsmen.

34. In case of remarriage the first bridewealth must be returned before a second can be accepted. To receive bridewealth for the same woman more than once is punishable. The fine is Shs.40/-. For exception see 90B.

35. It is a punishable offence for a father to receive payment of bride-wealth from two suitors for his daughter at the same time. Before receiving payment from a second man, he must return any instalment paid by the first suitor.

The fine is the same as in 34.

36. If a woman is living in concubinage (*butende*) the relative who is entitled to receive bridewealth for her is not allowed to open negotiations regarding her marriage with another man, nor is he allowed to receive a first instalment of bridewealth until the woman has definitely left the house of her lover.

NOTE (see also Note to 281). The family of a girl living with a man in con-cubinage (*butende*) is seldom hostile to him. After a child has been born, the lover is often half accepted into the girl's family. He may even come to the parents' house and help in field-work; but such a situation exists only where the lover is poor. If the lover or his family possesses property, the girl's family would never become friendly. The poor lover in the house is called *nkwilima wa bakima* (the son-in-law of women) indicating that the lover is not the legitimate son-in-law, but has been accepted as a necessary evil by the female members of the house.

In the Ntusu chiefdom the lover of a girl living in concubinage is never accepted by the family; he would never dare to come near the girl's home unless he wished to offer payment of bridewealth.

37. Both parties to a marriage agreement have the right to dissolve the agreement at any time prior to the wedding (see 97).

*Payment of bridewealth by maternal or paternal relatives* [1]

38. The maternal uncle, if he is a rich cattle-owner and has no son, may give his sister's sons cattle for the payment of their bridewealth. Sometimes it may happen that a man has inherited cattle from his mother and uses them to pay bridewealth, or a mother may give cattle to her son from her own property for the same purpose. A family founded with bridewealth of such origin, i.e. paid from maternal pro-perty, is called a *numba ya bugongo* and a wife of such a family is called *nkima wa bugongo*. A family founded in the usual way, i.e. with property derived from the father or paternal relatives, is called *numba ya buta* and the wife *nkima wa buta*.

[1] This distinction is made in all Sukuma chiefdoms except in those of SS, KS. In these chiefdoms no legal difference originating in the source of bridewealth is known.

NOTE. Elements of mother-right complicate many rules of the Sukuma Customary Law (591, 608, 320, 365 for instance). No trace has been found in the traditions of the people that mother-right was at any time the general rule, or that there ever existed an *ignorantia paternitatis*. Equally, no tradition could be found to support the theory that these elements are due to influences from outside. It may, however, be remembered that the Hamitic invaders had matrilineal succession (see Introduction). It can be stated as a fundamental condition of Sukuma social life that the maternal family, although as a rule of no legal importance, exercises great influence in all matters concerning the marriage and particularly the children of relatives on the female side. Maternal relatives are comparatively rarely mentioned in recordings of the customary laws, but this gives a wrong impression of their importance. If anything goes wrong with the marriage or if any economic difficulty arises, the maternal relatives are frequently called upon to arbitrate or to help. Children visit their maternal as frequently as their paternal relatives (often showing preference for the maternal uncles), especially if the mother has died; even in cases of divorce, the maternal relatives remain in close contact with the children. (Note to 346, 628.)

39. A family founded with property acquired by the husband is considered a *numba ya buta*.

40. The maternal uncle or other maternal relative is allowed to help the nephew with the payment of bridewealth, and thus to found a *numba ya bugongo*, only if the bridegroom's father agrees. In the same way a father can give cattle for payment of bridewealth for his son of a *numba ya bugongo* only if the maternal uncle agrees.

41. If the first instalment of bridewealth was paid either from *buta* or *bugongo* property any further instalment paid from any other source does not change the original category of the house.

NOTE. It would be possible for the following case to arise: A man marries his first wife with the help of his maternal uncle, making the house *bugongo*. The assistance of his maternal uncle is not adequate, however, for him to be able to pay the bridewealth in full and he is left with a debt of a few cattle. Later the same man inherits property from a paternal uncle and uses it, legitimately, to marry a second wife, the inheritance being adequate to cover the whole amount of the bridewealth, even leaving him with a surplus. He cannot use these remaining cattle, however, to pay off the debt on the bridewealth of his first wife, for his paternal relatives have the right to control this surplus, and would object to its use for a *nkima ya bugongo*.

42. The bridewealth for a daughter of a *numba ya bugongo* is received by the maternal relative who paid bridewealth for her mother or by his heir.

D.C.'s Appeal 9/44. Ibadakuli (Busiha). *Milembe v. Limi.*

Milembe's bridewealth was received by her maternal uncle. When he died his son inherited his property including the bridewealth cattle for Milembe; later when the son died his sister Limi became the heir. Milembe then claimed the cattle of bridewealth from Limi. The court held that Limi was the rightful heir of her brother's property and that Milembe's bridewealth belonged to her maternal relative. The court added that in the event of a divorce Milembe's husband would have to claim the return of bridewealth from Limi.

*Bridewealth paid for a Nsugwa (Bondsman)*

43. The institution of *nsugwa* has been abolished.

NOTE. The institution of *nsugwa* did not have its origin in slavery. Everywhere men may be found who are too lazy in mind to remain independent. They are incapable of carrying any responsibility; they are happy if they get food, here and there a piece of clothing, and perhaps, in good time, a wife—all without their own effort. At the same time they are not lazy workers. If, as frequently happens, such a man has no relatives, he may work for a rich man and adopt the rich man's house as his home. Originally the rich man inherited his widow and children when the *nsugwa* died, but as early as 1925, when Chief Chasama of Msalala claimed the inheritance of a widow and her children, the court recognized the right of inheritance of the *nsugwa's* brother. Cases which still sometimes come before courts are initiated not by a *nsugwa*, but by the son of a *nsugwa*, who refuses to allow the rich man or his heirs to take the bridewealth of his sisters. The abolition of the institution will terminate its legal consequences but not its existence. A rich man did not try to find a *nsugwa*, but a man whom he accepted into his house gradually acquired the status of a *nsugwa*. No doubt this will still happen. The rich man did not think of profit when he paid bridewealth for the *nsugwa*, but regarded it as an investment of capital. As a rich man looked for a reliable man with whom to place cattle in trusteeship, so he invested capital in the *nsugwa's* marriage; the security of the investment was better than in the case of trusteeship because it remained in the house. Appeals from court cases of this sort which reached European courts were usually returned for retrial as neither party attempted to explain the principles of the *nsugwa* situation.

44. If a rich man has paid bridewealth for a poor man it must now be regarded as a loan. If a rich man paid bridewealth for a *nsugwa* prior to the abolition of this custom, the payment must be considered as a loan repayable at the latest when a daughter of the *nsugwa* marries.

45. If the *nsugwa* should acquire property, the rich man is entitled to claim repayment of the loan before the daughter of the *nsugwa* marries.

46. The *nsugwa* cannot make a counter-claim in respect of work which he states that he has done in the house of the rich man.

NOTE. These rules (43 to 46) were decided upon by the chiefs of the Sukuma Federation and their people in 1949. Formerly it was a frequent custom for a rich man to pay bridewealth for a *nsugwa*, which payment entitled the rich man to receive bridewealth paid for the *nsugwa's* daughter.

NOTE. It is doubtful whether the gift of freedom is always understood by the *nsugwa*; a *nsugwa* who has acquired property may not agree to pay his debt, preferring to pay many times more when his daughters marry; or the *nsugwa* may try to evade payment by making a counter-claim for salary due in respect of the years when he worked in the rich man's house. The rich man will probably then present his bill for keep, doctor's fees, payment of tax, and for a pair of trousers and so on *ad infinitum*. The fact is that no contract was made and the *nsugwa* was always free to leave.

*Bridewealth paid on behalf of a man who is not a member of the family*

47. If a man pays bridewealth on behalf of another man who does not belong to the family (paternal or maternal) the latter becomes thereby a member of the former's family.

NOTE. Cases of this kind are not frequent and happen only in special circumstances, for instance:

D.C.'s Appeal No. 16/46. Ibadakuli (Uchungwa). *Ntima* v. *Shija.*

The father of Ntima, when a child, had been found and adopted by Humanga, whose name he took and in whose house he grew up. Humanga paid bridewealth for his marriage, of which Ntima was the offspring. Ntima claimed from Shija, a descendant by blood, a share in the property inherited from Humanga. The court ruled that Ntima must be regarded as a member of the family and entitled to a share of the property.

Basiha (Nyegezi) No. 69/46. *Magunga* v. *Holo.*

The court held that Magunga, who was a freed slave and for whom Holo's father had paid bridewealth, must be considered a member of the family.

### Bridewealth paid after the father's death

#### Monogamous household

48. If a daughter marries after her father's death her bridewealth is received by the *nkuruwabo* (first-born son).

#### Polygynous household

49. If a daughter marries after her father's death her bridewealth is received by her eldest full brother.

50. If one of the widows has no son the bridewealth for her daughter is received by the *nkuruwabo* of the deceased father, i.e. by the *nkuruwabo* of the whole polygynous family.

NOTE. He can use these cattle to pay bridewealth for any younger son of the family; he is the deputy of the father.

51. Usually the marriage-cattle of a daughter who has no brothers are kept by her mother, but the *nkuruwabo* of the family has the right of disposal.

52. If there are only daughters in the family the co-guardian and the mother receive the bridewealth (332).

53. If the bride is an adult and has no living male relative, her bridewealth may be accepted by any friend of her family, but he receives the cattle only in trust and the woman herself is the owner.

D.C.'s Appeal No. 85/41. Nyanza Federation (Bukumbi). *Bt. Nabesa* v. *Nbushi.*

When the father and uncle of Bt. Nabesa, both Ha tribesmen, arrived in Mwanza many years ago they formed a close friendship with Nbushi. They died before Bt. Nabesa married. When she did marry, Nbushi received her bridewealth of eight cattle. Bt. Nabesa now claimed the return of ten cattle as her property. Nbushi was an old man and she was obviously afraid that her cattle would be inherited by Nbushi's children after their father's death. The court held that the cattle had to be considered Bt. Nabesa's property, and that she therefore could dispose of them as she liked.

The African assessors stated: According to the native bridewealth law, the bridewealth must go to the senior male relative when the father dies and leaves a daughter who subsequently marries. If there is none, the recipients are the mother and the co-guardian. After the mother's death the daughter herself inherits these cattle. The cattle cannot become the property of a friend of the father no matter how great a friend he may have been.

## METHODS OF PAYING BRIDEWEALTH

A. The usual customary bridewealth is paid either in full before marriage, or in instalments, of which one is paid before marriage and the remainder afterwards.

B. In certain circumstances a nominal bridewealth is paid.

### A (i) *Bridewealth paid in full before marriage*

54. The total number of cattle is handed over in one delivery. Bridewealth is never paid in instalments before the marriage. The young wife follows her husband into his or his family's house after the wedding.

NOTE. This arrangement is seldom made except in SS, KS, and SM, where it is the usual one.

### A (ii) *Bridewealth paid in instalments before and after marriage*

55. Usually the wedding takes place after the payment of the first instalment, which seldom amounts to less than half the whole bridewealth. The instalments paid after marriage may be large or small. It is not the practice to fix the amount or to make any agreement or promise regarding the dates of later payments.

(*Magasa gatashilaga*—the debt of bridewealth never ends.)

56. The father of the bride has the right to claim payment of outstanding instalments by court action.

57. The father is not allowed to recall his daughter in the event of non-payment except in BSN, NF, UF, where the father may send for his daughter and forbid her to return to her husband until the rest of the bridewealth has been paid. The husband is allowed to visit his wife in her father's home; if he chooses he may come and live with his father-in-law. This situation is only possible if the son-in-law has not paid the *ng'ombe ya butigu* (26).

NOTE. Such cases are very rare; they may occur if the son-in-law has property and openly refuses payment.

58. If the non-payment of the *ng'ombe ya butigu* is obviously intentional, since the son-in-law has cattle, the court may decide that the son-in-law must pay the remaining instalments of bridewealth immediately.

NOTE. Cases of this kind are extremely rare, and in many chiefdoms the courts would refuse to hear such cases and would refer them to the family council. Litigation between close relatives is made as difficult as possible by the court functionaries, as the fact of having made the family quarrel public will itself militate against later reconciliation. Should a party insist on bringing the case to court, the court will not refuse, on principle, to hear it.

59. A father has no right to forbid his daughter to leave the district with her husband even if the bridewealth is not fully paid; a wife is free to follow her husband.

60. Any unpaid portion of bridewealth remains a debt to which no rule of limitation is applicable. If a daughter marries before her mother's bridewealth has been paid in full, the mother's father, or her nearest paternal relative, has the right to claim payment of the old debt out of the daughter's bridewealth.

61. If a husband dies, the kinsman who inherits the widow as his leviratic wife must complete payment of any outstanding portion of the bridewealth; he takes over, with the widow, all the obligations of the deceased husband.

62. If a wife dies before the last instalment of bridewealth has been paid, the husband must complete payment of the outstanding portion (*magasa*).

NOTE. This rule was decided upon by the chiefs of the Sukuma Federation and their people in 1949. Formerly different rules existed in the various chiefdoms.

(a) BD, KF, BS except SBS. The husband had to complete payment of the bridewealth as above.

(b) UF, NF, BSN, ZM, SM. Before 1939 the husband was entitled to claim repayment of bridewealth already paid (confirmed in D.C.'s appeal No. 33/43 of NF). Between 1939 and 1949 the husband did not need to complete payment but could not claim repayment of bridewealth already paid.

(c) SBS. If the wife who died left children, the husband had to complete payment of bridewealth. If there were no children, the husband did not have to complete payment.

(d) SS, KS. The father-in-law and the husband divided the bridewealth already paid into two halves, and each took one. For each child the husband had to leave his father-in-law the usual amount of cattle.

NOTE. Customarily, at the death of a husband or a wife, the family of the deceased must pay to the surviving spouse one head of cattle, called *ngombe ya ntwe*. In the case of the wife's death it is a cow; in the case of the husband's death, a bull, but the widow is only given the bull if she severs connexion with the deceased husband's family.

NOTE. In NF, UF, KF this custom is not known. In KS the present is a *mbuli ya ntwe*.

## B. *Nominal bridewealth*

63. Bridewealth amounting to only one to three head of cattle is paid in cases where the bride and bridegroom are considered too old to have children. If the husband dies, repayment of bridewealth cannot be claimed if the widow herself is not inherited, i.e. if she returns to her own family.

NOTE. This applies to a marriage between old people who marry for the sake of mutual assistance to keep a household going. If the woman should give birth to a child (no such case is remembered), it would belong to the husband. When the bridewealth is handed over, it is expressly stated before witnesses that it is a nominal bridewealth. The one or two beasts are called *ngombe ya lina*—cattle of the grave—because they are, figuratively, buried and will never return to the payer. Another expression is *ngombe ya kipya moto*—cattle of being burned by fire—because the woman can only expect to be hurt by fire but not by the virility of her husband.

## REPAYMENT OF BRIDEWEALTH

The man who pays back the bridewealth is called *njimuji*; the man who receives the repayment is called *njimulilwa*.

### General rules

64. The obligation of a father-in-law or his legal substitute to return bridewealth or a part of it arises in consequence of divorce or the return of a widow to her family.

NOTE. The rules concerning repayment of bridewealth in case of divorce are applied with great flexibility in individual cases. The particular circumstances, i.e. the cause of divorce, the personal relations between son-in-law and father-in-law, their economic positions, and the existence of children (sentimental, as well as legal factors being considered) often determine the use which is made of the legal possibilities. For instance, if father-in-law and son-in-law are on good terms and the wife's family has done its best to prevent the divorce, but the wife, who has borne a child, insists on it, the husband might take his child and give up all claim to repayment of the remainder of the bridewealth.

65. The amount of bridewealth due to be repaid and the procedure for repayment are determined by the court.

66. *Kujimula ng'ombe* is performed in public near the court house (*ibanza*). The father-in-law brings the cattle to be returned to the court house where they are taken over by the son-in-law and his party.

67. The son-in-law is not allowed to seize by force the cattle which the court has decided are due to him.

Nyanza Federation Appeal 41/43. Ilemera. *Court* v. *Lutenga.*

Lutenga was granted a divorce and return of bridewealth. He went to his father-in-law's village and took the cattle by force, i.e. he drove them off without waiting till they were handed over to him. He was fined Shs.25/-.

68. If the father-in-law does not possess the means to return the required number of cattle in accordance with the decision of the court, the unpaid balance becomes a common debt.

69. This is a preferential debt. If and when the former wife remarries it must be returned from the bridewealth paid by the second husband (100).

70. If the original cattle of bridewealth are still in the possession of the father-in-law, the son-in-law has the right to insist that they be returned.

NOTE. If the father has received a heifer and kept it in his herd until it becomes a cow, he must return this cow.

71. If the original cattle are not in his possession the father-in-law need not return beasts of the same quality as those he received. The length of time the couple have been married is taken into consideration, but the son-in-law can refuse to accept totally useless animals.

NOTE. It is explained thus: the cow may be old now, but so is the wife. For instance, if the son-in-law paid a heifer seven years ago among other beasts and it has been used by the father and is no longer in the herd, the father must return a cow which may be expected to calve once more.

72. If the son-in-law for the above or other reasons refuses to accept the cattle of bridewealth returned to him, and the court considers his refusal not justified, it can order him to accept the cattle. If he does not obey the order, the father-in-law can be told to bring the cattle to the court house and leave them there at the husband's risk.

NOTE. The following case confirms that the usual reason for a refusal is that the husband wishes to obstruct the divorce out of spite, so that his wife cannot remarry.

D.C.'s Appeal Case 65/45. From Ngambo Federation Court. *Mayige* v. *Kusakamala.*

Mayige claimed return of bridewealth from his wife's father. The latter had no cattle and it was decided that he should pay when his daughter remarried. She married Kusakamala who paid bridewealth for her, which the father sent to Mayige. Mayige refused to accept them because he disliked Kusakamala and the father returned the cattle to Kusakamala (obviously afraid to keep them, see para. 34); Kusakamala continued to live with his wife and Mayige filed a suit for adultery. The court held that Kusakamala must be considered a bona fide husband and that Mayige had no right to claim compensation for adultery.

73. The son-in-law can demand the repayment of bridewealth in the same commodities in which he paid it. For instance, if he paid cattle, he can ask that the father-in-law should pay back cattle. If the father-in-law has no cattle but offers repayment in money or goats, the son-in-law cannot be forced to accept such payment. He can wait at his own risk until the father-in-law acquires cattle (68).

74. The existence of tribal *bupugo* ('joking' relationship) between father-in-law and son-in-law does not debar either party from filing a suit against the other.

NOTE. Formerly special rules existed for repayment of bridewealth between men who had a *bupugo* relationship, but the following leading case expresses the present view.

D.C.'s Appeal 17/47. Usega Fed. Appeal 4/46. *Kabuli* v. *Nghelepe.*

The judgement (*in extenso*) says:

'The issue in this case for decision is as to whether the appellant is debarred under tribal law and custom from entering a suit for the recovery of bridewealth on the ground of *bupugo*. From inquiry in other parts of the district I gather that this custom was practised throughout NF, UF, but that it is now considered to be obsolete by most Native Authorities. In my opinion the sooner that it is extinct the better, as it appears entirely to conflict with British principles of common sense and justice.

'On these latter grounds I allow the appeal with costs and uphold the judgement entered in the court of origin.'

It has been confirmed that although it may still happen that one partner to a *bupugo* will not file a suit against the other, such an attitude is his private affair. Courts would hear such cases and would not acknowledge an argument of the defendant that a decision of the court in such a case would be *ultra vires*.

Characteristic of the Sukuma people is the *bupugo* which exists between members of certain families or between inhabitants of certain chiefdoms, for instance, between the following families: Siha and Golo; Binza and Kwimba; and between the following chiefdoms: Mwanza and Masanza I and II; Nasa and Nera, Bujashi; Beda and Bujashi; Busukuma and Msalala; Negezi and Bujashi; Bujashi and Negezi, Iwanda, Nyamhanda; Busmao and Busukuma; Buhungukira and Nasa; Luhumbo and Busukuma.

The *bupugo* between these groups of people in most cases originated in some event in the past, usually an alliance in tribal wars. The parties to a *bupugo* were not allowed to fight each other, but when they did fight, the man who shed the blood of his 'brother' was killed even if he had only wounded him. It was held that their property was held in common; for instance, if a Siha took a beast from a Golo, there was no case of theft; but he had to drive it away openly in the daytime and not steal it at night.

75. In all cases of repayment of bridewealth the offspring of the animals of the original bridewealth need not be returned, except that any calves which are still suckling have to be returned with the mother for good.

76. The repayment of bridewealth can only be claimed from the man who received the bridewealth or from his heirs.

77. If, after her father's death, a daughter should be granted a divorce, her divorced husband may claim repayment of bridewealth from the *nkuruwabo* of the deceased.

78. It is a legal obligation on all heirs to contribute towards repayment of bridewealth.

NOTE. This rule was decided upon by the chiefs of the Sukuma Federation and their people in 1949. Formerly it was within the discretion of the other heirs whether or not to help the *nkuruwabo* in making such payment.

NOTE. This rule may be considered as the logical consequence of paragraph 48 and as being in accordance with the provision of paragraph 621.

Although up to now occasions when brothers refused financial help have been rare, a case is remembered in which a number of brothers all inherited property from their father but later, when bridewealth had to be repaid for a divorced sister, one of the brothers, who was doing well as cook to a European, did not respond to the demand of the *nkuruwabo* for help.

Such cases may grow in number in future.

79. If a father leaves no sons and his daughters inherit the property, which may include their bridewealth, the negotiations concerning repayment of bridewealth take place between the husband of the divorcee and her nearest paternal relative.

## Repayment of ceremonial beasts

80. The rules differ in the various areas, but no attempt has been made to unify them because these payments are purely customary.

A. *Ng'ombe* or *mbuli ya maji* (24) is not returned if bridewealth is returned.

D.C.'s Appeal No. 27/48. Nyanza Federation. *Kabesa* v. *Milembe*.

The court stated in its judgement that a *ng'ombe ya maji* never has to be returned even if the beast has not been killed.

This applies in all chiefdoms except SBS, SS, KS, where it has to be returned.

B. *Mbuli* or *ng'ombe ya kilezu* (25) is not returnable if bridewealth is returned. All chiefdoms except KF, SS, KS, where it has to be returned.

C. *Ng'ombe ya butigu* (26) is returnable if bridewealth is returned— (NF, UF, KF, BSN); is not returnable if bridewealth is returned— (BS, SBS, SS, KS).

D. *Ng'ombe ya kugila* (27) is returnable if bridewealth is returned, but only if the husband's father paid it and the wife's father did not make the counter gift—(BS, SS, KS, BSN, BD, KF); is not returnable if bridewealth is returned—(UF, NF).

E. *Mbuli ya luswagilo* (28) is not returnable if bridewealth is returned.

F. *Tumbati or Shs.2/-* (29) is not returnable if bridewealth is returned.

## Repayment of bridewealth in case of divorce

81. The number of cattle which the father-in-law has to return to his son-in-law depends on:

(i) the reasons for the divorce, which have to be examined by the court.

(ii) the number of children of the marriage, whether living or dead.

### (i) *Reasons for divorce*

82. The rules relating to the guilt of either party are enumerated in para. 258.

### (ii) *Number of children*

83. The father-in-law is entitled to keep back from the bridewealth:

A. For each living child (male or female) five cattle.

B. In the chiefdoms of SM, for each child born fifty hoes or Shs.50/-.

C. In cases where either the father-in-law or the husband is a chief the rate is for each living child ten cattle, and for each dead child five cattle.

D. In cases where the husband or the father-in-law is a *ng'wanangwa*, *munang'oma*, a direct descendant of a chief, a regent, or a deposed chief the rate is for each living child six cattle, and for each dead child three cattle. Formerly the relevant rules differed in various chiefdoms.

1. In UF, NF, KF, BSN, BD, for each child two cattle were retained by the father-in-law.

2. In BS, SS the husband might choose either to take the children and lose the whole bridewealth, or to hand over all the children to the father-in-law and take the whole bridewealth.

3. In SBS, for each male child the father-in-law kept five cattle, and for each female child seven cattle.

4. In KS, for each male child the father-in-law kept two cattle, and for each female child three cattle.

NOTE. Formerly it was not the custom for a chief to claim repayment of bride-wealth if he returned his wife to her father, but only if she deserted him. This rule is no longer operative.

P.C.'s Appeal Case 61/42. Ngambo Federation. *Ntemi Chasama* v. *Dulumo*.

The court held that the chief was entitled to the repayment of bridewealth.

84. The father-in-law is entitled to retain two beasts from the bride-wealth for each child born alive but who subsequently died, for each still-born child, or for a foetus whose existence has been certified by a female relative of the husband (602B). Formerly the rules varied according to whether the children were alive or had died.

(*a*) NF, UF, KF, BD, BSN. Children born alive who had later died were taken into consideration.

(*b*) BS, SS, KS. Children who had died were not counted.

D.C.'s Appeal Case No. 5/45. Nyanza Federation. *Maria* v. *Dyonisi*.

Maria gave birth to three children, one of whom died as a baby. When later a divorce was granted, her husband disputed the deduction of two beasts from the bridewealth for the child who had died. The court held that the father-in-law had the right to deduct two beasts.

D.C.'s Appeal No. 2/42. Fulo (Mwanza). *Bt. Jeko* v. *Nyigombejo*.

Bt. Jeko had borne seven children of whom five had died. Bridewealth paid amounted to nine cattle. A divorce was granted and the court held that the father-in-law should retain four head of cattle for the two living children and five head for the five dead ones.

The second case shows that no father-in-law can demand more than the original number of cattle paid as bridewealth, however many children may be born as a result of the union.

NOTE. Rules 81–84 were decided upon by the chiefs of the Sukuma Federation and their people in 1949.

### *In case of return of widow to her own family*

A. *Childless widow*

85 A. If the widow refuses to be inherited, bridewealth has to be returned in full (603).

B. If the next-of-kin refuses to inherit the widow, i.e. if none of the kinsmen agrees to take her as his leviratic wife, half the bridewealth has to be returned (604).

NOTE. This rule was agreed by the chiefs of the Sukuma Federation and their people in 1949. Formerly the full bridewealth had to be returned in either case.

NOTE. The right of the heirs to claim return of bridewealth for a widow needs no justification in the Sukuma mind. As J. H. Driberg writes in *At Home with the Savage*: 'Although marriage is an affair between two individuals, it is also a contract between two groups, families or clans. The marriage contract between these two groups is not terminated by death. The rights implied by the levirate, however, cut both ways. The inheritance of a widow serves as much to ensure her maintenance as to assume marital rights over her. To deny the marital rights must logically absolve the husband's heir from the duty of maintenance. A precipitate change in these rules would work out to the disadvantage of the widows, although it might be intended to improve their fate.'

Cases are not rare in which an old widow who has never had children is returned to her family by the heirs of her deceased husband. Such action is not looked upon as unethical; its justification lies in the fact that as a rule—at least until recently—the bridewealth is paid with cattle from the paternal herd in order that the children of the marriage should belong to the paternal family. The bride's father receives the bridewealth, but his side of the contract is not fulfilled if his daughter produces no children. Therefore the husband's family has the right to return the daughter to her paternal family and claim return of bridewealth. The action of the husband in not returning his barren wife may be understandable, but it cannot determine the attitude of the rest of the family.

D.C.'s Appeal No. 13/39. Fulo (Bukumbi). *Salingu* v. *Mununa.*

In this case the original Native Court decided that bridewealth had to be returned. The Appeal Court gave the decision that no bridewealth had to be returned. Salingu's younger brother married Mununa's sister 27 years ago, and paid bridewealth of 9 cattle. After 27 years of married life, during which no child was born, the husband died. Salingu claimed return of full bridewealth from the wife's brother. The assessors stated: prior to 1922 the bridewealth had to be returned in full. From 1922 to 1933 the courts usually decided that no bridewealth was to be repaid in such cases as the deceased husband had presumably had value for his bridewealth. From 1933 onwards, however, the opinion of the courts varied, some deciding that bridewealth should be returned and some that it should not be returned.

Cases are also known in which the courts did not follow the rule, for instance:

D.C.'s Appeal No. 45/45. Fulo (Bukumbi). *Lweyo* v. *Ntemi Kisabo.*

Lweyo claimed return of bridewealth because, after his brother's death, the widow returned to her father when the heirs refused to inherit her. The widow remarried later and bridewealth was paid for her. Many years later Lweyo brought the case into court, and the Appeal Court was informed by a letter, DC/4/159 of 19.9.44 signed by several chiefs of the Nyanza Federation, that if the heirs of a deceased husband refuse to inherit (*kumpokea*) the widow and take responsibility for her maintenance they cannot claim return of her bridewealth. The court decided accordingly.

86. The relative who inherits the widow with the consent of the family council (600) is entitled to claim the bridewealth due if the couple should later separate, but only if the widow leaves her deceased husband's family and returns to her own family. If the widow or her leviratic husband decides to separate and the widow chooses another member of the same family by consent of its council, no return of bridewealth can be claimed by the first leviratic husband.

D

87. A widow has the right to refuse to be inherited by a distant relative if a nearer one exists.

NOTE. In the same way, the family of the deceased husband can refuse to allow the widow to be inherited by a distant relative.

88. If a change of leviratic husband has taken place the last husband, not the first, is entitled to receive the bridewealth which has to be paid back. This rule is confirmed in Appeal No. 38/46 of Ibadakuli SBS (Busiha).

B. *Widow with children alive or having borne children who subsequently died*

89 A. For each child alive five head of cattle are deducted from the bridewealth which has to be returned.

B. For each child who has died two cattle are deducted.

C. Any bridewealth remaining has to be repaid if the widow refuses to be inherited and/or refuses to remain with the deceased husband's family.

D. Half of any bridewealth remaining has to be repaid if the widow is returned to her family by the heirs (610).

NOTE. This rule was decided upon by the chiefs of the Sukuma Federation and their people in 1949. Formerly two head of cattle were deducted for each child.

90 A. If any of the close kinsmen of the deceased renounce their right to claim the return of bridewealth, or any part of it, a divorce certificate (*Nyaluba ya bushimbe*) must be issued before the widow or the paternal relatives can consider the matter settled (261).

B. After the issue of a divorce certificate the deceased husband's relatives have no right to prevent the remarriage of the widow. If the close kinsmen of the deceased husband have renounced their right to any part of the bridewealth and a divorce certificate has been issued, the father of the widow is allowed to accept bridewealth for her if she remarries.

91. If the widow is a *nkima wa bugongo* (38) the same rules as above are applicable, but the decision in the case of a refusal of the widow to be inherited, lies not with the paternal relatives of the deceased husband but with his maternal relatives, i.e. with those who paid the bridewealth for his wife who is now a widow.

### In case of sickness of wife

92. If a wife becomes insane or incurably sick the husband cannot return her to her family nor is he permitted to claim repayment of bridewealth.

93. If the wife falls sick with leprosy or epilepsy her husband is entitled to return her to her family, but he can only claim repayment of half of the bridewealth. If there are children the usual rules apply (83).

NOTE. These two diseases (leprosy and epilepsy) constitute an exception to the rule because they are considered to be hereditary (*busatu wa kibyalilwe*), unlike other diseases which could have been contracted during married life.

94. If the husband falls sick with one of the above diseases and his wife wishes to leave him, the husband is entitled to claim the return of the full bridewealth. If there are children the usual rules apply (83).

NOTE. The rules of paras. 93 and 94 were agreed by the chiefs of the Sukuma Federation and their people in 1949. Formerly no rules existed and the courts differed greatly in their judgements.

### In case of death of wife

95. If a wife for whom bridewealth, or any portion of it, has been paid dies, no repayment—either wholly or in part—is required.

NOTE. The husband is still liable to pay any portion of bridewealth still outstanding at his wife's death (62).

NOTE. Cases concerning repayment of bridewealth in the event of the wife's death are frequent although the law is very clear.

D.C.'s Appeal No. 64/45. Ngambo Federation. *Ntemi Nonga v. Singu.*

Nonga's wife died five years after their marriage. The court held that he was not entitled to claim return of bridewealth. The court stated: If this man wishes return of bridewealth he may first try and revive the dead and return her to her family. If he cannot do this, he cannot get anything.

D.C.'s Appeal No. 32/45. Nyanza Federation. *Mugaka v. Nyanda.*

Mugaka's son, an Askari, married Nyanda's daughter when on leave. After two nights of married life he returned to duty, and in the course of the next twelve months his wife died. His father now claimed on his behalf return of bridewealth. All the Nyanza chiefs agreed that a wife's death is no ground for the return of bridewealth. The court held that Mugaka's claim was unfounded. It was just bad luck that his son received so little value for his outlay.

Similar cases were decided in the same way:

D.C.'s Appeal No. 16/46. Nyanza Federation.

Demand for return of bridewealth after the wife's death was refused.

D.C.'s Appeal No. 5/46. Usega Federation.

The wife died after one month of married life and the court refused a demand for return of bridewealth.

D.C.'s Appeal No. 9/43. Bukumbi. *Sweke v. Kilesa.*

Sweke claimed return of bridewealth when his wife, Kilesa's daughter, died one month after marriage. The court held that no bridewealth had to be repaid.

Cases are known in which a wife has died before consummation of marriage was possible, although the marriage was validly celebrated. The difficulty of deciding such cases may be overcome by reference to the custom mentioned in the following case:

D.C.'s Appeal No. 22/46. Ibadakuli (Seke). *Mwandu v. Saganda.*

Mwandu paid bridewealth of twelve cattle for Saganda's daughter. When the girl arrived at the bridegroom's house she was taken ill, developed a high fever and died, after a few days, of smallpox. The fact that Mwandu did not shave his head, which would have been his unavoidable duty as a husband, decided the case in his favour and the court held that Saganda must return the bridewealth to Mwandu (97).

96. The cause of death is not taken into consideration, and death by suicide is included.

NOTE. Death by suicide is treated in the same way as natural death because the wife's suicide is nearly always motivated by dissatisfaction with her married life.
Wrong decisions of the courts are to be found. For example:
D.C.'s Appeal No. 14/41. Nyanza Federation. *Gagi* v. *Bulendu*.
Gagi's wife was Bulendu's sister. She committed suicide. The court agreed that half of the bridewealth should be returned to the husband.

## Repayment of instalments of bridewealth if the engagement is dissolved

97. If an engagement is dissolved by one of the two parties or if one of them dies, the instalments of bridewealth in cattle already paid are returned together with their offspring. If the girl dissolves the engagement, she must return all gifts which she has received from her bridegroom. If the bridegroom dissolves it, he cannot claim return of the gifts which he has given to his bride.

NOTE. It is a widespread custom for bride and bridegroom to exchange gifts; the bridegroom usually gives the bride one or more bracelets of beads or metal known as *isanga lyumu*—dry bracelet. If the bridegroom still has doubts about the feelings of his bride, and wishes to make the betrothal sure, he seeks to meet the bride and sleep with her. This intercourse is called the *isanga lidoto*—the wet bracelet—and is only permitted after the payment of the first instalment of bridewealth; the fiancé does not try to persuade the girl to have sexual intercourse with him before the wedding is definitely fixed. Such a demand might endanger the engagement as the girl would regard talk about marriage as no more than a ruse to persuade her. In the minds of the people proposals for a passing liaison and wooing for marriage are two quite distinct issues.

98. If a woman lives in concubinage and dies in the house of her lover who has begun to pay an instalment of bridewealth towards their intended marriage, the cattle of such instalment need not be repaid.

NOTE. An instalment paid towards bridewealth is regarded as compensation for the time the daughter spent in the lover's house.

## Repayment of bridewealth in case of remarriage

99. If the father-in-law has not completed the repayment of bridewealth after his daughter has been divorced he must pay his debt immediately on receiving bridewealth for her second marriage (69, 73).

100 A. This debt has priority over any other. The former son-in-law has the right to claim the amount which the father of his former wife owes him direct from any person to whom the father may have given the cattle of the second bridewealth.

B. If the father has used these cattle as bridewealth payment for one of his sons, his former son-in-law has the first claim on them and they must be handed over to him. This may cause the son's marriage to become a concubinage except in areas where a *ng'ombe ya maji* is paid. There the marriage would remain valid and the *ng'ombe ya maji* would be regarded as bridewealth.

### Repayment of bridewealth on demand of third party

101. Any paternal or maternal relative who has given cattle to a member of the family for payment of bridewealth has the right to claim the repayment of these cattle direct from the relative of the wife who received her bridewealth.

102. The donor has this right only when he has given cattle which he acquired himself. If the cattle he gave were inherited they are reckoned an unconditional gift to the bridegroom.

103. The only permissible reason for exercising this right and taking away cattle of bridewealth when the marriage has not been dissolved is if a gross breach of convention has been committed by the man on whose behalf the relative paid bridewealth; for instance, if he should beat the wife of the donor or cohabit with her. The donor is not permitted to exercise this right simply because he is in need of cattle.

104. If the donor, having given the full amount of bridewealth to his relative, should take it away the legitimate children would become illegitimate as a consequence of his action. (Cases are rare, but have been known.)

105 A. If a daughter-in-law refuses to obey the orders of her father-in-law or her brother-in-law (whichever is the head of the family) during the absence of her husband, his representative has the right to claim divorce and repayment of bridewealth, and this can be done without consulting the husband.

B. If the daughter-in-law becomes pregnant or gives birth to a child during the absence of her husband and it is obvious that the child cannot be that of the absentee husband, the representative of the absentee (father or brother) has the right to claim divorce and repayment of bridewealth.

C. The family representative of the absentee husband (father or brother) is entitled to claim divorce and repayment of bridewealth if he decides that on account of certain occurrences the family of the daughter-in-law are people with whom relationship by marriage is undesirable.

P.C.'s Appeal No. 3/46. Nyanza Federation. *Futi* v. *Malugu.*

The brother of Futi's wife had killed one of his brothers with a knife. Futi was absent at the time of the crime, but his father wished to sever all connexion with such a bad family and therefore claimed divorce on behalf of his absent son and return of bridewealth. A part of the bridewealth had already been repaid by the time Futi returned. The wife was then living with Malugu and Futi claimed compensation for adultery from Malugu.

The court held that the divorce was valid, although the husband was absent when it was granted, as the father was entitled to claim it on behalf of his son. No compensation was awarded.

## Limitations on filing a suit

106. Action for repayment of bridewealth can be brought before a court any time after a divorce has been granted, unless the legal claimant has renounced his right before witnesses.

# CHAPTER II

## MARRIAGE

### INTRODUCTION

AT the age of about ten years boys cease to sleep in their parents' house and move into the *maji* (in the south called *ibanza*). This is a simple hut, in no way distinguishable from the other houses of the village. In the north it is often situated within the boundaries of a homestead where the unmarried sons of the house and other boys of neighbours live together. The *maji*, however, is open to any man who wishes to sleep there. Boys, adolescent men, bachelors of any age, married men who have quarrelled with their wives and wish to punish them by their absence, and passing strangers may use the *maji* as a lodging-house.[1]

Girls do not sleep in their parents' house after the first menstruation. They have their own *maji* (*ibanza*) which is established in the house of an old married couple of the village. No special arrangements are made by the villagers for opening a *maji*. Often a girl goes to sleep in the outer room (*ibindo*) of her grandparents' hut where she is joined by a few girls of her own age, if the grandparents agree. Some old people like to have the *maji* in their house, because they like the laughter and liveliness of the young folk; others refuse because of the noise and the responsibility involved. If there are many girls in a village ready to join the *maji*, a special hut may be built for them, close to the homestead of a father with several daughters. Sometimes an empty hut in the village may be turned into a *maji*.

In the *maji* there is no leader, no special discipline, and no teaching. A girl cannot change her *maji* without good reason, but must remain in the one she first entered. The girls return early in the morning to their parents' house where they help their mothers in the daily work. The inhabitants of a *maji* are free to leave it at night, and not only the young men of the village, but married men also call at the house and frequently invite the girls to dances (*bina*). It is not good form for a man to enter the *maji* at night, but the evenings are spent in conversation and flirting (*wikologosha* or *nabalabya*). A community spirit prevails among the village youth which does not allow a young man, and especially a stranger, to interfere in the love affair of another man. The *maji* time, especially during the first few years, is a very happy phase, but sexual intercourse is in no way its sole purpose. In many cases the state of semi-virginity is retained for a long time. The behaviour of the girls is not criticized by

---

[1] This institution is not the same as the bachelors' and unmarried girls' houses, so often described by travellers in areas inhabited by Papuo-Melanesians. The *maji* never serves unmarried couples as permanent or temporary quarters.

the community as long as they observe the conventions of their position which demand not chastity but discretion.

As far as their relations with men are concerned, the girls have only one duty, which is to inform the 'lady of the house' if they change a lover. If changes happen too often, a girl is warned that she is likely to get a bad name for fickleness; but it is also not proper for a girl to consort with the same lover for any considerable time, because the parents fear that the girl and her lover may finally decide to live in concubinage, a step which would spoil the marriage prospects of the girl and deprive her family of an immediate payment of bridewealth. The ideal behaviour for a girl while living in the *maji* is to have a few lovers, so as to gain sufficient experience for a good wife, and to marry at the age of about 18 to 20 years. Sometimes, though less often than might be expected,[1] the sojourn in the *maji* ends with pregnancy. In such a case the 'lady of the house' can probably help to ascertain the father of the illegitimate child (for legal implications see 276 et seq.). Nowhere in Sukumaland is the human value of a female depreciated by an event which proves her ability to bear children.

Boys and girls enjoy a great measure of understanding on the part of older persons. They are not expected to take life too seriously, and they are not scorned if they dance during moonlight nights and sleep the greater part of the day. They often go to dances in distant villages and parents are not expected to persuade or command their boys and girls to stay at home working instead of dancing. Life for them is not all dancing and flirting, however. For considerable periods when field-work has to be done, no *mbina* takes place and young and old alike work in the fields. It will be noted (Introduction to Chapter IV) that a child learns early in life to handle a hoe.

As soon as a boy reaches the age of about thirteen years he is called into the *elika* of the *kibanda* in which he lives; he is told to come next morning to a certain holding and to participate in the communal work which has been arranged by a peasant of the village and the *nsumba ntale*. This very important step in the life of a Sukuma boy is taken without ceremony. From this day onwards, until he is called by the *banamhara* into the *ihane*, he remains a *nsumba* and is under the discipline of the village organization of his age group.

A few years later he may enter as a pupil into one of the many secret or dance societies, which are not only social clubs but have their special codes of discipline which the pupil is taught during his initiation. If a society of this kind has also a certain purpose, such as game hunting, snake-charming, or porcupine hunting, the young man is occupied with

---

[1] Certain contraceptive measures are common knowledge among women and the girls are instructed in them. For instance, *coitus interruptus*, no intercourse 5–6 days after menses, ablutions, and the use of decoctions prepared from leaves of *Aloe vulgaris* (*lukaka*) or from powdered roots of *Plumbago zeylanica* (*nshoto*); the first medicine is taken internally; the second is applied to the *os uteri*.

many duties in connexion with the magic aspects of his society; above all he has to obey the orders of the older members and observe the discipline which they demand from the pupils. Members of these societies also spend many days at field-work organized on a system of mutual help.

The organization of the women and girls of a village is less strict and does not play the same role in public life as does that of men. But there is no such thing as a young girl who does nothing. Not only does a mother expect her daughter's assistance in the house, but grandmothers, aunts, and other female relatives also expect help, now and then, from the young girls.

The foregoing description of the young people's life might suggest that marriage is a superfluous institution, but marriage here as everywhere else has its advantages, and both bridegroom and bride are well aware from the start of its social implications. The main points are:

A. Legitimacy of children (265).
B. A bachelor always occupies an inferior place in the public life of the village. He cannot be chosen for the posts of *nsumba ntale* or *munyampara*.
C. Economic advantages (Introduction to Chapter III).
D. By marriage the circle of relatives is widened and the security of the individual is thereby enhanced (Introduction to Chapter I).
E. Regularity of life becomes at a certain age a desirable object.
F. Public approval of the matrimonial status as such.

Marriage is taken as seriously in Sukumaland as anywhere else, even though a considerable number of divorces occur, because the advantages of marriage once attained are not lost, whatever the fate of the parties to the union. The house is built, the family is founded, and changes in it do not greatly affect the status of the people concerned. As a matter of fact, existing conventions take into account the insecurity of a customary marriage, as is shown by the attitude of a wife towards her family after marriage and theirs towards her; she remains in close contact with them and in case of distress the family will hardly question whether she is right or wrong, but will support her.

## FORMS OF MARRIAGE[1]

### I. *Kulunja*

107. This is the common form of customary marriage in which the preliminaries and the ceremonies themselves follow the prescribed customary procedure.

108. If a man has serious intentions he tries to make the acquaintance of a girl during the day—on the roadside, in the market, or by waiting

---

[1] Variations in the preliminaries leading to customary marriage exist, and further variations of detail occur in different areas. In the following description minor differences are not mentioned.

for her on her way to fetch water. Or he may make a visit to a friend or a relative and have a look round for any available girls. Sometimes meetings may be pre-arranged by parents or relatives, but it is a very strict rule that no pressure is exerted by the girl's parents in favour of any one suitor. The young people themselves must first agree to marry, and then the girl gives the young man permission to arrange the next steps. The father will always ask for a definite decision before he accepts bridewealth. This procedure is customary whether a man is single or is already married and wishes to take a second wife.

After the two young persons have agreed to marry, the man informs his father, though the girl may delay telling the news to her parents until she sees whether the man keeps his promise. Thereupon the negotiations regarding bridewealth and other details of the marriage can start.

NOTE. In a court case a girl said, with the anger of violated right in her voice: 'My father did not allow me to marry the man I love; he refused to have him as a son-in-law. He wished to choose my husband for me. I did not agree and thus I finally left my father's house and went to live with my lover.' The court and listeners sympathized with the girl and found the attitude of the father improper.

109. The first step, if the two families do not know each other, is to send delegates (*babuja ba shikalile*) who make inquiries about the other family: their clan and taboos, their popularity with their neighbours, and whether there is any history of disease, particularly leprosy or epilepsy. If the information secured is satisfactory, the father of the prospective bridegroom sends two *babuja ba winga* (also called *balunja*) to the house of the girl's father; he is not warned beforehand of their coming, though the mother may have been informed by her daughter. After the conventional greetings the *babuja* explain: 'We came here to look for a woman to cook food for us (*Twizaga kuchoba nkima wa kutuzugila*).' This is a standard formula and the father knows at once the purpose of the visit. He then calls some of his neighbours, a meal is prepared, and the conversation leads up to a few remarks about the position of the suitor and his family.

### Kulya Bukombe

110. If the girl's father is pleased with the proposal for marriage, he prepares a feast to which he invites his own relatives and neighbours and the relatives of the bridegroom. The purpose of the feast is to inform the public about the proposal, and thus give an opportunity to other suitors to increase their efforts and compete in the number of bridewealth cattle (Note 1. C to 10). After a short time the man's father gives a feast to which he invites neighbours and a number of the girl's relatives. The latter (called *bakombe*) are headed by a near relative, preferably a paternal uncle, of the prospective bride; before leaving they have been given full instructions with regard to the amount of bridewealth. During this visit the two parties try to come to an agreement. The discussion some-

times lasts many hours, as the parties begin with extremely low offers and extremely high demands. If they fail to agree, the *bakombe* may return home and later bring a new offer. If no agreement is finally reached the matter is closed without causing any embarrassment to either party. The failure of negotiations never debars other suitors from trying their luck. If the negotiations lead to an agreement, the girl leaves the *maji* and any temporary liaisons have to be severed.

In the agreement a date for the handing over of the marriage-cattle— either the first instalment or the full amount as the case may be—is fixed.

111. On the day fixed the *bakombe* come to fetch the cattle. They are received with pleasure, and a goat or a bull (*kitinde*) is slaughtered to entertain them. The *bakombe* usually stay the night in the house of the bridegroom's father. When the cattle herd comes home in the evening the beasts of the bridewealth are selected. If the father is a rich man, another bull or goat (*luswagilo*) is slaughtered, and many inhabitants of the village participate in the celebration and are given portions of the meat. In some areas this beast is slaughtered by the *bakombe* on the wedding day. The *bakombe* leave next morning and when they arrive with the bridewealth cattle at the house of the girl's father, the father kills a goat or ox (*tumbati*) the meat of which is given to the *bakombe* and also to many inhabitants of the parish. No invitations are issued; whoever appears receives a piece of meat. The girl's father has the right to return a beast if he does not consider it suitable, even though it has been accepted by the *bakombe*.

112. The cattle or goats which are slaughtered on these various occasions are not counted in the bridewealth, and do not have to be returned if the engagement is dissolved or if a divorce takes place later. The purpose of these feasts is to collect as many witnesses as possible for each phase of the procedure.

### Kuangalucha

113. After a few days the bridegroom (*ntoji*) visits the girl's father for the first time and they fix the date of the wedding. In some areas the future son-in-law is told that he must build a small hut containing the bridal chamber in the homestead of the girl's father before the wedding takes place.

### Kutola or Lushiku lwa Kutola

114. Great preparations are made for the wedding because many guests are expected. The father of the girl has to provide the feast. When the day arrives the girl's father sends for his future son-in-law (*kushika nkwilima*), who arrives at about 6 p.m. accompanied by his friends, the *bakwilima*. They are received by two young men (*batongeji*), who lead the visitors to the future home of the young couple, or to the house where

they will spend their first fortnight. The *bakwilima* are feasted and leave the house at about 9 p.m. when friends and female relatives of the bride enter to prepare the bridal bed. The bridegroom has to give a goat (*mbuli ya ng'wambi*) for this service. The bride is then told by her father: 'It is late now, go to your master.' The bride thereupon enters the hut where the bridegroom is waiting, and the friends leave them shortly afterwards. The guests may dance (*nyaloha*) the whole night and the next day, but the newly married couple do not participate. The girl is asked next morning by her mother's sister whether the marriage has been consummated. If the answer is in the affirmative the *ng'ombe ya maji* is slaughtered (in those areas where this custom is followed (22)), and the husband and wife go about each wearing a garment belonging to the other. In some areas it is the custom for the friends of the couple to look through holes made in the walls of the bridal hut, and mark the consummation of the marriage with an outburst of great rejoicing.

115. The young couple spend their first fortnight in a house belonging to the girl's father and situated in his homestead (*kaya*). According to custom a husband cannot take his wife from her father's house into that of his own father until he has paid the full bridewealth or the *ng'ombe ya butigu* (26, 58). It is within the discretion of the girl's father to allow her husband to take his wife home before the full bridewealth or the *ng'ombe ya butigu* has been paid. If a man marries a second wife he cannot take her home until he has paid the full bridewealth, but may only visit her in her father's house. If the bridewealth has been paid in instalments, a feast is held when the final instalment is handed over, after which the husband takes his wife to their new home. During the journey the husband has to present trifling gifts to his wife before she agrees to cross a stream, or pass a cross-roads, before she enters the house, before she sits down for the first time, and before she prepares the first meal for him.

### Bupinda Mbele or Butula Nzoka

116. One month after the wedding, a further ceremony is performed, *kusanja makono na sobuko*—to join hands with the father-in-law. The parents of the wife brew beer and call the son-in-law to drink it in their company. From then onwards the husband is allowed to enter the house of his father-in-law. A meal is prepared later which is shared by both, and this is the first meal they take together. In many houses the two men eat together regularly after this first common meal.

NOTE. It is considered extremely tactless for a man to address his mother-in-law directly or look straight into her face while talking, and the same applies to her. Observance of this rule is relaxed after the birth of a few children; but a son-in-law even then usually avoids meeting his wife's mother. The same rules apply to the wife and her father-in-law.

## II. *Kulehya*

The form of *kulehya* practised in the north differs from that in the south.

### A. *Kulehya* (*north*) (NF, UF, KF, BSN, BD, KM)

117. The girl, having failed to obtain her father's permission to marry, elopes with her lover in order to force her father to consent to her marriage.

The man brings the girl to the house of one of his relatives, sometimes even to that of his father, and it is his duty to inform the girl's father of this at once. The girl's father, especially if she is very young, often succeeds in compelling his daughter to return. The abductor must pay one head of cattle (*ng'ombe ya kupeleja*) to the girl's father (151). Often the delegates sent by the father return, bringing the cow and not the daughter. If the father of the girl agrees to accept the *ng'ombe ya kupeleja*, negotiations about bridewealth and marriage may commence forthwith.

118. The *ng'ombe ya kupeleja* is not included in the bridewealth and is therefore not returnable in the event of divorce.

NOTE. *Kulehya* has advantages for the lover which may counter-balance the loss of one head of cattle. Thus a rich cattle-owner may prefer to shorten the customary procedure; on the other hand, a man who has only a small number of cattle may think that the payment of one head is a good investment, in the hope that the father will agree to accept a smaller bridewealth than in the case of *kulunja*. The father knows that if he asks for too much bridewealth he may get nothing, because the couple may decide to live in concubinage (*butende*). *Kulehya* with intention to marry remains, however, a risk, as the lover can never know whether the father has enough authority over his daughter to recall her.

119. During the negotiations in connexion with bridewealth the girl lives in her father's house and the wedding is arranged in the usual manner (Note to 146B).

120. While the negotiations are going on, and even after payment of the *ng'ombe ya kupeleja*, the couple are not regarded as married. The man cannot claim compensation in case of adultery by the girl, but he is nevertheless liable to pay *misango* and *njigu*.

### B. *Kulehya* (*south*) (BS, SBS, KS, SS)

In the south two forms of abduction are known which are both expected to lead to legal marriage: 1. *Kulehya*, 2. *Kupumula*. There are also two forms of *kulehya*.

#### 1a. *The original form of Kulehya*

121. A man who possesses only a small number of cattle, which he knows would not be considered sufficient as a first instalment of bridewealth, offers them to the girl's father after abducting her. (One of these cattle is called *ng'ombe ya kulehya* or *ng'ombe ya kugija*.)

122. If the father agrees, the man receives the girl in a form of 'official' concubinage. At this time the amount of bridewealth is not fixed. It is a matter of arrangement whether the couple live in the father's house or whether the girl follows her lover into his house. If the lover acquires further property in due course he sends his *balunja* to the girl's father and negotiations for the payment of bridewealth begin.

123. In BS and SBS the cattle already paid, including the *ng'ombe ya kugija*, are counted as an instalment towards the total bridewealth payment. In all other chiefdoms the cattle already paid, excluding the *ng'ombe ya kugija*, are counted as an instalment towards the total bridewealth payment.

124. If the relationship between the lovers comes to an end the *ng'ombe ya kugija* is not returnable. If other beasts besides the *ng'ombe ya kugija* have been given by the lover to the girl's father they must be returned.

Ibadakuli Appeal -/42. *Machibya* v. *Bungulu*.

Machibya had paid seven head of cattle to Bungulu. The court stated that customarily only one head of cattle can be called the *ng'ombe ya kugija*, and that the others must be returned if and when the liaison of the lovers should be dissolved.

(The original Native Court gave judgement that all cattle are *kugija* and that therefore none of them have to be returned.)

125. *Misango* and *njigu* are payable if occasion arises. Cattle paid in *kulehya*, except the *ng'ombe ya kugija*, are counted towards these payments.

D.C.'s Appeal 6/44. Ngudu (Nera). *Magengeli* v. *Tungu*.

Tungu had paid seven cattle to *ng'wanangwa* Magengeli—not as bridewealth but as *ng'ombe ya kugija*. The girl became pregnant but the child died at birth. The court held that Tungu had to pay *misango*. In this case the father of the girl had returned all the cattle before the case started.

D.C.'s Appeal 8/43. Ibadakuli (Tinde). *Mayunga* v. *Masanja*.

Five head of cattle were paid by Mayunga to Masanja as *ng'ombe ya kugija*. When the couple dissolved their liaison, the man claimed the return of all five beasts, but the father refused to return any cattle whatsoever as one child had been born to the couple. The court held that the actions must be separated. The father must return all the *ng'ombe ya kugija* except one, and the lover must pay *misango*.

NOTE. For example: a man paid four head of cattle in *kulehya* and the woman died in childbirth; as he then owed eleven cattle for *njigu*, there remained a debt of eight head of cattle.

126. The children born of such a liaison belong to the maternal family like those of any couple living in concubinage.

1b. *Harusi kabunga. A new form of Kulehya*

127 (a) The preliminaries are the same as those described in para. 121.

(b) The bridewealth is fixed from the beginning and only a very small first instalment is paid. This includes the *ng'ombe ya kugija*.

(c) When the delegates of the woman's father, who are always village elders (*banamhara*), not relatives, arrive at her prospective father-in-law's house to take over the few cattle of bridewealth, one beast, one goat, or a sheep (*luswagilo*), is killed to feast them, and the delegates are anointed with ghee (*kubilwa maguta ga ng'ombe*). The couple is then considered to be married.

NOTE. There is actually no difference between the *harusi ya kabunga* and the *kulunja* forms of marriage, except that in the first case only a very small instalment of the bridewealth is paid. This new form of marriage has become so popular in recent times that it is even performed when the full amount of bridewealth, or a great part of it, is handed over before the wedding. It saves a great deal of the expense customarily incurred for wedding festivities. The invention of this form of marriage is obviously a reaction against the exorbitant amount of bridewealth payable in the south. At the present time the *harusi kabunga* is often practised in SS and KS, while the original form of *kulehya* (121) is still popular in BS and SBS.

## 2. *Kupumula*

128. The lover, having no cattle for bridewealth, goes to the girl's father and requests that he may be accepted into the household as the acknowledged lover of the girl with the intention of marrying her later. It is within the discretion of the father either to accept the suggestion or to send him away at once. The former attitude is often adopted by a father of a *nkuleji* or *nshimbe*.

No agreement about the amount of bridewealth is concluded at this time; such talks are postponed until the lover, by industry or luck, is in a position to start payment of bridewealth. The procedure is thenceforth the same as in *kulehya*, and the legal position is similar (121, 122).

NOTE. Fathers may agree to this form of 'legal concubinage' because they know that, if they do not agree, the couple may simply elope and live in *butende*.

## III. *Kugumira*

129. A man, in the presence of witnesses whom he has brought with him, throws strings of beads over the girl of his choice, or throws a piece of cloth over her in public, usually on the occasion of a dance (*mbina*). The lover has not previously announced his intentions to the girl.

NOTE. *Kugumira* is now seldom practised; its chief advantage was that the lover achieved a short cut to the negotiations with the girl's father. As a man of means he was sure of obtaining the father's assistance in influencing his daughter, while he might be doubtful about securing the girl's agreement after a trial of the usual courtship. Moreover, he might be aware that the girl had a suitor already and instead of entering into competition for the favour of the girl, he showed by *kugumira* that he wished to marry her.

Formerly *kugumira* was often practised by the *banang'oma* when they wished to procure a wife for the chief. In addition to the wives of official status (*ngole*) a chief usually had many other wives. It was rare for the chief to keep women other than his legitimate wives in the *ikuru*, nor was it customary for him to ask a girl to become his wife or invite a woman to live temporarily in the *ikuru*. A

chief led a very secluded life, seldom leaving his residence and then always surrounded by his *banang'oma*, *banikuru*, and by a number of *rugaruga*. Thus, if it
was considered advisable for the chief to have another wife, a few *banang'oma*
took the chief's lion-skin or his string of beads and threw it over the girl they
had selected, on the occasion of a dance, or when she was fetching water. The
girl was then taken at once to the residence. In this case neither the consent of
the girl nor that of her father was considered necessary. No one dared to resist
the *banang'oma* and the royal insignia. The girl on arrival in the residence was
handed over to the other wives of the chief or to one of the women living in the
*ikuru*, by whom she was instructed about her position in the royal household and
her duties; for instance, she was adjured to abstain from all intrigues, and never
to tell outsiders about events in the *ikuru*. Often a long time passed before she
saw the chief, her husband, for the first time.

The chief paid bridewealth but no customary marriage ceremonies were performed. If a chief was found by his courtiers with a girl met casually, he had to
pay a fine (*chenya*).

130. The string of beads or the piece of cloth is then brought to the
girl's father, who is usually pleased, because only a man of property will
choose this method of wooing in which the full bridewealth must be
paid before marriage. If a poor man should try *kugumira* the people present would consider it a practical joke.

131. If the girl or her father dislikes the man, the beads or cloth are
returned; if they agree to the marriage, the usual procedure as in the
case of *kulunja* is followed.

In NF the usual method of obtaining the girl's consent to a marriage
is now called *kugumira*. The suitor goes with a friend to the girl's house
where he is met by the girl, also accompanied by a friend. (The two
negotiators are called *bashindekeji*.) Although this meeting is not pre-
arranged, its purpose is very clear to everyone, and whether or not the
girl or her family are pleased is immaterial; it is the custom to receive
the two men cordially. The friend of the suitor informs the girl's friend
of the purpose of their visit, solemnly announces the desire of his friend
to marry the girl, and hands over a present for her. The answer to the
proposal is not given verbally. If the girl accepts she accompanies the
two friends to the door of her home; if her answer is in the negative she
turns back into the house at once. The gift will be sent back later.

## IV. *Kwingila*

132. This is the form of marriage between a widow and a relative of
her deceased husband (Note to 610, 612).

The widow and the relative whom she has chosen to be her husband
agree on the date for their legal union. Relatives of both families are
invited and a goat, the *mbuli ya kwingilila*, is killed and its meat consumed by the guests. The bed on which the consummation of the union
is to take place is cleaned with the contents of the goat's stomach (*kweja
ndili*). The ceremony is the same whether the widow remains in the
house of her deceased husband or follows her new husband to his house.

In some areas the goat is called *mbuli ya kweja kaya*. Its ear is pierced and the blood is allowed to drop on to the bridal bed. The goat is then killed and the meat consumed by members of the woman's family. If she has children by her first husband, his heir has to give her a goat (*mbuli ya kwinja bana hagati*). In the event of a widow being inherited by a step-son (601), the latter has to present her with a cow (*ng'ombe ya buchaminala*).

133. If the bridewealth had not been fully paid by the deceased husband, the relative who inherits the widow is obliged to pay whatever is outstanding. It is customary for him to pay at least one beast out of what is due on the occasion of *kwingila*.

134. The new husband of the widow takes over the duties and the rights of the deceased husband towards the widow's family.

## V. *Kumpa mgeni*

135. This form of marriage is only known in SS and KS (223B). If a wife dies and she has an unmarried sister their father can decide to give this unmarried daughter, if she agrees, to the widower as a substitute for the deceased wife (sororate). The widower has to pay an additional bridewealth of two to five cattle according to what is agreed between the parties. No wedding ceremonies take place.

## VI A. *Remarriage of a divorced woman*

136. If a divorced woman who has had a child by her first husband marries for a second time, the ceremony of *bupanda bupu* has to be performed. The new husband has to provide a goat which is killed when the first visit of the child of the first marriage is expected. The contents of the stomach of this goat are scattered on the floor, marking a path from the door to the bed. The child is called in and told to walk upon the *bupu*. From now on the child can visit its mother without fear of harm and can sleep in the house.

## VI B. *Remarriage of a divorced couple*

137. It sometimes happens that a divorced couple wish to remarry, especially in cases where the wife has had to leave her children. The husband then has to return the bridewealth which had been returned to him when the divorce was granted. If any instalments of bridewealth remain outstanding from the first marriage, the husband must acknowledge the debt (*magasa*) when remarrying.

138. If no cattle were returned to the husband after the divorce there is no ceremony to mark the legal remarriage of the couple, the presence of relatives and neighbours as witnesses being considered sufficient.

139. In cases where a divorce certificate has been issued, it is necessary for the couple to go to the court (*ibanza*) to cancel it. Otherwise the situation would be complicated if a question of adultery arose, in so far as the divorce certificate would refute the evidence of witnesses to the remarriage.

## VII. *Kukindikila* (SS, KS) or *Dimeli* (BSN)

140. This custom is known only in the areas mentioned above, and even there it rarely occurs. Two fathers make a mutual agreement regarding the future marriage of their minor children.

NOTE. The reason for such a contract may be poverty but is sometimes friendship.

141. The total bridewealth is agreed upon and a few cattle, often only a cow and a bull, are paid immediately after the conclusion of the contract between the parties.

142. The children remain with their parents and, when they come of age, the remainder of the bridewealth becomes payable and the young couple marry. The offspring of the beasts which were handed over as the first instalment are not counted as part of the bridewealth.

143. If one of the couple dies before the marriage takes place or refuses to marry, the instalments of bridewealth already paid have to be returned. If the father of the girl has no property the debt has to be paid at the latest if and when the girl marries another man.

## VIII. *Kuhanira*

144. This and the custom of *kuhaha* (see below) are only known in BSN, ZM during times of famine. A father sends his 10 to 12 year-old daughter to a rich cattle-owner and receives from him five beasts as the first instalment of bridewealth. When the girl reaches marriageable age, the amount of the final bridewealth is fixed. If the girl dies the bridewealth already paid becomes a common debt.

## IX. *Kuhaha*

145. In a case of pressing debt or in time of famine the father of a daughter pledges her against the loan of one or two head of cattle, promising to return the loan when the girl marries. At the time of the loan the girl may be a very small child and she always remains with her parents. Very often it happens that the loan is increased in course of time. If so, the girl's parents bring her up with the idea that she will have to marry into the creditor's family. If she refuses to do so, or if she dies before reaching marriageable age, the loan, which was never regarded as bridewealth, has to be repaid.

NOTE. The practices described in 140–5 do not belong to the category of child marriages; their motive is not so much the desire to marry young girls, but rather to invest cattle in a secure form; for the father of the girl it may be the last expedient resorted to for saving the family from starvation.

## PROCEDURE FOR LEGALIZING A MARRIAGE

146 A. *Kulunja* (107) and B. *Kulehya* (117).

The consummation of marriage during the *lushiku lwa kutola*.

NOTE. In all cases of *kulehya* and of marriage following on many years' concubinage, the woman returns for a few days before the wedding to her parental home where marriage rites of some sort will be performed, in particular the formalities of the *lushiku lwa kutola*.

C. *Kulehya* and *Kupumula* (121 et seq.).

The payment of bridewealth.

NOTE. Cattle paid after the amount of bridewealth has been agreed, not cattle which may have been given to the girl's father at the beginning of the connexion.

D. *Harusi kabunga* (127).

The killing of the *luswagilo* beast and the anointing of the delegates with ghee.

NOTE. The union is legalized by the killing of the *luswagilo* beast and the anointing with ghee, despite the fact that the young people themselves are not present.

E. *Kugumira* (129).

The consummation of marriage during the *lushiku lwa kutola*.

F. *Kwingila* (132).

The killing of the *mbuli ya kwingilila*.

G. *Kumpa mgeni* (135).

The payment of the additional bridewealth or, if none is to be paid, the entrance of the sister into the widower's house.

H. *Remarriage* (136, 137).

Payment of bridewealth or, if none is paid, the witness of relatives and neighbours, or a declaration in the *ibanza* and the return of the divorce certificate.

I. *Dimeli, kuhanira, and kuhaha* (140, 144, 145).

The consummation of marriage during the *lushiku lwa kutola*.

147. The following marriage rules were proposed by the chiefs of the Sukuma Federation and their people in 1949 (Appendix II):

(*a*) Particulars of all customary marriages shall be reported to the Native Court of the area in which the bride is domiciled.

(*b*) The following persons shall be required to appear before the court as witnesses to the marriage:
  1. the husband and the wife;

2. the father of the wife or his deputy;
3. one independent witness for each party.

(c) All relevant particulars shall be recorded in a register kept by the court and on certificates issued by the court to the parties.

(d) Such particulars shall include full details of the total bridewealth agreed upon by the two parties, and shall show all payments made and outstanding in this respect. All further payments made shall be reported to the court, and entered both in the court register and on the certificates.

(e) The fee for registration shall be Shs.2/-.

(f) Application for registration as described in rule (a) above shall be made within one month following the ceremony legalizing the marriage according to tribal law. Failure to do so will render the responsible party liable to a fine not exceeding Shs.6/-.


## POLYGYNY

### *Kupalika* or *Kutola Mhali*

148 A. The number of wives is not restricted.

NOTE. The position of the first wife in a household is distinct from that of the others, although the visits of the husband to each of his wives take place at regular intervals; he visits each one in turn every other day, or every three to five days. If a man keeps separate homesteads (*kaya*) the visits may last a fortnight or more if the homes are in different chiefdoms. In all other ways the first wife holds a commanding position in the household and the other wives obey her and even like to do small services for her. In a peaceful house her authority is acknowledged without being enforced. The other wives call the first wife not by her own name, but 'the mother of [her child]', for instance 'Mama Juma'; if she has no child, they call her 'Mama'. The internal work of a house is organized by the first wife, though she would never exclude herself from the work. The only difference may be that she sits on a stone or a low stool, during such common tasks as husking ground-nuts or grading cotton, while the other wives sit on the ground. The first wife is often married with the father's property (Note to. 2) and her family has to undergo a stricter scrutiny than that of a second wife whom the husband has married with his own means.

It is the general opinion that it is not difficult to keep peace in a polygynous household. The wives compete with each other in work and good behaviour, and the husband enjoys the benefit of it. Disharmony is generally due, not to incompatibility of character among the wives, but to the stupidity and partiality of the husband.

Polygyny is so deeply rooted in the conventions of society, and the adaptation of the family's organization to it is so complete, that the wives of one household harbour no feelings of jealousy amongst themselves; but, on the other hand, the feeling of envy between them is very acute. They consider it entirely natural that their husband should divide his affections among several wives; but that one of them should receive more strings of beads or brass rings than the others would be more than they could endure.

B. A man wishing to take another wife usually tries to obtain the consent of his first wife, although this is not absolutely necessary. The custom is for the husband to present the first wife with a goat (*mbuli ya nkima ntale*) when he takes a new wife. The first wife has no right to demand this goat in court but she may do so before the family council.

NOTE. The husband usually discusses the question of another wife with his first wife and if she objects he tries to persuade her. He may even send for his sister or another female relative to help him in convincing her of the advantages of the second marriage. The acknowledged advantages of polygyny, as far as the wives themselves are concerned, are the following:

1. If a man has several wives he is not inclined to indulge in costly liaisons outside his house.
2. In a monogamous household the wife is often alone; the neighbours' homesteads are not always in the immediate vicinity. A second wife means company for the first wife.
3. Within the routine work of a household there are many tasks which can be better accomplished by several people working together.
4. Very often a man marries a second wife after his first wife has given birth to a child. The young mother has no objection as she believes in the general superstition that unfaithfulness by the husband may endanger the life of the baby.

C. Usually, but not necessarily, the wives live in separate houses; if they are good friends or if circumstances make it necessary the whole family may live in one room.

NOTE. Plenty of conversation, laughter, and jokes and also serious discussion may take place while the husband is lying in bed with one of his wives and the other one is lying in her own bed, if both wives live in one house. The knowledge of such details may be necessary for the understanding of court cases. For instance, in a court case in NF (Nasa), it appeared that conversation in the room became very emotional, and when the wife who was alone demanded the blanket from the laughing couple, the husband threw it to her, as she thought, a bit too powerfully. The ensuing struggle ended outside the hut with the result that each wife lost an ear [*sic*].

D. Each wife has allotted to her a number of fields which she cultivates with the help of her children; the husband gives his help in turn to each of the households. Whether the wives live in the same house or on the same holding in different houses the harvest of each household is kept separate (405, 584).

149. If wives are living in different villages or chiefdoms contact between the households remains as close as possible. Often children of one house live for weeks in one of the other houses. The father encourages this contact, knowing that there is always the possibility that the children of the several houses will have to solve many common problems after they have grown up.

## CONCUBINAGE

### (*Butende*)

150. The institution of concubinage is related to that of marriage in the Sukuma mind. It is widespread and no moral stigma is attached to it.

NOTE. A chief wished to protect concubinage by imposing a fine for adultery committed with the female partner of a *butende*. This proposal could not be recommended for general acceptance because to protect concubinage means to reduce the importance of marriage. Further, so long as the right of the woman's father to claim *misango* and *njigu* from the lover is acknowledged, the latter can have no legal right to the woman and therefore compensation in case of adultery cannot be granted to him.

The following case, however, illustrates the attitude of lower courts towards concubinage.

D.C.'s Appeal 40/37. Ngudu. *Maganda* v. *Ng'wanangwa Mahonda*.

Maganda lived with a woman in concubinage. *Ng'wanangwa* Mahonda was found at 10 p.m. by Maganda behind the house and when asked what he was doing there, he answered that he had visited his sweetheart in the house. The original court fined Mahonda 20/-. The native appeal court sentenced Mahonda to one month's imprisonment, because he had been found at 10 p.m. on the premises of another man, and because as a headman he should know the law. In the D.C.'s appeal court both convictions were quashed and the case was dismissed. It was stated, however, that the attitude of the headman was provocative and deserved punishment, but that this cannot be imposed by the court which must follow the existing provisions of the law.

The frequency of concubinage varies in the different chiefdoms; it is least frequent in BSN, while the greatest number of people living in concubinage may be found in SS and KS. It is popular in NF, UF, but comparatively rare in BF and BD.

## *Kupula, kulehya,*[1] *kuswesula*

151. These are the names given in different areas to abduction without immediate intent to marry. If a man incites a woman to leave the house where she is living with her next-of-kin and to live with him in concubinage, he must pay *ngwekwe* or *ng'ombe ya kupeleja* (one cow and one goat) to the woman's nearest paternal relative (117).

NOTE. The term *ngwekwe* exists only in NF, UF, KF, BSN, BD, KM, SM. In SBS, KS, BS the payment is called *ng'ombe ya kufumira*. In these latter areas a *mbuli ya ngwekwe* is paid to the *bakombe* who come to the house of the man or of his father to fetch the bridewealth cattle (110).

152. If the woman was not living with her next-of-kin before going to live in concubinage, no *ngwekwe* is payable by the man.

153. If the man wishes later to marry the woman, the beasts of the *ngwekwe* payment are not counted as part of the bridewealth. Therefore, in case of divorce the *ngwekwe* does not have to be returned.

In Nasa (UF) *ngwekwe* is counted as part of the bridewealth and must be returned in case of divorce.

154. The payment of *ngwekwe* creates no legal rights for the lover.

155 A. In UF, NF, BSN, BD *ngwekwe* need only be paid once by the same man if the girl, after having returned home, decides later to return to his house and live there with him.

---

[1] The word *kulehya* is used both for the practices described in paras. 118 and 123 and for the procedure described in para. 153.

B. In SS, KS *ngwekwe* can be claimed by the girl's family a second time from the same man if the woman, after having been persuaded to return to her parents, decides later to go back to her lover.

156. The *ngwekwe*, in case of a *ng'wanangwa*, *munang'oma*, regent, direct descendant of a chief, and a deposed chief, amounts to two head of cattle and one goat. In the case of a *ntemi* it amounts to five head of cattle and two goats.

157. The property of a couple who have been living in concubinage is divided as follows when they decide to separate:

A. If a man and woman have started a common household together the property which has been acquired by common effort, i.e. such items as cattle or money, is divided into two equal shares.

The hut is given to the man while the woman receives the cooking utensils.

Food in store is divided as follows:

| The woman receives as shilandi: | The man receives |
|---|---|
| all kinds of beans; | millet and sorghum; |
| half of the maize; | cassava; |
| sweet potatoes; | cotton; |
| half of the ground-nuts. | rice; |
| | half of the maize; |
| | half of the ground-nuts. |

B. If the woman has followed the man to his house and settled down there and both have worked the holding, the woman can only take with her: her private property, cooking utensils, the *shilandi* as above.

NOTE. Rules A and B were decided upon by the chiefs of the Sukumaland Federation and their people in 1949. Formerly the rules differed in the various local federations.

UF, NF, BF, BSN, BD, SM. All food in store was divided equally between the man and woman.

BS, SBS. The man received three-quarters and the woman one-quarter.

SS, KS. The woman took nothing except her cooking utensils.

C. If the man has followed the woman into her holding he can take nothing with him except his private property, unless he has expressly arranged for a division of the fields before cultivation (cf. 252).

158. In all cases the woman is entitled to take with her gifts which she has received from her lover.

## RESTRICTIONS ON MARRIAGE
### 1. *Consanguinity*

159. Persons who can trace their descent from a common ancestor (agnatic or uterine) are prohibited from marrying.

NOTE. Rules restricting marriages are no longer so strictly observed as in the

past. Public opinion enforces them only in cases where transgressions are de-
nounced by a diviner as the cause of some ill fortune which may have befallen
the community.

160. Two persons belonging to the same clan are allowed to marry if
they cannot discover a common ancestor.

NOTE. As already mentioned, it is the custom for *babuja bas hikalile* to investigate this point (109), but with regard to consanguinity their research is very
superficial. (Their main concern is with leprosy and epilepsy.) If the families are
not aware of any relationship it is assumed that they are unrelated. If a common
ancestor should be discovered, the man or his father has to give to the girl's
father one head of cattle (*ng'ombe ya budugu*) which the receiver may keep or kill
for a feast to which he may invite the relatives of both sides. This beast has also
to be paid if it is discovered after the wedding that the newly married couple are
related. Thus people observing the same taboos are allowed to marry. In any case
taboos (*migilo*) inherited from the father are obligatory for the offspring, those
from the mother are voluntary. In a family very often the taboos of both father
and mother are observed. Cases are known in which the matrimonial peace has
been disturbed by a husband who refused to acknowledge the wife's taboo. If a
wife wishes to adopt the taboo of her husband and to relinquish her own, a
simple rite is performed the main feature of which is that she eats—with special
magical precautions—the food forbidden to her.

161. If two persons, who are regarded as belonging to the circle of
relatives for whom intermarriage is prohibited, should have sexual intercourse resulting in the pregnancy of the girl, the man has to pay the
*ng'ombe ya budugu*. The child belongs to the maternal family.

NOTE. No exact definitions of the expressions 'near relative' and 'distant relative' exist. It is sometimes stated that near relatives are not allowed to marry but
distant relatives are. The term 'near relative' is in this case interpreted as a person who has remained in close contact with the family. For instance, if a grandfather's brother has emigrated and nothing has been heard of him, so that his
name has fallen into oblivion, cousins of the second generation could marry,
perhaps after payment of the *ng'ombe ya budugu*. The relatives would not have
agreed to the union if the grandfather's brother had not emigrated and if his
descendants were still living in the same village.

## 2. Affinity

162. A man is not allowed to marry his wife's sister so long as his wife
is alive, nor is he allowed to marry his step-daughter so long as her
mother is alive (135, 223). A man cannot marry the persons whom he
customarily has to avoid, e.g. his mother-in-law or his daughter-in-law.

## 3. Blood brotherhood (lusalago)

163. A blood-brother is treated as a natural brother; he can therefore
marry the widow of his blood-brother, but not the sister.

NOTE. These rules are not always strictly observed.

## 4. A curse (kizumo)

164. *Kizumo* is the name given to a relationship of enmity between
two persons belonging to two different clans, originating in an event in

the past; a member of one such clan cannot marry a member of the other.

NOTE. Hindi and Lenge are two clans in the Mwanza chiefdóm (NF). One of two brothers belonging to the Hindi clan was in the habit of questioning his wife whether she had been faithful to him during his absence. Once when he returned home unexpectedly he saw his brother leaving his house. He followed him and killed him with a spear in a fury of jealousy. Their father cursed the murderer exclaiming: 'Whosoever of the Hindi clan shall talk to the murderer or to his descendants will die.' The son left the village and settled in another area, where he was called Nlenge, and became the founder of the Lenge sub-clan. On account of that curse members of the two clans are afraid to intermarry,

Members of the Hindi and Bayungu clans are also exogamous. When Lemi, the ancestor of the Hindi clan (which is the clan of the ruling chiefs), left Buha and arrived on the shores of Lake Victoria, he and his followers continued their journey by boat. His brother Muyungu was in another boat and, when the moon rose over the lake, he saw the moonlight reflected in the water. He had never before seen such a phenomenon and he ordered one of his sons to fetch the light. The young man jumped overboard and was never seen again. When Lemi heard of this foolishness he was very offensive to his brother, who became angry, left him, and returned to the shore and settled in an area nearby. When he heard later that Lemi also had returned to the shore he declared solemnly: 'Lemi is not my brother any more; he laughed and cursed me when my son disappeared. Any descendant of my family who marries a descendant of Lemi's family shall die.'

## 5. Profession

165. In former times a number of clans were forbidden to intermarry with families of blacksmiths and potters. This rule was never general and is now obsolete.

NOTE. The blacksmiths of the area belonged to the Longo tribe which had immigrated from alien countries (Ruanda). They settled down where ironstone (mbale) was to be found and it is said (but this tradition may be only a local version) that they had their own chief in SM. The Tuta (Ngoni) raided the area but the Longo chief was so engrossed with his smithies that when the drums of war sounded he was unprepared and many Longo were killed. The survivors fled in all directions without leaders, but in course of time groups of them settled again where they found mbale; others made themselves independent of the mineral and collected old hoes, smelted them and made new ones from the material. The trade in hoes was very important in Sukumaland and hoes were in many parts the common currency of the people. The smiths were neither cattle-breeders nor agriculturists; they bartered hoes for corn and cattle but consumed the latter and did not keep them. The blacksmiths' way of life was fundamentally different from that of the rest of the population and depended on different factors. They therefore developed different rites. For instance, the agriculturist makes sacrifices and prayers to ensure rain in times of drought, while the blacksmith can work better in the dry than in the wet season. The Sukuma themselves give this as a reason for the earlier prohibition of marriage with smiths.

# CHAPTER III

## DIVORCE (*KULEKANA*)

### INTRODUCTION

THE dissolution of a marriage did not and does not make any considerable change in the social and economic status of either of the two people concerned.

Formerly, if a man was tired of living with his wife he went with her to her father and claimed return of bridewealth; on the other side, if a father-in-law began to dislike his son-in-law he sent for his daughter and returned the bridewealth. If a divorce took place the children were always given to the father, and no concern was felt regarding the feelings of the mother. If a man was tired of living with the mother of his children, no provision of any kind existed within the law which would enable the mother to keep her children.

Adultery was seldom considered grounds for divorce, nor was it regarded as a reason for terminating conjugal life. An adulterer had to pay compensation to the husband (note to 170).

Such was the conception of the law, and it has not changed much except in one important particular. Native courts and elders called as arbitrators do not immediately agree to dissolve a marriage. They grant a divorce only after many attempts to reconcile husband and wife. A decision or final judgement is delayed as long as possible, especially in cases where one party demands divorce while the other is willing to continue married life, and in all cases where no acknowledged reason for divorce is forthcoming.

There are not many reasons why a man should divorce his wife. Sentiments are not complicated, life is simple, and economic extravagance on the part of the wife is impossible. Changes in the physical appearance of a woman in the course of years, or love for another woman, are never the hidden reason for domestic trouble started by the husband. The legal institution of polygyny, as well as the husband's legally and socially acknowledged right to extramarital liaisons, afford him opportunities for satisfying his aesthetic feelings. Men take great pride in possessing more than one wife; a polygynous household proves that the master is a man of means and authority. Further, a divorce is troublesome and the material gain for the husband, especially when there are children, may be small. It may also happen that the father-in-law has used the cattle of the bridewealth and is not in a position to return them. The most important factor which makes a husband reluctant to claim a divorce will be discussed later.

The situation of a wife is very different. There is no opportunity for her to meet other men without incurring censure; she readily exaggerates in her own mind any unpleasant quarrel at home, as this is the centre of nearly all her activities; and she may succumb too easily to temptation in the form of illusory promises of a life of more intense emotion with another man. Even the existence of children does not influence her decision if she has fallen in love with another man.

It would be wrong to assume that an African woman is a bad and heartless mother. It would appear rather that she remains all her life primarily a 'woman', reluctant to give up any natural rights in favour of motherhood, except during the infancy of her child, when it is completely helpless. Two factors may have influenced this attitude although it may be difficult to ascertain cause and effect in this matter. Firstly, a mother knows that she will keep her child only as long as she lives with her husband; she may lose her child at any time without being at fault; for instance, if her husband becomes so brutal or completely indifferent that she cannot endure life with him any longer. In all circumstances a father can claim possession of his children. Secondly, children themselves soon become independent of their mother. From their earliest days they are accustomed to have many 'mothers', i.e. female members of the family, as well as neighbours. Thus what a child may lack in individual care and love is often compensated for by the collective sentiment of the family and even of society. It may be said that a Sukuma child of three or four years old does not need its mother to the degree which is elsewhere considered essential for the child's well-being and for the building-up of its character.

Though a woman's legal status is inferior to that of her husband, in fact the value of her work, in the home and in the fields, secures for her an unassailable position in the household on account of which she enjoys considerably greater freedom than would appear to be the case. And in spite of the fact that the law allows extensive rights to the husband, most divorces are initiated by the wife.

Moreover, there is always a possibility that a divorced woman will remarry, even at an advanced age; in fact marriage, divorce, and remarriage are regarded as customary stages in a normal life-cycle. A woman's value is not diminished by sexual intercourse, and her right to a normal life (*bulambu*) is acknowledged.

### GENERAL PROCEDURE

166. A marriage contract can be dissolved:

(*a*) In BSN, UF, BS, KF by mutual consent of the parties concerned without the intervention of a court but before a council of village elders. A case is only brought to court if there are quarrels and complications.

(*b*) In NF, BD, SBS, KS, KM by a judicial decree at the suit of husband or wife.

167. The council of elders can only arbitrate, they cannot enforce their decision. Either party may refuse to accept it and may bring the matter before a Native Court.

NOTE. Wherever councils of elders deal with divorce cases there is a marked tendency to have the decision registered in the *ibanza*, i.e. to pay the fee and have the judgement issued by the *ibanza*, although the hearing takes place before the elders.

168. Should the decision of the elders be accepted by both parties and subsequently one of them fail to fulfil a condition of the judgement, an action can be filed against the delinquent before the Native Court. The decision of the elders would be recognized by the court as valid in law.

169. Should a husband or wife fall sick during the negotiations and discussions about a divorce all procedure is stopped at once, and no judgement can be pronounced until the sick party has recovered.

## RECOGNIZED GROUNDS FOR DIVORCE

### SUIT BROUGHT BY HUSBAND

#### I. ADULTERY (*Bushihya*)

##### General Rules

170. Adultery by a wife constitutes grounds for a divorce.

NOTE. The following is a description of the ancient procedure in cases of adultery:

In some chiefdoms, for instance in NF, UF, adultery was a punishable offence and suspicion was sufficient for the filing of a suit. The ultimate aim of the procedure was to obtain a confession from the defendant. Testimony of the wife or of other persons, even if supported by indirect evidence, was not considered decisive for a conviction. For the satisfaction of the judges and of public opinion the accused had to admit his guilt. A persistent denial in the face of a threatened ordeal or curse could secure the acquittal of the defendant. The amount of the fine varied, but usually consisted of a bull and a cow or fifteen goats or sheep. The court knew the accused and his means, and did not hesitate to increase or reduce the fine accordingly.

If a man had no property, any one of his relatives could be held responsible for payment. The fine was sent to the chief. The plaintiff and defendant each had to pay two goats as court fees, which were received by the *ng'wanangwa* and shared with the assessors of the court.

If the defendant suffered injury when caught *in flagrante delicto*, he had to pay just the same. If he was killed, no blood-money (*njigu*) was payable. In other chiefdoms, for instance in BSN, adultery was not acknowledged as grounds for filing a suit.

171 A. A man cannot claim compensation on account of his wife's adultery more than twice during their married life.

B. If a wife lives in adultery with several men the husband can only sue the man with whom his wife is living when he finds her. He cannot sue more than one person in a single legal action (212).

C. The payment of damages for adultery confers no rights to any illegitimate child of the union.

172. No accusation of adultery or claim for damages can be supported unless there is direct or indirect evidence of sexual relationship between the man and the woman accused (exceptions 190, 209).

P.C.'s Appeal No. 48/44. Liwali's Court, Mwanza. *Saidi* v. *Maganga*.

Saidi claimed compensation for adultery from Maganga because his wife was seen by witnesses riding on the carrier of Maganga's bicycle. The claim was refused.

173. A charge of adultery can only be brought before the court:
A. by the husband, or
B. in the absence of the husband, by his nearest male relative.

D.C.'s Appeal No. 13/48. Ibadakuli (Shinyanga). *Kawili* v. *Ntwege*.

The court dismissed the appeal because it was ascertained that the plaintiff, Kawili, who claimed compensation for adultery from Ntwege, was neither husband nor brother-in-law of the woman with whom Ntwege had sexual intercourse.

D.C.'s Appeal No. 31/41. Fulo (Bukumbi). *Madadila* v. *Henry*.

Madadila accused Henry of committing adultery with his sister-in-law, whose husband, Mushimbe, Madadila's brother, had been away from home for about two years. The woman was four months gone with child. Compensation was awarded to the brother of the absentee.

NOTE. A brother is not entitled to bring his married sister and her lover to court. It is also unknown for a father to lay a charge of adultery before a court citing his son or vice versa; further, no case is known in which a brother has cited a brother or half-brother. Customarily, relatives do not cite each other in court, but the adulterer must pay one head of cattle (*ibengwe*) to the relative whom he has wronged. The beast is killed and consumed by a gathering of members of the family.

174. The court is entitled to refuse to hear a charge of adultery which has been unreasonably delayed by the petitioner after he has obtained full knowledge of the matter. If the husband had no knowledge of the fact until he acquired it through the birth of a child, the claim for compensation cannot become time-barred by the delay.

D.C.'s Appeal No. 11/41. Fulo (Burima). *Leo* v. *Kazungu*.

Leo had divorced his wife and the bridewealth had been returned to him when he laid a charge for adultery against Kazungu and claimed damages, on hearing that his former wife had given birth to a child which must have been conceived before she was divorced. Kazungu, corroborated by the woman, admitted paternity. The court therefore ruled that Kazunga had to pay damages of five beasts although at the time of the hearing the divorce was legally valid.

175. A wife cannot be convicted of adultery if the identity of her partner is unknown; for instance, if he escaped unrecognized by his pursuers and the wife refused to disclose his identity.

*Amount of compensation in case of adultery*

176. A man convicted of adultery has to pay compensation. The amount varies according to the social position of the superior in rank whether he is the husband or the adulterer.

NOTE. This rule was agreed by the chiefs of the Sukuma Federation and their people in 1949. Formerly the rule was one-sided: a tribal dignitary received from an adulterer more cattle than he himself would have to pay as adulterer. The damages to be paid varied in the different local federations and in different cases. For instance, in D.C.'s Appeal No. 19/48, the adulterer in a case brought by a village headman had to pay damages amounting to eight cattle, while in the same kind of case, Bukumbi No. 9/47, the adulterer paid five cattle.

177. Damages are payable to the husband as follows:
A. in case of a commoner: 5 head of cattle (4 cows and 1 bull).

NOTE. This rule was agreed by the chiefs of the Sukuma Federation and their people in 1949.
Formerly in all chiefdoms damages of 5 head of cattle were payable, except in BS, SBS, and KS, where damages amounted to 3 cattle (2 cows and 1 bull).

B. in cases of *banangwa, banang'oma*, direct descendants of chiefs, and deposed chiefs: 10 cattle (8 cows and 2 bulls).

C. in the case of a regent (*neji*): 15 cattle (12 cows and 3 bulls).

D. in the case of chiefs: 25 cattle (20 cows and 5 bulls).

NOTE. These rules (B, C, D) were agreed by the chiefs of the Sukuma Federation and their people in 1949.
NOTE. The new rules mean that a man who commits adultery with a chief's wife has to pay damages of 25 cattle and a chief who commits adultery with a commoner's wife also has to pay damages of 25 cattle. Previously the tendency was for an officer of the Native Administration or a tribal dignitary to expect a special rate of compensation as an injured party (plaintiff) while paying the commoner's rate as an offender (defendant). This inequality of payment was applied in cases of 151, 176, 271, 300B, 313B. The commoners were not always satisfied and the NF and UF issued rules of reciprocity in 1939. These rules were not invariably applied as the following court cases show:

D.C.'s Appeal 3/47, Usega. *Makemelele v. Malangwa.*
Malangwa caused the pregnancy of Makamelele's daughter and, as Makamelele was a chief's son, the court awarded a *misango* (300B) of five head of cattle.

D.C.'s Appeal 2/44, Usega. *Petro v. Kamina s/o Ntemi Bahebe.*
Petro was not satisfied with the two head of cattle which the court awarded him as *misango*, because Kamina was a chief's son. The native appeal court stated that it had never been the custom for a commoner to demand five cattle from a commoner. (The court chose to ignore the fact that Kamina was a chief's son.) If in this case the defendant had been a headman, he would have had to pay five cattle in accordance with the rules promulgated in 10/11/39.

The bias in favour of a chief's family, shown in both these cases, although no longer legal in view of the rules issued in 1939, has a certain justification in that traditionally, as mentioned above, differing rates of payment according to whether a man was a commoner, a chief, or a tribal dignitary were recognized.
Cases in which a commoner disturbed the domestic life of a chief or other tribal dignitary were rare. For instance, no recent case is remembered in which a man was charged in court with adultery with a chief's wife. The fixing of com-

pensation for adultery at twenty-five cattle is therefore arbitrary, but as the reciprocity had been accepted this high rate of compensation was not debated. There have, however, been a few cases of a man living in concubinage with a chief's unmarried daughter and causing her to become pregnant. For instance, a man of Ng'wagala (BD) had to pay twenty-five cattle as *ngwekwe* (151) for living in concubinage with a daughter of *Ntemi* Masanja. This payment cannot be considered excessive when it is remembered that in earlier times a man causing the pregnancy of an unmarried daughter of a chief or committing adultery with a chief's wife was killed outright and all his property was sequestrated. If he had no property his family, and sometimes even the whole village, had to pay for the outrage; even cattle paid as bridewealth were liable to be seized. The daughters, sisters, and wives of a *ntemi* (and also those of *banangwa*) lived a very secluded life. They were never allowed to leave the residence (*ikuru*) without an escort of other women and courtiers. It was one of the duties of *banang'oma* to escort female members of the chief's family when they went visiting. The daughters of *banangwa* did not join the *maji* in the village. Not only were these women guarded by their own people, but the family of any man who showed signs of being interested in them would have him closely watched also, for fear he might do something to provoke the chief's displeasure.

Acceptance of rules 176 and 177 by the chiefs was preceded by lengthy discussions, and some of the chiefs from KS and SS especially were of the opinion that these rules were likely to diminish the prestige of the chiefs.

The following alternative proposal was put forward during the discussions: 'The right of chiefs and tribal dignitaries to higher compensation is acknowledged; but if a court finds that a chief's or dignitary's daughter or sister has behaved in a manner calculated to lead to an illegal liaison, payments should not exceed those imposed in case of commoners.' This proposal takes account of the fact that the control of the female dependants of chiefs and dignitaries has now been generally and considerably relaxed, and there is therefore no reason for a man to be specially penalized for contracting a liaison with one of them, if she behaves in a provocative way. In a case of this kind the prestige of the chief's family is diminished whether a heavy penalty is imposed or not.

Finally, the chiefs unanimously accepted the provisions of rules 176 and 177.

178. If the court comes to the conclusion that the wife in a case of adultery is to be considered guilty to an unusual degree, it can order that, of the five cattle payable by the adulterer as damages, the wife has to pay one cow.

NOTE. This rule was agreed by the chiefs of the Sukuma Federation and their people in 1949. Formerly rules regarding the punishment of the wife varied in the different chiefdoms, but nowhere was she liable to pay damages.

The scales of punishment in the different chiefdoms were as follows:

(a) KF (Sima): Shs.40/-;
(b) KF (Nera): Shs.40/-, but only if the woman was found to be chiefly responsible;
(c) NF, KM: Shs.20/-, but only if the wife ran away with a lover, not if she committed adultery while separated from her husband;
(d) UF, BSN, BD, SS, BS: at one time a fine was imposed, but the penalty had been abolished.

The rule that a wife should share in the payment of damages, instead of paying a fine as formerly, was made because it was considered inequitable that the woman should pay a fine and the man damages; a situation might then arise in which, if neither the woman nor the man were able to pay the amount required the woman might be imprisoned while the man remained free. A wife may be considered liable to pay damages if, for instance, it is proved that she has deluded her lover into believing that she is not married.

The following is an example of another case in which it may seem justifiable that the wife should participate in the payment of damages:

D.C.'s Appeal 3/43. Shinyanga (Mwanhini). *Magaji* v. *Magoge.*

Seven days after Magoge had been convicted and ordered to pay compensation for adultery to Magaji, Magaji's wife came to him again and was found there five days later by her husband. Although witnesses testified that Magoge had tried to expel her, he was ordered to pay compensation a second time, because his efforts to drive her away had not been successful.

### Proof of adultery

179. Two types of evidence are admissible in cases of adultery: (1) direct evidence; (2) circumstantial evidence.

### 1. *Direct evidence*

180. Any person assisted by at least two witnesses is entitled to catch a married woman *in flagrante delicto* and inform the husband about the act of adultery. If the husband is absent one of those persons who have the legal right to file a suit in his stead may be informed.

NOTE. The usual person is the husband and he needs witnesses as does anyone else. It is seldom that other people have any interest in this matter or will take the trouble to prove the fact to the husband. Such a case happens sometimes if the wife makes a journey to visit relatives or friends, and is then caught *in flagrante delicto* by the wife of her paramour. The husband at home, when he hears of the fact and can obtain proof, has a good case for claiming compensation for adultery.

181. The witnesses must declare their presence to the guilty couple at the time. Their testimony is considered inadmissible if they watched the occurrence from a hiding-place without revealing themselves.

### 2. *Circumstantial evidence.*

182 A. Whether a situation in itself is considered sufficient evidence of adultery or requires corroboration must be left to the discretion of the court.

B. Corroboration is not necessary if the available circumstantial evidence excludes any interpretation other than that of adultery.

C. Corroboration is necessary if the only available information is insufficient to prove adultery. In such an event the cumulative weight of a number of incidents indirectly suggesting adultery is admissible.

D.C.'s Appeal 28/47, NF. *Manoni* v. *Sumuni.*

Manoni accused Sumuni of adultery with his wife. After he had caught the couple *in flagrante delicto* in the open, the husband gave the following evidence in court:

1. he produced clothes belonging to the defendant;
2. he had brought the defendant naked to the house of a witness;
3. together with the witness he had reported the case at once to the village headman;

4. he had gone from there to the father of the defendant and had reported the case to him;
5. the village headman had dispatched people to the spot where the adultery was alleged to have taken place, and marks likely to be caused by the act were found.

The court awarded compensation to the husband.

NOTE. Examples where corroboration is not necessary:

I. A husband returns to his house at night earlier than was expected. He hears the voices of his wife and a man inside the house. He barricades the door from outside and calls witnesses, in whose company he enters the house. They find a man, fully dressed, who explains, when asked to give a reason for his presence, that he came to ask the husband for quarters for the night, or perhaps to borrow an axe. No man is supposed to enter a house in the husband's absence except a relative or a very intimate friend, and the court would therefore not accept the excuse and would consider the adultery to have been proved.

II. D.C.'s Appeal 1/44. Fulo, Mwanza. *Sumuni* v. *Lukugabilu.*

Sumuni searched for his wife who had left him in the morning and found her in Lukugabilu's house. It was already night and neither Lukugabilu nor the wife could give any plausible explanation of the situation. Sumuni had four witnesses with him.

The court held that no proof of actual adultery was necessary and awarded damages to the husband.

III. A husband sees his wife and another man disappear in a field of sorghum. He calls witnesses and when he returns with them, finds the man already back on the path while the wife appears a moment later coming out of the field. The witnesses enter the field and find certain proofs of cohabitation. The court would find that adultery had been proved.

IV. A husband hears that his wife has entered a house with a man. He calls witnesses and with them forces an entrance into the house where they find the couple alone, but not *in flagrante delicto*. The court would consider it unnecessary to ascertain whether adultery had been committed or not. The situation, which cannot be explained otherwise, would be considered sufficient proof of adultery.

V. D.C.'s Appeal 63/44. Ngudu (Nera). *Sefu* v. *Sangija.*

Sangija stated in public that he had slept with Sefu's wife. The court held that this statement, made before several witnesses, did not require corroboration and awarded damages to the husband.

183. The most usual evidence requiring corroboration is the following:

1. if property of the alleged adulterer is produced;
2. if the wife confesses;

D.C.'s Appeal 20/44. Fulo (Ilemera). *Johanna* v. *Petro.*

Johanna's wife had confessed that she committed an act of adultery with Petro. No other evidence was forthcoming and the court refused to award damages to the husband.

D.C.'s Appeal 16/47. Ibadakuli (Shinyanga). *Kini* v. *Burchard.*

Kini's wife having admitted that sexual intercourse had taken place between her and Burchard, Kini claimed damages from Burchard who denied the charge; when it was shown that statements made by Kini's wife concerning Burchard's physical characteristics (circumcision) were incorrect, the court ruled that no damages were payable.

3. if the alleged adulterer has been injured;

4. if the alleged adulterer omitted to file a suit when publicly in-insulted or beaten by the husband.

D.C.'s Appeal 1/46. Ibadakuli (Mondo). *Madede* v. *Nyangindu*.

Madede claimed compensation for adultery from Nyangindu; he had no eye-witnesses, but he produced a bicycle and a broken bottle, the property of the defendant, and he had witnesses who had heard him chase the defendant down a path. The court held that this was sufficient corroboration and added that the defendant, who is a *ntwale*, would without doubt have arrested the plaintiff if he had not been guilty. As the *ntwale* had done nothing to defend his reputation the court awarded compensation to the husband.

### Infection with venereal disease

184. Evidence of infection with venereal disease is counted among cases where corroboration is required.

D.C.'s Appeal No. 3/45. Ibadakuli (Lohumbo). *Luhende* v. *Luwayi*.

Luwayi was sued by Luhende for compensation for adultery, because his wife had been infected with syphilis and had named Luwayi as her lover. Luwayi suffered from syphilis, but as this was a known fact in the village, the statement of the wife without further corroboration was not held to be sufficient to warrant the award of compensation.

185. If husband and wife both have venereal disease and no adultery can be proved, no divorce can be granted on the grounds of infection alone.

NOTE. Additional evidence is required because the Sukuma is aware that venereal disease can be contracted without sexual intercourse. Infection of a wife by her husband (*kasogone*, *kashwende*) is no ground for divorce even if adultery by the husband can be proved; divorce may be granted on account of the wife's adultery, but not on account of adultery on the part of the husband.

186. If adultery is proved, the hearing is postponed until the infected person is cured, as in a case of injury.

187. If a wife should die of venereal disease the husband is not entitled to claim *njigu* from her lover, even if it can be proved that he infected her.

NOTE. This rule was agreed by the chiefs of the Sukuma Federation and their people in 1949. Formerly a husband could claim *njigu* in BSN and BS.

NOTE. It is realized that only gross neglect of the disease by the infected person could cause his or her death in normal circumstances.

### Damages payable in case of infection with venereal disease

188 A. A man who has infected a married woman must pay to the husband five cattle as compensation for adultery, two cows as damages for infection, and Shs.50/- fine.

B. A man who has infected an unmarried woman must pay to her father, her brother, or to the woman herself, two cows as damages and Shs.50/- fine.

NOTE. It must be left to the discretion of the court to decide whether or not the guilt of a person in all these cases is proved beyond reasonable doubt. As a matter of fact, such cases are frequently brought to court and a decision given, as the infecting person often admits the charge. In the D.C.'s appeal 13/42, Fulo, the lover declared: 'I agree that I have this disease. I thought that I would not infect the girl. I do not know where I contracted the disease myself, perhaps from my concubine who has left me. These are my words, it is up to you to decide.'

This confession shows the kind of attitude on the part of a defendant which is frequently met with in such cases. As sexual intercourse is not considered immoral, and as the mechanism of infection, especially the incubation periods of these diseases, is not clearly understood, an infection is just 'bad luck'.

C. A woman who infects a man is liable to pay the same damages and fine as in 188B.

NOTE. These rules were decided upon by the chiefs of the Sukuma Federation and their people in 1949. Formerly different rules existed in the various chiefdoms:

(188A). In KF, NF, BD, BS, SBS, KM, UF the husband was not entitled to compensation for the infection of his wife, in addition to compensation for adultery. In BSN, KS, the adulterer had to pay a fine of Shs.50/-.

(188B). The man who infected the woman had to pay:
damages of 1 cow, no fine (BS, SBS, BD);
,,  ,, 2 cows, fine of Shs.50/- (BSN);
,,  ,, 3 cows, no fine (KS, KF (Nera));
,,  ,, 2 cows, no fine (NF, UF);
,,  ,, Shs.60/-, fine of Shs.40/- (KM, KF (Usmao, Sima)).

In BSN, UF, KM, KS the same compensation was payable if a woman, married or unmarried, infected a man.

In BD, NF, BS, KF, SBS a woman did not have to pay compensation.

NOTE. The rule imposing the same penalties on men and women was accepted unanimously. If few women are in a position to make a payment of two cows as damages, there are also men who possess nothing. Women can inherit property and the payment may be postponed indefinitely. The fact that a fine can now be imposed is important. It was considered advisable that if a woman were unable to pay the fine she should be imprisoned, since this would prevent an infected woman becoming a danger to the public, and furthermore while in prison she could be compelled to undergo medical treatment.

189. If a husband has been infected by his wife or vice versa, no damages are payable by either party (Note to 185).

### Adultery during husband's prolonged absence

190. If a husband, after an absence from his home, returns and finds his wife living with another man in concubinage, he can file a suit for divorce and can claim damages for adultery without producing any further proof.

191. If he returns to find his wife pregnant or having borne a child which cannot be his child because of the length of his absence, several courses are open to him:

1. he can claim damages for adultery, refuse to accept the child as his, and forgive his wife;

2. he can claim damages for adultery, acknowledge the child as his, and forgive his wife;
3. he can claim damages for adultery, divorce his wife, and claim return of bridewealth in full. The child then belongs to the maternal family (284);
4. he can acknowledge the child as his (286);
5. if the man who is named by the wife as responsible for the pregnancy refuses to accept responsibility, the provisions of paras. 275 to 279 are valid.

NOTE. The lover has to pay compensation for adultery only; he cannot be held liable for the payment of *misango* and *njigu*, except when the husband returns during his wife's pregnancy and is granted a divorce. In this case the lover may be liable for payment of damages to the husband and of *misango* to the woman's father, or even of *njigu* if the case arises. If the husband only claims compensation for adultery and does not claim a divorce, he cannot demand return of bridewealth if the wife dies during pregnancy or in childbirth; by receiving damages and omitting to claim divorce he acknowledges wife and child as his.

192. If a husband, after his return, obtains proof that his wife has had sexual intercourse or has lived with another man during his absence, but had broken off the connexion before she knew of his return, He cannot claim compensation for adultery and the fact is not considered a ground for divorce.

NOTE. This rule was agreed by the chiefs of the Sukuma Federation and their people in 1949. Formerly this rule was applied in all chiefdoms except in BSN and BD, where the husband could claim damages and could obtain a divorce.

NOTE. The next-of-kin of the husband is entitled to claim damages from the adulterer at the time when the adultery was committed (173B). The notion underlying this, and many similar rules and customary views, is that the law cannot be expected to correct nature and impose chastity on a healthy person. If the husband is absent for any length of time, he has no right to examine the conduct of his wife after his return; his next-of-kin has the right to object to the adultery of the wife, because he is the recognized substitute for the husband.

193. If the husband returns and hears that his wife has died in the house of her lover or during a pregnancy caused by a lover, he is entitled to claim compensation for adultery but he cannot claim return of bridewealth from his father-in-law. If the wife dies during childbirth, the child belongs to the husband.

Confirmed in D.C. Mwanza's Appeal No. 11/47—*Tungu* v. *Ngunya*.

### Cohabitation with a widow (610)

194. If a widow, who has not been inherited but has remained in her deceased husband's family, cohabits with a man, he cannot be required to pay compensation for adultery; because she cannot be considered a married woman.

NOTE. This rule was agreed by the chiefs of the Sukuma Federation and their people in 1949. The rule has been generally accepted from 1927 onwards except in NF, UF, where the lover of the widow had to pay damages for adultery.

D.C.'s Appeal No. 12/44. Ibadakuli. *Munyo v. Mwika.*

Munyo's son was married to Nyamuke and died after a few years. Munyo failed for two years to arrange a leviratic marriage for the widow. Nyamuke went to live with Mwika and Munyo claimed compensation for adultery. The court held that no compensation was payable, as Munyo had failed to arrange for Nyamuke to be remarried to a member of the family.

195. If a widow, having lived for a time as a leviratic wife with a relative of her deceased husband, leaves him and cohabits with another man, her lover is liable to pay compensation for adultery to the next-of-kin of the deceased husband.

NOTE. In the situation described in 194 the widow is no man's wife after her husband's death until she is inherited and remarried by a relative of the deceased husband. In the situation described in 195 the widow has become the legal wife of the heir and, whether she lives with him or apart from him, her status as wife is unchanged.

## Adultery in ignorance of wife's status

196. It is the duty of a man to ascertain that a woman with whom he sleeps or whom he marries is eligible. Any statement which the woman may have made to the man has no legal value, and the man cannot use it in his defence if accused of adultery, even if such statement was made before witnesses.

D.C.'s Appeal No. 41/42. Fulo (Bukumbi). *Maliyabwana v. Abdullah.*

Maliyabwana's wife left him and was subsequently found by him living with Abdullah, whose defence was that he did not know that the woman was married; this was not accepted by the court, which ruled that a man is responsible for ascertaining whether a woman with whom he has intercourse is or is not married.

D.C.'s Appeal No. 11/47. Usega (Masanza I). *Tungu v. Ngunya.*

Tungu claimed from Ngunya damages for adultery. Ngunya stated: 'The woman came to my home at Masanza I, and I took her and lived with her. I questioned her as to whether she was married and where she had come from. She denied having been married, and stated that she had come from Kwimba and wished to find a home and a husband.' The court gave judgement in favour of the husband.

NOTE. The two cases are representative of many others. Whatever the circumstances (except 199), the law always supports the husband against the adulterer. A man who takes a woman as his concubine or invites her to follow him temporarily into his home, or who follows a woman temporarily into her home, must remember that he runs the risk of being charged with adultery.

The native courts consider only the injury to the husband and take no cognizance of the possibility of ignorance on the part of the adulterer.

197. If a man discovers that the woman with whom he lives is the wife of another man, he must sever the connexion at once, i.e. he must expel the woman. If he continues to live with the woman but goes to the headman and reports the situation, he is liable to pay damages when the husband claims them (212).

198. If the man who is found by the husband sleeping with his wife

can prove that she has become a prostitute, the husband cannot claim damages.

NOTE. The man must be in the position to prove this fact; if he cannot do so and merely states that the woman has the reputation of being a prostitute, he is liable to pay damages. The fact that he proves that he gave a present to the woman in money or kind does not absolve him from responsibility. Other people as witnesses must prove that the woman lives by prostitution.

199. If circumstances prove that it was in fact impossible for the man to discover the truth about the woman's status, he cannot be charged with adultery.

Examples:

A. The husband is reported to have died on the coast, and the family performs the usual rites. The widow remarries and the second husband pays bridewealth. The first husband reappears later; the rumour of his death was false.

B. If a man marries a Sukuma woman abroad and pays bridewealth to a 'relative' he cannot be charged with adultery by her husband later. The court will have to ascertain whether the relative acted in good faith, but the man himself cannot be charged with adultery.

NOTE. It is for the court to decide whether or not the father of the wife should be held responsible in a case as described in 199A. If the husband dies, his brother is entitled to take the widow as his leviratic wife. If this solution is not accepted, the widow's father should return such portion of the bridewealth as is due to the family of the deceased husband before accepting a second bridewealth. Thus it may be contended that the father should be fined, and the second husband acquitted.

200. If neither of the two husbands agrees voluntarily to waive his claim to the wife, it is left to her to decide with whom she chooses to continue the marriage. The husband who is not chosen is given back his bridewealth. If the loser is the father of a child, he can take the child with him and the usual deduction is made from the bridewealth which has to be returned.

NOTE. As a matter of fact, the usual choice of the wife is her first husband.

## II. DESERTION (*Bupeji*)

201. Desertion by a wife is grounds for divorce.

202. The husband is entitled to claim divorce and return of the bridewealth if he knows where the wife is living, or if he can prove by direct or indirect evidence that the wife ran away with intent not to return. When a divorce has been granted in the absence of the wife, the bridewealth should not be returned until six months have elapsed.

NOTE. This rule was agreed by the chiefs of the Sukuma Federation and their people in 1949. Formerly a man could claim divorce and return of the bridewealth only if he knew the new domicile of his wife.

NOTE. It was considered advisable to require a delay of six months for repay, ment of bridewealth, in case the wife should later decide to return to her husband. Sometimes special obstacles may have prevented her immediate return. For instance: A couple quarrels and the husband insults his wife; so she leaves the house and returns to her parents or goes to friends. The man follows her and asks her to return, but she refuses him exclaiming: 'I will not return; I shall never re-enter the door of our house. If ever you see me naked again, I shall die. Sleep with whom you like but never with me.' These words are spoken in the heat of the moment and as time passes, the wife, persuaded by mediators sent by her husband, feels inclined to return to him. She is, however, prevented by her oath, which she now regrets. A *nfumu* must be called to remove the spell. He asks for a goat and, after he has formed a figurine out of clay representing a couple having sexual intercourse, he invites the husband, the wife, and a few friends to follow him into the bush, where he digs a small hole, kills the goat, smears the blood on the figurine, and buries it in the hole saying: 'The bad words are buried here. This man and his wife may again sleep together without evil consequences.' The goat is roasted on the spot and consumed by those taking part in the ceremony.

In present conditions, especially in view of improved means of communication, the old law seems to be obsolete. Formerly the argument used by the father-in-law was that as long as the son-in-law could not show where the wife was living, it was possible that he had murdered her. In the olden days when an unhappy wife could go hardly anywhere except to one of her relatives, such an argument may have had some justification; today it seems to be far-fetched.

203. It is not considered to be desertion if the wife leaves her husband and goes to a relative.

204. If the wife goes first to a relative and, after staying a short time with him, leaves and goes elsewhere, her husband can file a petition. In this case he is not obliged to make a statement about her whereabouts.

205. Any man who hides a married woman and denies her presence in his house when the husband comes in search of his wife is punishable, unless he is her father or brother. The fine would not be less than Shs.20/- (*Bugobya*).

206 A. Neither a relative nor any other man can be held responsible or incur penalties for giving shelter to a woman, or for not informing her husband (if he knows him) about the arrival of his wife.

B. But, if a man, especially a non-relative, is asked by a woman for shelter, he should bring her to the village headman, if he wishes to avoid the risk of being involved in an adultery case.

NOTE. Rule 205 was agreed by the chiefs of the Sukuma Federation and their people in 1949. Formerly this rule was generally followed except in the chiefdoms of NF, where even the father or brother of the wife was liable to pay one head of cattle if he concealed the truth about a wife's whereabouts from her husband.

207. Although a husband very often follows a wife who has deserted him, it is not held to be his legal duty to do so.

NOTE. Sometimes courts applied a great measure of equity, sometimes they followed rigorously the letter of the law. An example of the first attitude:

Busule (Shinyanga) case 54/46. *Nholi* v. *Nyumbu*.

Nholi had lived apart from his wife for two years, during which time he neither looked after her nor cared for her. Nholi had inherited her after his brother's death, and had abandoned her completely after a few short visits. When he heard that his wife had settled down in Nyumbu's hut, he went there and claimed damages. The court held that Nholi 'has acted like a trapper who is out to catch game' and refused to award damages.

### An example of the second attitude:

D.C.'s Appeal -/46. Ibadakuli (Busiha). *Nkinga* v. *Shinji*.

Ten years before the case Nkinga had separated from his wife Kulwa and handed her over to his brother Masele who took her as wife for some years and then in turn separated from her; she then returned to her parents' home. Masele came one day with the proposal that Kulwa should move to a third brother's house. Kulwa refused and when she was later found living with Shinji, Nkinga claimed damages from him. The lower court awarded damages on the ground that bridewealth had never been returned.

The appeal court held that the procedure adopted by the husband and his brothers was highly immoral and contrary to law and custom. The appeal court refused damages to the husband on the grounds that 'ex turpi causa non oritur actio'.

208. A husband whose wife runs away and later returns cannot claim damages if he hears that she has committed adultery. He can demand divorce and return of bridewealth if he does not wish to have her back.

Confirmed in D.C. Mwanza's Appeal No. 24/46.

### *Elopement*

209. If a man persuades another man's wife to leave her husband and elope with him, the husband can claim a divorce. The case is treated as adultery, and no further proof of the fact of adultery is necessary in the following circumstances:

A. if the couple are caught in the act of elopement;

NOTE. If a husband meets his wife with another man and the wife has her personal belongings with her, it is an adultery case if the husband can prove that the man and his wife intended to elope together and that it was not a chance meeting. But if the husband hears from others or with his own ears that his wife intends to elope with another man, he cannot file a suit against this man.

B. if the couple are found in the new domicile either living in a common household or in separate quarters. Proof of sexual intercourse is not necessary in either case.

210. It is not accepted as an excuse if it can be proved that the wife followed the lover uninvited.

Confirmed in D.C. Shinyanga's appeal No. 3/43.

211. Any person who gives shelter to a couple whom he knows to have eloped is liable to a fine of Shs.20/- (*nalicha*).

NOTE. This rule was agreed by the chiefs of the Sukuma Federation and their people in 1949. Before that time this rule was in force in all chiefdoms except those of BS.

212. If a wife elopes with a man who later leaves her, and then goes to live with another man, where her husband finds her, the man with whom she is then living has to pay the damages for adultery. If the wife is not living with another man, the man who eloped with her is liable to pay damages (171B).

NOTE. This rule was decided upon by the chiefs of the Sukuma Federation and their people in 1949. Formerly some courts followed this rule, while others made the first man responsible for damages, even if he had left the woman and another man was living with her.

NOTE. It was held that the relative guilt of the two men is not in question. The only consideration is the wrong suffered by the husband, for which the law provides that he shall receive damages. The man who originally eloped with the wife may have gone away and it may, therefore, be difficult for the husband to claim damages from him.

### Refusal to accompany husband

213. A wife cannot be forced to accompany her husband to a new domicile inside or outside Sukumaland. But if the wife refuses to follow him, the husband can claim a divorce with return of the bridewealth and possession of his children.

214. If the bridewealth has not been fully paid and the wife agrees to follow her husband, the father-in-law is entitled to withhold the children until the remainder has been paid.

### III. INJURIES INFLICTED BY WIFE

215. Any injury inflicted on her husband by a wife, or even the mere fact that she has struck him, is considered grounds for divorce.

### IV. NEGLECT OF DOMESTIC DUTIES

216. Continual neglect of domestic duties, such as cooking, carrying water and fuel, and field-work, or habitual drunkenness of the wife, are acknowledged grounds for divorce. (A neglectful wife is called *ng'wolo*.)

### V. IRREGULARITIES WITH REGARD TO BIRTH OF CHILDREN

#### A. *Abortion (Kufunda funda)*

217. 1. If it can be proved that the wife has taken an abortifacient successfully, the husband is entitled to claim a divorce.
2. Should bridewealth be returned, no deduction may be made for a foetus deliberately aborted.
3. The husband is entitled to claim *njigu* from the practitioner who assisted in the abortion (308).

#### B. *Causing death to a child during birth (Kukandikija ng'wana)*

1. If a mother by reason of her fear or pain disobeys the orders of the midwife and by so doing kills the child during labour, the husband

can claim a divorce. But it is conceded that he can only do so after it has happened twice.

2. If the bridewealth has to be returned the usual number of cattle for a child who has died are deducted.

## VI. REFUSAL OF CONJUGAL RIGHTS

218. If the wife refuses to have sexual intercourse with her husband, her attitude is grounds for divorce.

## VII. USE OF MAGIC MEDICINE

219. If a wife, without having obtained the permission of her husband, consults a practitioner and undergoes treatment, the husband is entitled to claim divorce.

NOTE. An exception is the use of love philtres or love amulets.

220. The practitioner is fined one head of cattle.

## VIII. INFERTILITY OF WIFE

221. This is a cause for divorce irrespective of the number of years of married life, but the court must consider in each case whether the husband is using the infertility of his wife as a pretext for claiming a divorce, or whether he considers it a genuine and decisive defect in his married life. Infertility of the wife is not held to be a cause for divorce if, after several years of childless married life, the husband decides that he wishes to divorce her because she is barren (*ngumba*). On the other hand, infertility of the wife must be considered a cause for divorce if the couple have tried all possible remedies of native or European science without result.

NOTE. The fact of a wife's infertility is taken very seriously by all concerned. It is the duty of the couple to ascertain the reason. The first step is to consult a diviner who is expected to indicate the cause of the defect. Here follow a few examples of alleged causes:

1. It is revealed by divination that husband and wife are related. A goat is killed and a strip cut from its skin. The husband is told to hold one end and the wife the other end of the strip, while an elder cuts through it, exclaiming that thereby all family connexion which may exist between the two is for ever severed.

2. A girl has been persuaded by her parents to marry a certain man, but she loves another one. Before the wedding she swears to herself 'I will marry this man but I shall never love him. I shall sleep with him but I shall not bear him any children.' The couple duly remain childless, but after she has been married for some time, the wife comes to like her husband and she wishes now to have children but is prevented by her oath. A *nfumu* is consulted to remove the spell.

3. Sometimes a husband chooses a more practical method of finding out the cause of sterility. He selects one of his nearest relatives and asks him to sleep with his wife, choosing a man who has had many children, preferably by several wives. If the experiment proves unsuccessful the husband knows

that the failure is due to the wife. If the experiment is successful the husband pays one head of cattle to the relative.

222. It is possible for the husband to claim return of bridewealth and to continue married life. In this case the ceremonial beasts, and especially the *ng'ombe ya maji*, are regarded as bridewealth when the remainder of the bridewealth has been returned, so that the marriage shall remain legally intact.

D.C.'s Appeal No. 52/47. Fulo (Beda). *Jenu v. Mahyila.*

Jenu claimed return of bridewealth from Mahyila, his wife's father, because his wife was barren. The assessors of the case stated that it was good Sukuma customary law for the bridewealth to be returned to the husband of a barren wife, even though husband and wife remained living together. The headman should be informed that the bridewealth has been returned, but that the union continues by mutual consent.

NOTE. The return of bridewealth should enable a man to take a second wife and thus give him the chance of a family. At the same time the original couple may like each other and wish to remain together.

## SUIT BROUGHT BY THE WIFE

### I. ADULTERY

223 A. Adultery of the husband is no ground for divorce except if committed with his daughter or step-daughter.

NOTE. Adultery committed by the husband is not condemned by the family or by society and is not regarded as transgressing any moral convention. It does not normally endanger the domestic peace for any length of time, although the clamour at the time of the occurrence may be considerable. Many cases are known in which a husband brought a concubine into the house and, if she behaved herself with the expected degree of servility and respect towards the legitimate wife, the two women lived side by side in peace. Even if the husband were to bring home a woman for a few days, the family of the wife and the public would think such behaviour incorrect, but would not consider it sufficiently serious to warrant a divorce.

B. Adultery committed with the wife's sister is not considered grounds for divorce except in KS and SS (135).

224. If a divorce is granted on account of incest, the court can order that the children be given into the guardianship of a paternal relative. If there is none, a maternal relative may be appointed as guardian. In every case the children remain the children of their father and he is entitled to receive the bridewealth for his daughters when they marry. If a reliable guardian can only be found in another district, the mother cannot refuse to allow the children to be handed over to him, even though it may be difficult for her to visit them frequently.

NOTE. The court might also try to persuade the father to accept repayment of the whole bridewealth, if no suitable paternal guardian can be found. If the father agrees the children would then belong to the maternal family (244); but the court has no right to order such procedure.

## II. DESERTION

225. If a man is absent from home for more than two years without special reasons, such as imprisonment, military service, sickness in hospital, the wife is entitled to claim a divorce.

NOTE. This rule was agreed by the chiefs of the Sukuma Federation and their people in 1949. Formerly no such rule existed but several chiefs had already made proposals for the introduction of this rule in the local federations. The chief of Buduhe (BS) had adopted it already and judgements were given accordingly. Further, in one case (D.C.'s Appeal No. 29/46 Shinyanga) the Native Court of Busule acknowledged that after two years' absence of the husband a wife could consider herself divorced.

NOTE. It often happens, if the husband goes to work outside Sukumaland, that he never returns or not for many years, although his initial intention was to stay only a short period. The man becomes accustomed to and begins to like the life of a detribalized African; he may join an Islamic or Christian community; sometimes he marries and founds a family. In the beginning he may have provided for his wife at home, although even that is the exception rather than the rule, but soon he forgets his family at home altogether. It is rare for a man to ask his wife to follow him, after a time, into a foreign area, when he decides to settle there. All this time the wife at home is waiting for her husband's return. She often becomes a loose woman whom no one can control, and no one can blame her or produce arguments against her conduct, since her husband himself shows by his prolonged absence that he does not care; alternatively she may give birth to a few illegitimate children while living with another man in concubinage.

Although the husband's family has the legal right to interfere (105, 173B), it seldom uses the right which applies mainly to cases in which the absence of the husband is limited in time. Generally the courts were, and still are, reluctant to grant a divorce in the absence of the husband.

226. If the domicile of the husband is known, he must be contacted and warned that a divorce will be granted to the wife if he does not explain his intentions with regard to his matrimonial life and does not give a date for his return.

227. If a divorce is granted to the wife on the grounds of desertion the father has to return the bridewealth to the husband's nearest relative.

228. If a man, before his departure, left his wife in the care of his brother or a near relative and has not returned after two years, the wife is entitled to claim a divorce.

NOTE. Rules 226 to 228 were agreed by the chiefs of the Sukuma Federation and their people in 1949.

NOTE. A woman is not held to be the legal wife of such a trustee, as would be the case if her husband were dead. In the latter case she would have been invited, and have agreed, to be inherited by the heir in levirate marriage.

### III. INJURIES INFLICTED BY HUSBAND

229. The courts consider only severe injuries to be grounds for divorce. Generally the following injuries are considered sufficiently severe to warrant the granting of a divorce:

A. Any wounds inflicted by a spear, knife, bush-knife, or any sharp instrument; biting, fractures, permanent maiming, permanent disfigurement, for instance, by throwing a fire-brand into the face.

B. The following acts of violence and their consequences are not generally regarded as grounds for divorce: minor blows, beating with a stick (even when causing bruises or swellings), pushing, kicking, throwing household goods at the wife.

Note. The usual procedure in court is to call for the wife's father or brother and discuss the matter with him. If the father states that he objects to his daughter being beaten and that he wishes to return the bridewealth, divorce will be granted. But if the father does not regard the matter as serious or thinks the beating well deserved, the court will accept his point of view.

The court concerns itself primarily with the question of the injury. The case is adjourned until the wife is cured or at least until her health is restored so far as possible. A fine may be imposed and if the man has no property he may be imprisoned in default. Compensation for the injury is assessed and if the man has no property, it may remain a debt.

230. In both cases, whether divorce is granted or not, a wife is entitled to compensation (*igwegwe*) for injuries. A wife can claim compensation without claiming a divorce and the court is entitled to impose a fine as well.

Note. It is the unanimous opinion that the payment of compensation and fine will not imperil the continuance of married life. There is no reason to presume that the wife after an action in court would be in danger of repeated and perhaps increased violence from her husband. In most cases the injury is inflicted in a state of drunkenness or rage, and the punishment is looked upon as a logical and merited consequence. All parties concerned consider the affair basically as a misfortune rather than the outcome of a bad disposition. If a husband should be of a dangerous disposition, the wife and her family will insist on a divorce.

231. The following is the scale of compensation:

A. One head of cattle to be paid as compensation by the husband to his wife: in case of fracture of finger, loss of tooth, minor wound inflicted with sharp instrument, injury to part of outer ear, any fracture which has completely healed.

B. Five head of cattle in case of any fracture which has not healed perfectly, any kind of permanent maiming, loss of eye, loss of ear, any permanent disfigurement of face.

Note. This rule was agreed by the chiefs of the Sukuma Federation and their people in 1949. Formerly scales of compensation varied slightly in the various chiefdoms.

Note. The scale is the same as that used generally in cases of injury.

232. The cursing of his wife by a husband, and vice versa, is not considered a ground for divorce; but if such a case is brought before elders they usually require a small payment to be made to the injured party.

Note. In some parts of the country the insulted wife invokes the help of the women's organization of the village. The members may then decide to organize a procession to the house of the offender and claim from him the payment of *masumule*, for instance a big pot of beer.

## IV. NEGLECT OF CONJUGAL DUTIES

233. If a husband intentionally neglects his wife for more than six months, this fact is considered a cause for divorce.

NOTE. This rule was agreed by the chiefs of the Sukuma Federation and their people in 1949. Formerly no such rule existed, but various courts gave judgements in which neglect of conjugal duties by the husband was acknowledged as grounds for divorce. For this reason the chiefs of SS proposed the above rule to the other chiefs who accepted it unanimously.

NOTE. The domestic life of the Sukuma is not conducted behind walls and closed doors. Therefore even in such difficult problems as proving intention in case of neglect, the court may find sufficient evidence to give judgement. For instance, the fact that a husband, without plausible reason, ceases to sleep in the same bed with his wife will assume great significance in such a case. This rule, however, was introduced mainly to provide for the frequent cases in which a leviratic wife is neglected by the heir of her deceased husband. As she often lives in a separate house, the visits of the heir are witnessed by many persons.

A wife will often accuse her husband in court of neglect of conjugal duties with no desire to obtain a divorce, but because she feels that it may lead to a reconciliation if both partners have an opportunity of airing their grievances in court, rather than continuing a series of fruitless quarrels at home.

Chief's court 52/44. Mondo (BS). *Binti Malele* v. *Mnyankali.*

The two are wife and husband. The wife Malele explains: 'I file a suit against my husband because he does not want me, he wishes to drive me out of the house. He claims repayment of bridewealth from my relatives, but I still love him. Thus I consider it a good thing to accuse him before you. Here he may explain the cause of his attitude towards me.' The husband Mnyankali answers: 'It is true I asked for repayment of bridewealth, because my wife told me I was impotent. Thus I thought it right to ask for my property as she considers me impotent.'

After considerable discussion the parties agreed in court to continue their married life in peace. In a case of this kind the court is approached by the parties as though it were an assembly of village elders whose aim is to arbitrate and reconcile. Neither party desires a judgement to be given. The hearing gives the wife an opportunity to confess that her feelings for her husband are still strong, while the husband's refusal to go home with his wife would look like an avaricious desire on his part to obtain return of bridewealth.

## V. IMPOTENCE

### (*Atigwaga buthiku*) (*Ng'osha atimaja*)

234. A divorce may be granted to the wife if it can be proved:

A. that the husband was impotent at the time of marriage, i.e. during the wedding night and during the following days;

B. that the man, after years of married life, has become impotent;

NOTE. If the husband contradicts the statement of his wife, the court can order them to retire for a night to a house where a witness will be placed to ascertain the truth. If the statement of the wife proves to be true, a divorce is granted.

C. that the man has become impotent, although children were born before he became so.

NOTE. Cases of this kind are rare because an impotent husband usually closes his eyes to any irregular conduct of his wife as long as she does not neglect her household duties. As the wife has children, she is reluctant to break up the household.

## VI. INCAPACITY TO BEGET CHILDREN

235. A husband's incapacity to beget children is grounds for divorce.

NOTE. A wife's legal position within the husband's family changes in her favour considerably as soon as she has given birth to a child, for the following reasons:

1. One possible ground for divorce is eliminated (221).
2. In the event of a divorce only part of the bridewealth has to be returned.
3. In the event of the husband's death the widow with children can choose her status within the husband's family (609).
4. A mother of children can consider her matrimonial life stable as long as she herself does not break it up (Introduction to Chapter III).

For these reasons the wife is given an opportunity in law to dissolve a union in which she is prevented, through no fault of her own, from attaining the most advantageous status possible for her.

## VII. IRREGULARITIES OF SEXUAL INTERCOURSE

236 A. Bestiality, sodomy, or the insistence on any abnormal form of sexual intercourse are held to be grounds for divorce.

NOTE. Such cases very seldom come into court; a divorce is arranged before a council of members of both families. Sexual irregularities, other than those mentioned in 236A, are looked upon as forms of insanity. They are not punished and, as long as they do not injure anyone, no damages have to be paid. In a case of bestiality the animal has to be killed and the evil-doer has to pay its price. Irregularities of any kind are very rare in Sukumaland.

B. Ejaculatio praecox (*mwangu giti ng'oko*) is considered grounds for divorce.

NOTE. Although the difficulty of obtaining reliable evidence is recognized, many cases are known to have been decided by councils of village elders or by councils of members of the families concerned.

## VIII. NEGLECT OF MAINTENANCE (*Bugumanija*)

237. Intentional gross neglect of the family, accompanied by general misbehaviour, is considered grounds for divorce. Lesser signs of neglect such as failure to provide clothing, female accessories, or relishes are not considered grounds for divorce.

NOTE. As in para. 233 the husband is often brought to court for the sole purpose of being taught a lesson. A divorce will be granted only if the husband is known to be a waster and provides neither clothing nor other necessities of life for his family.

238. In case of divorce on grounds of gross neglect of the family, the court has the right to make provision for the guardianship of minors.

The father cannot be deprived of his children, but he can be deprived of their guardianship (224).

NOTE. This rule was agreed by the chiefs of the Sukuma Federation and their people in 1949. Formerly no rule existed.

## IX. INCOMPATIBILITY

239. If husband and wife both express a definite decision to terminate their marriage, a divorce is granted.

NOTE. If the wife's family declares its readiness to return the bridewealth, the procedure is simple and a divorce is granted forthwith. If the question of return of bridewealth cannot be settled at once, the court tends to prolong the procedure and to ascertain the true reasons for the incompatibility of the partners. Finally, if all efforts of the court to reconcile the parties fail to change their resolution, the court grants a divorce in order not to aggravate the situation. If the husband is the plaintiff a refusal to grant the divorce may drive him to improper actions, i.e. to create 'grounds for divorce' on purpose. If the wife is the plaintiff she may very likely run away if a divorce is refused. In either case the result would be divorce.

The provisions of paras. 239 and 240 may seem to make the enumeration of acknowledged grounds for divorce irrelevant, since divorces can be granted without them. In practice, however, a divorce is only granted if the court ascertains the cause of the trouble and comes to the conclusion that it is irreparable. Incompatibility is acknowledged as a ground of divorce, but only after prolonged and critical deliberations.

The force which operates behind the letter of the law is public opinion, which supports the party who abides by the law, and will not favour the transgressor. Public opinion exercises the greatest influence in the close circle of the family and of the Sukuma village community. It derives its strength from knowledge; every incident has its witnesses and every loud conversation its uninvited listeners. No person who desires to remain within the circle can disregard public opinion. Everywhere the court is the forum where public opinion finds its most outspoken expression—not only within the canon of the law, but even more so in its interpretation. The procedure in native courts differs from that in others in that visitors intervene and put questions to witnesses, and the public does not hesitate to express agreement or displeasure with the attitude of the parties or the statements of witnesses. This atmosphere in court is more noticeable in divorce cases than in any others, because the human element and the general understanding of the implications of a case tend to make every spectator a judge. Thus, under the impact of public opinion, a court will hardly grant a divorce and a party will hardly insist on demanding one without stating adequate grounds.

240. If one partner to a marriage definitely, and after repeated attempts by the court to bring about a reconciliation, insists on a divorce, a divorce is granted.

## CASES WHERE NO DIVORCE IS GRANTED

241. If husband or wife is sentenced to imprisonment, this fact is not considered grounds for divorce. It is held that a wife cannot obtain a divorce without the consent of her imprisoned husband.

NOTE. Even if a person should be sentenced to a long term of imprisonment, it is not possible to know beforehand whether the term may not be considerably shortened.

242. Illness, chronic or acute, such as crippling, deformation, blindness, insanity, is not acknowledged as grounds for divorce (93).

## LEGAL EFFECTS OF DIVORCE
### Rules referring to children

243. The children always belong to the father, but the amount of bridewealth which has to be returned (83) is reduced by five head of cattle for each living child and two head of cattle for each child which has died.

NOTE. This section contains some repetition of previous paragraphs but it has been considered useful for practical purposes to assemble them again under the above heading.

244. The father has the right to renounce possession of his children, in which case he can demand return of bridewealth in full.

NOTE. The usual motive in this case is not greed but the father's difficulty in finding a home for the children. If the father's parents are still alive this problem is easily solved, but if he has no suitable relatives, he may prefer to leave the children with their maternal family. It may also happen that, in the first bitterness of feeling, he wishes to break completely with the past. Frequently such a man leaves the locality for a time.

245. Neither the father-in-law nor any other member of the maternal family has a right to demand that the father should agree to receive the full amount of bridewealth and renounce his right to the children, even if it can be proved that the father is not a fit person to look after the children (224).

246. The father is permitted to demand his children at any subsequent date, and the maternal family cannot refuse to hand them back if the father is prepared to return the cattle which he received in respect of them (see para. 243) when the bridewealth was returned. The maternal family then has the right to demand payment for the children's maintenance while under their care.

The amount claimed for maintenance must not exceed one cow, irrespective of the number of children maintained.

NOTE. This rule was agreed by the chiefs of the Sukuma Federation and their people in 1949. Formerly the amount payable for maintenance varied in different areas:

A. In UF, NF, KF, BSN, BD a token payment of a blanket and perhaps Shs. 10/-.
B. In KM, KS one head of cattle.
C. In BS, SS, SBS the whole bridewealth, irrespective of the number of children.

NOTE. A number of chiefs proposed very high—almost prohibitive—amounts to be paid for maintenance by fathers. This was not generally accepted and finally the limit was set at one cow. It seems that the proposal for a high amount took into consideration the points of view of the father and maternal grandfather, but not the fate of the children. Such children are only minor heirs of the maternal family with whom they are living, while they would become their father's main heirs (*nkuruwabo* and *nzuna*).

The law distinguishes between the amounts payable by a father who claims his legitimate child (246) and by a father trying to legitimize his illegitimate child (269). The payment of a large amount for the purpose of legitimization operates to prevent a father, who has not cared about his daughter for many years, attempting to enrich himself from her bridewealth.

247. A father is not allowed to take some of his children with him and leave the rest with the maternal family, taking in their stead a part of the bridewealth. He must either take all his children or leave them all.

248. A father-in-law cannot ask for more cattle for the children than the original amount of the bridewealth.

NOTE. For example: if the total bridewealth was ten head of cattle, and was returned in full, three children being left with the maternal grandfather, the father, if he later asks for the return of the children, will be required to pay only ten head of cattle plus maintenance.

249. An infant in arms remains with the mother until it is weaned and no maintenance can be demanded by the maternal family when the father comes to fetch his child.

D.C.'s Appeal No. 29/47. Msalala (KM). *Msuka* v. *Barabara.*

When Msuka obtained a divorce from Barabara's daughter, their child was not yet weaned and was therefore left with the mother, but the usual number of cattle was deducted when the bridewealth was returned. After five years Msuka demanded his child but Barabara wanted one head of cattle for the child's maintenance. The court held that no maintenance was payable and the child must be returned to his father. The elders held the view that Barabara could not claim for the child's maintenance, just as Msuka could not claim the produce and calves of the cattle he left with his father-in-law when the bridewealth was returned.

250. It is within the discretion of the husband to allow the mother and her children to visit each other; he cannot be coerced into giving such permission.

NOTE. The rules regarding the domicile of the children in case of divorce are usually treated very liberally by the father after his first rage at the time of the divorce case has given place to a cooler judgement of the whole affair. The children often spend months in the house of their maternal grandfather, uncle, or mother.

### Rules referring to maintenance

251. The maintenance of a divorced wife (*nshimbe*) is a charge on her relatives and never upon her husband and his family.

### Rules referring to property

252. A wife must be allowed to retain possession of her private property, i.e. property she brought with her from her father's house,

inherited property, clothing, gifts from her husband, and gifts from members of her own and her husband's family.

253. The wife takes with her all kitchen utensils of native make. She is not entitled to implements which have been bought in a shop (aluminium pots, kettles, &c.). Mats made by her are her own property.

254 A. Property acquired by the wife through her skill as practitioner, midwife, potter, beer-brewer, &c., is her property if the husband has not paid the practitioner's fee, which amounts to one heifer (ng'ombe ya mhela).

NOTE. The fees of practitioners vary according to the gravity of the disease and the duration of the cure. A doctor's fee (mhela) seldom exceeds one cow for a female patient and one bull for a male patient. The practitioner can only expect to be paid his or her fee if the patient recovers; but the payment of simba nti and shilatu is required from every patient; these fees usually amount to one or two shillings.

B. This heifer has to be paid by the husband, even if his wife's skill has been acquired during married life, if he wishes to obtain the right to the property acquired by the wife.

C. If husband and wife have jointly purchased cattle, house, or commodities, these possessions become the property of the husband, if no agreement before witnesses has been concluded.

255. The divorced wife has no claim to food in store or to crops in the field.

NOTE. This rule was agreed by the chiefs of the Sukuma Federation and their people in 1949. Formerly the divorced wife was entitled to the shilandi (wife's share in the harvest),[1] except in KS and SS where she got nothing.

NOTE. It was the custom for the wife after her marriage to bring seed for the shilandi crops from her father's home. Nowadays many of the crops which comprised shilandi are planted for sale, the fields for them are prepared by ploughing, manuring, and by employing communal labour. Therefore the wife has lost her claim to shilandi because the crop is no longer brought from her home; moreover, shilandi has lost its meaning, because it originally consisted mainly of crops used for relishes and for consumption in the house and not of cash crops. During the last few years there has been a tendency to give the divorced wife less and less from the crops.

The village elders[2] were usually influenced in their decision regarding shilandi by consideration of the grounds of divorce. If the wife had deserted her husband or was guilty of adultery she got nothing; but if the divorce was granted because of the husband's neglect of maintenance (238), she was awarded a share of the shilandi, because she had probably done all the field-work.

If shilandi was awarded to the wife, the following rules were applied:

A. If some of the shilandi had been sold during the year of the divorce, the wife could not claim a share of the proceeds nor could she claim a share of anything bought with the proceeds.

B. The crops in the field were divided in the same way as the food in store.

---

[1] The word shilandi is unknown in KS and SS.
[2] No lawsuit relating to the division of property after a divorce is recorded.

C. If the *shilandi* crops and the husband's crops were interplanted, the cleaning of the field was the responsibility of both wife and husband even after divorce. If one of them neglected the work, the other was entitled to take the whole harvest. The court could award to the lazy party a share of the harvest in consideration of the work done before the divorce.

D. The division of crops into *shilandi* and husband's crop was not affected by the actual work done in the field. For instance, even if the wife looked after the cotton field by herself, the cotton remained the husband's crop.

The new rule 255, now accepted everywhere, seems to be hard on the wife, but since the great majority of divorce suits are initiated by the wife, the rule expresses public opinion.

### Rules referring to return of bridewealth

256. It is the duty of the court to ascertain the degree of guilt of husband or wife, and to assess accordingly the amount of bridewealth which has to be returned, after the customary deduction for children has been made (81).

NOTE. Court judgements for many years past have given evidence of the careful consideration devoted to determining guilt in divorce cases.

Fulo Appeal Case 13/44. *Yamunda* v. *Kacheyeki.*

Yamunda claimed divorce and return of bridewealth from his wife's father Kacheyeki, without giving any grounds for his demand. The court decided that a divorce should be granted, but no bridewealth should be returned because the husband repudiated his wife without giving any reasons for his attitude.

Latterly the chiefs of KS and SS agreed to introduce the question of guilt into divorce cases and to deduct two cows if bridewealth had to be returned and the court had found the husband to be the guilty party.

Opinion was unanimous in favour of the adoption of rules introducing the question of guilt into divorce cases. It was felt that the most frequent cases, in which the husband must leave cattle for maintenance, would be those of 'neglect of maintenance' (238) and 'neglect of conjugal duties' (233) concerning mainly levirate wives.

257. If the court finds that the wife is the guilty party, the whole bridewealth has to be returned. If the court finds that the husband is the guilty party, the maternal family is allowed to keep two cows.

258 A. Full bridewealth has to be returned if the court finds that any one of the following grounds for divorce has been established: adultery by wife (170); desertion by wife (201); injuries by wife (215); neglect by wife (216); irregularities by wife (217); refusal by wife (218); use of magic medicine by wife (219); infertility of wife (221); desertion by husband (225); impotence of husband (234); irregularities by husband (236); incapacity of husband (divorce claimed by wife) (235); incompatibility (divorce claimed by wife) (240).

NOTE. It may seem surprising that paras. 225, 234, and 236 are included in the list of cases where full bridewealth has to be returned, but the possibility of remarriage as well as the degree of guilt of either party are taken into consideration.

B. Two cows can be retained by the wife's family in case of: adultery by husband (223); injuries by husband (229); neglect by husband (233);

neglect of maintenance by husband (237); incompatibility (divorce claimed by husband) (240).

NOTE. The payment of compensation, as in the case of injuries inflicted by the husband, should not be confused with the payment of two cows in case of divorce. The court may impose both payments if it finds them justified.

C. The two cows do not have to be returned if the wife should re-marry.

D. The two cows are reckoned as payment for the wife's maintenance and are handed over to that relative who received the original bride-wealth, or his heir.

259. If, in consideration of the number of children, no bridewealth has to be returned and the court finds that the husband is the guilty party, he has to pay two cows.

NOTE. Rules 256 to 259 were decided upon by the chiefs of the Sukuma Federation and their people in 1949. Formerly the following rule existed every-where: In any case of divorce, bridewealth, or a portion of it, depending on the number of children born to the couple, had to be returned to the husband irre-spective of the grounds for divorce.

260. If, in case of divorce, the amount to be deducted for children is greater than the amount of bridewealth which the husband has paid, he must either leave the children to the maternal family or, if he wishes to take his children, he must pay the balance of the bridewealth.

## WHEN A DIVORCE BECOMES LEGALLY EFFECTIVE

261. Divorce rules have been proposed by the chiefs of the Sukuma Federation and their people (Appendix II):

Particulars of all decrees of divorce shall be entered in a separate regis-ter kept by the court, and divorce certificates shall be issued to either party on application.

The above-mentioned particulars shall include full details of the amount of bridewealth, if any, which is repayable. Any payments made in execution of the decree shall be reported to the court and entered in the register and on the divorce certificate. The fee for registration of a divorce shall be Shs.4/-, payable by the plaintiff in each case.

If the divorce case has been decided by arbitration before the village elders, the case must be registered at a Native Court and divorce certi-ficates must be issued.

Formerly a divorce became absolute:

1. When the husband received repayment of the whole, or one instal-ment of, the bridewealth; the number of cattle handed over is ir-relevant; payment of one beast makes the decree absolute.

Ibadakuli Appeal No. 35/42. *Nhoja* v. *Nhindilo.*

Nhoja was granted a divorce and the wife's father returned to him five of the original eleven cattle of the bridewealth, leaving the rest to be returned later.

Nhindilo took the woman as his concubine, whereupon Nhoja claimed compensation for adultery. The court held that the wife should be considered a divorced wife after the first instalment of repayment of bridewealth had been made. Therefore no compensation was due to Nhoja.

For a similar case see D.C.'s Appeal No. 18/48 Usega Federation, *Nzumbi* v. *Ntemi Ndalahwa*.

2. When a divorce certificate was issued by the court. The issue of this document was not obligatory.

NOTE. For several years the issue of a divorce certificate has been demanded by the parties in nearly all chiefdoms and in nearly all cases after a divorce has been granted in court. Despite this it was considered necessary to make the issue of a certificate obligatory because certificates have not been demanded in the very cases where the issue of one was most important. In such a situation it was sometimes difficult to find witnesses after many years to prove the fact that a divorce had been granted although no cattle had changed hands.

A. NF, UF. No divorce certificate was issued until the first instalment of bridewealth had been repaid.

B. BD, BSN, SS, BS, KS, KM. A divorce certificate could be issued independently of arrangements regarding the repayment of bridewealth.

3. If no bridewealth had to be repaid or could be repaid, the judgement of the court or the final decision of village elders accepted by the parties concerned made a divorce absolute.

## ELIGIBILITY FOR REMARRIAGE OF A DIVORCEE

262. As long as a wife is not legally divorced she must be considered married to her legal husband.

263. If she lives with another man she commits adultery. If she wishes to marry another man it is the duty of the woman, or her father, or her father's heir to claim a divorce first.

D.C.'s Appeal No. 29/46. Ibadakuli (Usule). *Nholi* v. *Nyumbu*.

Ng'wanangwa Nholi had separated from his wife who went to live with her parents. After about two years, during which time Nholi had not looked after his wife, she decided to live with Nyumbu. When Nholi heard of it he claimed damages. The court held that the rule according to which a wife is bound to her husband until the granting of a divorce holds good, and awarded Nholi damages for adultery.

264. A woman is still considered to be married during negotiations for a divorce or during the time that a civil suit which may lead to a divorce is pending.

# CHAPTER IV

# CHILDREN

## INTRODUCTION

As soon as a child (*ng'wana*) displays understanding (a Sukuma says: 'it will bring water if you ask for it'), it is treated by kinsmen and neighbours in a manner which does not differentiate between children of three, seven, or even more years of age. The same happens with regard to older children from ten or twelve years onwards; thus adults consider rather the age group[1] to which a child belongs than its individual age. A child of three or four years is usually addressed like one of ten years and sometimes even like an adolescent person.

Boys and girls begin to help in field and house at an early age. The boys' duty is to herd cattle, goats, and sheep. There is now little danger from wild animals except in a very few areas, and thus herds of thirty or forty beasts may be seen with a shepherd not much taller than a young goat. Girls help their mothers in all tasks of domestic routine, but are also frequently sent with the cattle. All children help in the fields at times when hands are urgently needed.

The children's education, which covers a very small field, is in the hands of the mother. Orders are given without sharpness, questions are put without menace, and obviously parents and other grown-ups remember the time when they themselves were children. Therefore it seems that the children are treated with understanding and their faults are readily pardoned. Small children and even those of more advanced age are seldom punished; at least not methodically as a measure of education. A child is punished usually only when an adult person has been provoked to short-lived anger. Examples of persistent ill treatment of children are very rare and are looked upon by everyone as symptoms of madness. Children are regarded by their parents and families as an asset not a liability; only a madman will destroy or damage valuable property of his own.

There is very little systematic teaching and the mothers of a village do not have individual ideas about the education of small children. The child can hear and see everything, but it only assimilates what it understands. The bringing up of children is conditioned not so much by strict

---

[1] Although age-grades are not an obligatory institution, their principle can be traced —to a certain degree—mainly in the *Sumba* and *Namhara* organizations. The following terms for age and sex are much in use:

| | |
|---|---|
| *Balele* (pl.), infants. | *Bashimbe* (pl.), widows or divorcees. |
| *Byanda* (pl.), boys up to puberty. | *Bajaha* (pl.), men of 40 to 50. |
| *Baniki* (pl.), girls up to puberty. | *Bashike* (pl.), women of 40 to 50. |
| *Basumba* (pl.), young men. | *Banamhara* (pl.), old men. |
| *Banhya* (pl.), young women. | *Bagikulu* (pl.), old women. |

conventions as by natural dangers; for instance, if parents object to their children coming home late in the evening from their play, the roaring lion in the not too far distance impresses the child more than does a lecture from the father about punctuality. The dangers of ordinary life make it essential that children should become independent of parental care as early as possible. Therefore children are precocious. By the time a Sukuma child is five years old it already has a considerable knowledge of life.

Nothing human is strange to children. The bedroom of a hut is small and parents in talk and action pay little attention to their children's presence. Limitations of space have given rise to very strict rules of discretion, even in matters where discretion is not necessary. It may be said that a question put to a child concerning its home is never answered; the child would not even consider whether it was harmless or not.

At an early stage children begin to imitate the life of adults, and the Sukuma word for this game is *mambulia*. They build little huts, pretend to possess many cattle which they form from clay, cook imaginary food in pots made from the same material, and go 'to bed' after a day's heavy work. Such games are not played everywhere, but they are widespread. Parents take no notice of the children's play and never forbid it; thus the children often get tired of it, since it is a game like any other, and prefer catching birds or doing nothing. Since restrictions are few, there are few transgressions and fewer psychological problems.

There are plenty of sickly children, but cripples and imbeciles are rare, owing to the methods formerly employed for dealing with them. A child born crippled (*kisembo*), for instance, without hands or legs, was killed at once by the midwife. Flour and water were forced into its mouth and it died within an hour. No cases are known to have been taken to court.

An idiot child (*nelenele*), when the symptoms became apparent, was drowned during the rainy season. The village may have guessed what had happened, but no one would report the matter. The people say: '*babyala inoga*—they gave birth to a hollow ground-nut.'

A child with a hump back (*kigembe*) was also killed, but as this deformity often does not become apparent till later in life the method of murdering the child was different. For a time it might be hoped that a disease which would not be fatal to a healthy child would kill a weak one. If such a natural end was too long delayed, an opportunity might occur if the child contracted any sort of illness; then one evening the father, after the mother had been sent off on some pretext, prepared a rope with a noose. This was put round the neck of the sleeping child and the rope end thrust outside through a small hole (*kengerezi*) or other aperture in the wall. The father left the room and pulled the rope end, thus strangling the child. The rope was taken away and no sign of the murder remained. The loud lament of the mother when she came home was genuine and the neighbours were told that the child died suddenly of the sickness.[1]

## LEGITIMATE CHILDREN

265. Children born in wedlock belong to their father.

NOTE. As a rule all the children living in a house receive the same treatment from the grown-up persons, whatever may be the reason for their membership in the family. For instance, a grandfather will pay school fees for the illegitimate child of his daughter as he would for one of his own sons. No discrimination is made between an illegitimate and a legitimate child, and this attitude is understandable if one considers that a legitimate child may become illegitimate (244) and an illegitimate child may be legitimized by its father (269).

Should a father neglect his child, his kinsmen or the child's maternal relatives would strongly object. Very likely the child would run away to them and remain with them. If a father remarries after he has been divorced from his first wife and sees that her children are unhappy in the house, he will send them to his parents or to one of his married siblings.

## II. STEP-CHILDREN

266 A. If a child remains with its mother in the house of its stepfather, it can never become an heir to the latter's property.

B. If the father remarries after a divorce from his first wife, in which he kept the children, these children retain their position as *nkuruwabo*, &c., even if their step-mother gives birth to children.

## III. ILLEGITIMATE CHILDREN

*(Ng'wana wa nda ya bu or ng'wana wa butende)*

### 1. General rules

267. Children not born in wedlock belong to the maternal family.

268 A. If the illegitimate child is a boy, he is entitled to a share in his maternal grandfather's estate.

B. If the maternal grandfather has sons, the illegitimate child follows his maternal uncles in the sequence of heirs.

C. If the maternal grandfather has no sons, the illegitimate child becomes the *nkuruwabo* of his grandfather.

NOTE. If a father has only daughters, one of whom becomes pregnant without being married, he may not insist on finding the man who caused the pregnancy; he may wait and see whether the child is a boy, in which case he has obtained his *nkuruwabo*.

D. If the illegitimate child is a girl, the bridewealth for her is received by her maternal grandfather or his heirs.

D.C.'s Appeal 1/47. Ibadakuli (Shinyanga). *Wande d/o Nhola* v. *Nhola*.

Wande was the illegitimate daughter of Nhola who had never paid bridewealth

---

[1] This method of killing was obviously considered a kindness to the victim because it was applied also to a chief who had become acutely and incurably ill.

for her mother. When Wande married, her bridewealth was received by her grandmother. Nhola took the cattle away from the old woman. At her grandmother's death, Wande, as her heir, claimed the cattle. The court held that the father had no right to keep the cattle and that he must hand them over to his illegitimate daughter.

## 2. *Legitimization* (*Kikindikamata* or *Kukwang'wana*)

269. A father has the right to legitimize his illegitimate children at any time:

A. by paying bridewealth and marrying their mother;

B. by the payment of cattle for each child and compensation for rearing the child;

C. by paying bridewealth on behalf of an illegitimate son.

### A

270. The lover may start negotiations about marriage and payment of bridewealth as soon as he is informed of the pregnancy. It is the custom everywhere for the father of the woman to accept the bridewealth and agree to the marriage, but he is not bound to do so (294).

### B

271. The father can legitimize his children after he has broken off relations with their mother by making payments for each child as follows:

| | |
|---|---|
| where the father or grandfather is a commoner . . | 5 cattle |
| where the father or maternal grandfather is a village headman, regent, *munang'oma*, direct descendant of a chief, or a deposed chief . . . . . | 6 ,, |
| where the father or the maternal grandfather of the child is a chief . . . . . . . . | 10 ,, |

272. Only the man who has been named as father by the mother of the child and who has paid *misango* (288) has the right to legitimize the child.

273. It is within the discretion of the maternal family to accept or refuse the offer of the child's natural father.

274. The maternal family is entitled to compensation for the upbringing of the child. The amount of the compensation varies from two to ten head of cattle according to the sex of the child and its age when the father makes his offer of legitimization (compare 246).

### C

275. A special kind of legitimization, sometimes but not always recognized by the courts, may be effected by the father's payment of bridewealth on behalf of his illegitimate son. The son belongs to his maternal

family, but if the latter agrees to the father paying bridewealth for him, the son becomes a member and heir of the paternal family.

D.C.'s Appeal 4/45. Ibadakuli (Shinyanga). *Shilinde* v. *Kibonela.*

Since his father (Gindo) had not paid bridewealth for his mother, Kibonela was illegitimate and belonged to his mother's family. When he wished to marry, his father, with the consent of the maternal family, paid bridewealth for him and thereby legitimized him. On Gindo's death the children of Kibonela inherited the property. Their right to do so was contested by Shilinde, a distant relative of Gindo; the court decided in favour of the children of Kibonela.

### 3. *Illegitimate child of an unmarried woman*

276. The man whom a woman names as father of her child must admit paternity, unless he can prove that he had no sexual intercourse with the woman.

NOTE. Sexual intercourse with unmarried girls is considered natural and desirable (Introduction to Chapter II); consequently the pregnancy does not cause embarrassment to the man or to the girl or her parents; the girl is not disgraced, and the birth of her child does not prejudice her chances of an early marriage (Note 1C to 10). Every child is an asset and not a liability to the family to which it belongs.

277. If she has had many lovers, the one whom the woman names is the father of her child.

278. If the man insists that he has never had sexual intercourse with her and produces some sort of proof, the woman may be required to prove her assertion by giving details regarding place, hour, physical characteristics of the man, &c.

279. If the man named had intercourse with the woman within the period during which conception could have taken place, which is considered to be about two months, no argument about paternity can be admitted.

NOTE. A refusal to admit paternity was rare, even when proof of paternity was not beyond reasonable doubt. Although the man took upon him certain obligations, pride outweighed material considerations. To be chosen as the father of her child, especially by a young girl, was looked upon by the man himself and by the world as a proof of her feelings for him. Therefore, the man would not refuse to admit paternity if he had ever had sexual intercourse with the girl.

In recent times more cases of disputed paternity have come before the courts, possibly because girls now have more opportunities for taking lovers who are not Sukuma men. Investigation in such cases is becoming more thorough, especially if the suspected father is a stranger or has left the country.

280. If the woman names as father of her child a man who can prove the falsity of her statement, the question of paternity would be closed; the woman would not be allowed to name another man.

281. If an unmarried woman becomes pregnant, her father or, failing him, her nearest paternal relative, sends two relatives to the lover or his father who announce that the woman has named the lover as the father

of her child. This procedure is called *kutwalilwa nda*, and takes place when the pregnancy becomes obvious. If the lover agrees he hands over an arrow or some tobacco as token of his consent.

NOTE. In some areas the pregnant woman is sent to her lover, accompanied by two friends. Thus the whole village becomes witness to the *kutwalilwa nda*. Sometimes the lover comes to live with the woman's family during her pregnancy (*kulela nda*). He helps in all kinds of work, but he gains nothing except that he lives as the husband of the pregnant woman. As soon as the woman gives birth to a child, he has to leave the house.

282. If the woman is living in her lover's house, no *kutwalilwa nda* takes place, but this does not affect the legal liability of the lover. It is considered obvious in this case which man is responsible for the pregnancy. If the lover wishes to deny paternity, it is up to him to prove his case.

283. The lover is not held responsible for any expenses connected with the pregnancy, except those mentioned in 300 and 313.

### 4. *Illegitimate child of a married woman*

284. If a wife has conceived a child during the absence of her husband, the latter can, after his return, either acknowledge the child as his own or refuse to do so, in which case the child is considered illegitimate and belongs to the wife's family (190, 191).

NOTE. Nowadays the younger generation shows a tendency to be more strict in questions of paternity, and absent husbands after their return now make a lot of 'fuss' which the older generation considers excessive. The conservative element argues that the majority of absent husbands do not worry about providing for the maintenance of their wives at home. Absent husbands, moreover, do not keep their promises, made before departure, about the length of their absence from home. In view of these signs of negligence, the 'fuss' made on their return is disproportionate.

285. If the pregnancy has been caused by a relative of the absent husband, it is the general custom to acknowledge the child as legitimate.

286. If a husband, after a lengthy absence from home, returns and finds that his wife is pregnant or has borne a child during his absence of which he cannot be the father, he must decide at once whether to acknowledge paternity of the child or not. If he has once acknowledged paternity and resumed married life, he cannot later disown the child.

NOTE. Cases have occurred—especially if the illegitimate child happens to be the only son and therefore the *nkuruwabo*—of a subsequent change of mind on the part of the husband. If the husband takes a second wife who has a child, or if his first wife later has a child, he may wish to have a son of his own as *nkuruwabo* and try to disown the son of another man.

287. If the husband after his return makes no decision and resumes married life, it is understood that he acknowledges paternity. If he dis-

owns an unborn child or a child already born, he must do so before witnesses.

NOTE. The rules in paras. 286 and 287 were agreed by the chiefs of the Sukuma Federation and their people in 1949. Formerly no rule existed regulating the question of paternity; some courts acknowledged the father's right to revoke his first decision and disown the child at any time; other courts considered the first decision of the husband to be final.

### Misango and Njigu

The legal consequences of an illegitimate pregnancy are *misango* and *njigu*. These institutions do not exist in the chiefdoms of the Mweli Federation except in KM.

### 5. Misango

288. *Misango* is the payment made by a lover to the father of an unmarried woman as compensation for causing her to become pregnant; the woman in question may be an unmarried girl, a divorcee, or a widow in respect of whom bridewealth has been returned.

289. The obligation to pay *misango* is the immediate consequence of the *kutwalilwa nda* and is also payable in cases mentioned in 282.

D.C.'s Appeal No. 53/43. Fulo. *Edward v. Mwinula.*

Edward refused to pay *misango* because he had not been officially informed of the woman's pregnancy. The court held that the payment of *misango* is not dependent on information but on the paternity of the unborn child, which in this case was clearly his, because he had been living in concubinage with the girl, Mwinula's sister.

290. *Misango* is also payable between men who are blood-brothers if they belong to two chiefdoms whose people consider themselves blood-brothers. The tribal blood-brotherhood has been broken by the man who has caused the pregnancy of his blood-brother's daughter (74).

NOTE. Rules based on custom rather than on a moral code have been applied by agreement:

NF Appeal No. 18/45. Fulo (Bukumbi). *Shimba v. Nghelela.*

Ujashi and Negezi, the two chiefdoms to which the parties belong, have a *bupugo* relationship and between the inhabitants of these two chiefdoms no *misango* is claimable. The court acknowledged the validity of this argument and held that the plaintiff had no right to claim *misango*.

291. The payment of *misango* gives the lover no rights over the child.

D.C.'s Appeal No. 7/45. *Geha d/o Malami v. Kasulende.*

Kasulende lived with Geha in concubinage and paid *misango* for three children. The court held that the children belonged to the maternal family unless bridewealth were paid for their mother.

D.C.'s Appeal No. 6/44. Fulo. *Machibya v. Isabiga.*

Isabiga paid six cattle after having lived with Machibya's daughter and had two children by her. He considered that the children belonged to him, but the court ruled that if he wished to have the children, he must pay another four cattle, since four cattle of the first payment counted as *misango*.

NOTE. Incorrect judgements have occurred:

D.C.'s Appeal 38/44. UF (Nasa). *Phillipo* v. *Mabula.*

The court held—after consultation with two assessors—that since no special arrangement with regard to the child had been made at the time of the marriage, the child was the property of the father who paid the *misango* at her birth.

292. If *misango* has been paid and bridewealth is subsequently paid, the number of beasts paid as *misango* is not deducted from the bridewealth.

293. If the father of the girl agrees to accept the payment of bridewealth from the man who made his daughter pregnant he cannot later claim *misango*.

D.C.'s Appeal No. 31/44. UF. *Ntemi Bahebe* v. *Bulegi.*

Bulegi's father offered to pay bridewealth for his son who had caused the pregnancy of Bahebe's daughter. Bahebe refused to accept the bridewealth as he considered it too small. He claimed *misango* and returned the cattle which Bulegi's father had already sent. The court held that·Bulegi must pay *misango* and that Bahebe had a right to claim it, although it is seldom that a father follows this procedure.

NOTE. By accepting bridewealth before claiming the payment of *misango*, the father of the unmarried woman renounces his claim to *misango*. If he requires the payment of *misango*, he must claim it before he receives the bridewealth.

D.C.'s Appeal No. 28/44. KM (Msalala). *Misamo* v. *Mayuki.*

Mayuki had two children by Misamo's aunt. Afterwards he paid five cattle and three more children were born. All the children grew up in the house of Mayuki. When two of the girls were to be married, Misamo claimed that their bridewealth should be paid to him, as the senior representative of the maternal family, because the five cattle were payment for *misango* and the girls were illegitimate children and therefore belonged to the maternal family. The court held that the five cattle must be regarded as bridewealth (after so many years no witnesses were produced by either party) because the woman's father, during the eight years before his death, had never claimed *misango* for the children born after the first two, and had also left them living with their father, an unusual procedure in the case of illegitimate children.

294. A father who pays *misango* and later bridewealth has legitimized his child by these payments; he is not required to make further payments for the maintenance of the child.

NOTE. Rules 293 and 294 were agreed by the chiefs of the Sukuma Federation and their people in 1949. Formerly rule 294 was followed in BD, SBS, SS, KS. In KF, BSN, UF, NF the father had to pay two head of cattle, in addition to *misango* and bridewealth, in order to secure possession of his child.

295. Although liability for the payment of *misango* is established by the procedure of *kutwalilwa nda*, the actual payment has to be made after the birth of the child.

296. In the event of a miscarriage *misango* has to be paid. After a mis-

carriage, a female relative of the lover is called to make an examination, very often in the presence of the wife of the village headman as witness. Only if the existence of a foetus is proved does *misango* have to be paid.

NOTE. This rule was agreed by the chiefs of the Sukuma Federation and their people in 1949. Formerly it was followed in all chiefdoms except SS, KS, KM, where *misango* was only payable for a child after it had been brought out of the house for the first time.

297. If part of the bridewealth has been paid, but the wedding ceremony has not yet been arranged, the bridegroom must at once pay the rest of the bridewealth if there is a pre-marital pregnancy. Otherwise the father-in-law can postpone the wedding and claim the payment of *misango* first. The father-in-law must then return, for the time being, the cattle which he has already received as the first instalment of bridewealth.

NOTE. No court cases are remembered in which a father has, in these circumstances, broken up the marriage. The usual solution, found in a council of the two families concerned, is a compromise by which the son-in-law makes an immediate payment of a further instalment and then marries the girl.

298. *Misango* is payable for each illegitimate child, even if a woman has several illegitimate children by the same man.

NOTE. This rule was agreed by the chiefs of the Sukuma Federation and their people in 1949. Formerly rule 298 was followed in NF, UF, KF, BSN, BD, BS, SBS. In SS, KS, KM *misango* was payable only for the first child of an unmarried couple.

P.C.'s Appeal No. 41/43. Fulo. *Ikingo* v. *Madundo*.

Ikingo paid Shs.10/- as *ng'ombe ya maji* (23) (first instalment of bridewealth) for a woman with whom he was living in concubinage and by whom he already had three children. The court held that this was bridewealth and not *misango*. Ikingo had paid *misango* after the birth of the first child and had paid nothing since. When he paid Shs.10/- after the birth of the fourth child, it could not be regarded as an instalment of the *misango* for the second child.

299. At the birth of illegitimate twins, only a single *misango* is payable.

NOTE. This rule was agreed by the chiefs of the Sukuma Federation and their people in 1949. Formerly, a single *misango* was payable in NF, UF, BSN, BD, SM, KM; double *misango* was payable in KF, SBS, SS, KS.

*Amount of misango payable*

300. The following compensation is payable:

A. in the case of a commoner 2 cattle (1 cow and 1 bull).

NOTE. This rule was agreed by the chiefs of the Sukuma Federation and their people in 1949. Formerly it was followed in all chiefdoms except those of SS and KS, where *misango* amounted to three head of cattle.

B. in the case of *banangwa, banang'oma*, direct descendants of a chief, or a deposed chief . . . 5 cattle
in the case of a regent . . . . . . 8 „
in the case of a chief . . . . . . 10 „

C. The amount of *misango* payable is determined by the social position of the superior in rank whether he is the lover or the father of the girl.

NOTE. This rule was agreed by the chiefs of the Sukuma Federation and their people in 1949. Formerly no reciprocity of payment was acknowledged.

NOTE. Details of the rules for reciprocity of payment in cases between tribal dignitaries and commoners are given in the Note to 177.

301. If the *misango* is paid in money the usual rates of exchange are valid (5).

302. The lover must pay *misango* in cattle if he has cattle. If he has no cattle it is within the discretion of the father to accept money or sorghum or wait until the lover acquires cattle.

303. If the lover has no property, the *misango* payment becomes a common debt.

### 6. Njigu

*Njigu* is the word used generally for any payment of compensation in cases of homicide. The following paragraphs refer only to *njigu* payable in connexion with pregnancy and childbirth.

304. *Njigu* is the payment made by the lover to the father or the nearest paternal relative of a woman (his concubine) who has died during pregnancy or childbirth. The woman in question may be an unmarried girl, a divorcee, or a widow in respect of whom bridewealth has been repaid.

305. The paternal relatives of the deceased woman must declare their intention of claiming *njigu* immediately after the *isabingula* (ritual cleansing after a death.)

D.C.'s Appeal No. 28/46. Ibadakuli (SBS). *Kushaluka v. Shija.*

Kushaluka claimed *njigu* from Shija because his daughter had died in childbirth and Shija was the father of the illegitimate child. The court held that it is the custom to state after the *isabingula* whether it is intended to claim *njigu* or not. As no such claim had been made at the time by the deceased girl's relative, it must be assumed that the relatives believed then that the girl had died from a cause other than childbirth. In fact the claim for *njigu* was only made after some weeks had passed. No *njigu* was awarded.

306. A man's liability to pay *njigu* begins after the *kutwalilwa nda*, and ends when his concubine has recovered from her confinement and resumed her usual domestic duties.

D.C.'s Appeal No. 18/44. Ibadakuli (Busanda). *Swale v. Isengo.*

Isengo had caused the pregnancy of Swale's daughter. At birth great difficulties arose; the girl had to be taken to a European hospital and the child removed by operation. Her father took her away two days after the operation and the girl died two months later, never having completely recovered. The court awarded *njigu.*

D.C.'s Appeal No. 36/43. KM (Msalala). *Ndila* v. *Mayeyema.*

Mayeyema caused the pregnancy of Ndila's niece who was comparatively well four days after the birth of the child but then collapsed and died two days later. The court held that very probably puerperal sepsis had supervened and the death was due directly to the fact of having given birth four days before the fatal disease set in. *Njigu* was awarded to the uncle.

NOTE. If a woman dies two months after childbirth and has been ailing, going from one doctor to another during this time, the lover is liable to pay *njigu*. But if a woman who, only one week after childbirth, has been seen fetching water, falls sick and finally dies, the lover does not have to pay *njigu* whatever the cause of the woman's death.

307. *Njigu* is only payable by a man if the death of his concubine is directly connected with pregnancy, abortion, or childbirth.

P.C.'s Appeal No. 6/43. D.C.'s Appeal No. 7/43. Fulo (Beda).

*Mapalala* v. *Kilangabana.*

Kilangabana caused the pregnancy of Mapalala's daughter with whom he was living in concubinage. During her confinement, immediately before the birth, the girl died of cerebro-spinal meningitis. The Beda Native Court did not award *njigu* because the girl had died of a disease and not of childbirth. The NF Court awarded *njigu* because the girl died during childbirth. The two European Appeal Courts upheld the judgement of the Beda Court.

308 A. If a woman uses medicines for abortion and dies, the person who gave her the medicines, not the lover, must pay *njigu*.

B. If the woman herself, without the aid of another person, causes an abortion and dies, no *njigu* is payable.

NOTE. Rules 306, 307, 308 were agreed by the chiefs of the Sukuma Federation and their people in 1949. Formerly many differences existed in the various chiefdoms:

In NF, UF, KF, BD the responsibility of the lover lasted until about one month after birth.

In BSN the responsibility lasted until about two months after birth.

In KS, SS, BS, SBS the responsibility ceased a few days after birth.

In UF, NF, KF, BSN, BS *njigu* was payable for death from any cause, such as snake bite, pneumonia, smallpox.

In SS, KS, KM, SBS *njigu* was payable only for death connected with childbirth, pregnancy, or abortion.

NOTE. *Misango* and *njigu* cases are frequent everywhere and courts tend to vary their judgements in individual cases. The reason is that in different parts of the country different rules were in force and a certain amount of confusion arose.

309. If a widow living with her deceased husband's family becomes pregnant (610) more than nine months after the husband's death, her husband's family can expel her and claim repayment of bridewealth due. If she dies of a cause connected with childbirth, her father can claim the payment of *njigu* from the lover. If the widow remains within her deceased husband's family, no *njigu* is payable.

310. The fact that a woman dies in the house of her lover does not

make him liable to pay *njigu* unless she dies of a disease connected with childbirth, pregnancy, or abortion.

NOTE. This rule was decided upon by the chiefs of the Sukuma Federation and their people in 1949. Formerly, in the chiefdoms of KM, SM, BD, BSN, *njigu* was payable by the lover in all circumstances if the woman died in his home.

NOTE. The strict rules which formerly existed in some chiefdoms were designed to discourage concubinage; most people, however, consider that they have not proved effective, for these reasons:

A. The number of people living in concubinage in BD and BSN is no smaller than that in other chiefdoms.
B. It is not always the man who prefers concubinage to marriage. Very often a woman refuses to be married but agrees to live with a man in concubinage. Moreover, it is poverty rather than irresponsibility which most often causes a man to live in concubinage.
C. Concubinage is so common that it must be considered a socially approved institution (122, 150).

311. If part of the bridewealth has been paid but the celebration of the wedding has been delayed, the bridegroom must pay *njigu* should his bride die as a result of pregnancy (297).

312. In this case the father of the bride must return the instalment of bridewealth already paid. If the father does not return the instalment the bridegroom does not have to pay *njigu*.

*Amount of njigu payable*

313. The following compensation is payable:

A. In the case of a commoner: 11 cattle (8 cows and 3 bulls). One of the bulls, called *sungamata*, is slaughtered and the meat divided among both families concerned.

NOTE. This rule was agreed by the chiefs of the Sukuma Federation and their people in 1949. Formerly it was followed in all chiefdoms except those of SS and KS, where *njigu* amounted to 15 cattle.

B. In the case of *banangwa, banang'oma*, direct descendants of a chief, or a deposed chief: 15 cattle.

In case of a regent: 20 cattle.
In case of a chief: 25 cattle.

C. The rules contained in paras. 300c (including the Note), 301, 302, and 303 apply also to the payment of *njigu*.

NOTE. It is customary for the family to help in the payment of *njigu*. Formerly the whole family of the debtor was held responsible for its payment. Even if the debtor has plenty of cattle, he usually applies for help to his family: the family would consider it an insult if the debtor paid the *njigu* with his own cattle. It happens sometimes that more than eleven cattle are collected by the family. The surplus is slaughtered and consumed by the relatives who have assembled for the handing over of the *njigu* to the deceased's family. If a relative, who is considered by the others liable to help in the payment, refuses to pay his share, the family may decide to ostracize him.

But such a refusal was very rare, just as a lover very seldom made any difficulty over paying the *njigu*. The lover and his family considered themselves in danger if the payment of *njigu* was delayed. *Njigu* is blood-money and was paid to avoid a blood feud. The lover was deemed 'the murderer of the girl, and her relatives, if not appeased by payment of the blood-money, were regarded as acting within their rights if they took revenge on a member of the murderer's family. These notions are still prevalent and even today the murderer's family is afraid. In the olden days the whole family fled into the bush on hearing that one of its members had committed murder, and only returned to their homes when the payment of *njigu* had been effected. But although open murder will probably not be committed nowadays in this connexion, murder by magical means, including poison, is still dreaded. Public opinion would take sides with the girl's family, i.e. with the avenger, and the lover's family could never hope to establish its case without the help of the community. Thus it is obvious that the whole family of the lover will be concerned to arrange immediate payment of the *njigu*, and members of the murderer's family hand over their share of *njigu* cattle with surprising alacrity. They seem positively glad to get rid of a few cattle from their herds; and indeed they are happy because they live in constant dread until the *njigu* is paid.

*Misango* and *njigu* represent the Sukuma method of exercising control over the consequences of the sexual liberty allowed by custom. It would be unwise to abolish these payments before the fundamental conditions of Sukuma life have changed, and different conceptions have begun to influence Sukuma social institutions.

314. The chiefs of the Sukuma Federation agreed in 1949 to forgo the one cow out of the *njigu* payment which they had formerly received as their due. (*De facto* this payment had not been claimed by the chiefs for many years.)

315. The final decision about the payment of *njigu* must be recorded before a court.

NOTE. This rule was decided upon by the chiefs of the Sukuma Federation and their people in 1949. Even before then it had been usual to file a suit in court for obtaining payment of *njigu*, irrespective of whether the lover agreed to pay or not.

# CHAPTER V

## GUARDIANSHIP

### INTRODUCTION

CASES concerning questions of guardianship are seldom brought to court. Complaints by widows against their co-guardians, or vice versa, and consequent changes, demands for the dissolution of a leviratic marriage in order to contract another, are customarily decided by the family council, and considerations of equity have much weight with members of the family when arbitrating between guardians, co-guardians, and wards. The law is often so vague that different courts belonging to the same local federation are inclined to differ in their interpretation of similar cases. There seems to be no clear conception of the extent of the responsibility of a guardian for the property of his ward. Apart from fundamental laws which are generally observed, each case is judged according to its merits.

It would have been contrary to the principles adopted in this recording of the customary law, as well as injurious to the efforts to achieve a much needed unification, to interfere with the existing situation to the extent of creating rules where there are none.

Especially in the matter of guardianship, any undue pressure or interference might endanger the existence of highly beneficial native institutions. No good purpose would be served by trying to formulate strict rules regarding responsibility of guardians for the property of their wards. In the majority of cases the guardians are next-of-kin who willingly incur financial sacrifices for their wards by helping them, when they are grown up, with the payment of bridewealth if the father has left no property. There are more poor than rich men in Sukumaland. Also it may be assumed that a father who leaves minor children has died a young man and has had little opportunity to acquire property.

If guardianship were to be regularized on a more business-like footing, with a clear definition of the responsibility of the guardian for the property of his ward, entailing an obligation to render an account when the ward became of age, and a limitation of rewards accruing to the guardian, the probable result would be that relatives of rich wards would be reluctant to act as guardians on account of the financial responsibilities involved, while relatives of poor wards would refuse because they could derive no advantage from it.

### I. GUARDIAN OF MINORS

#### A. *Choice of co-guardian by widow*

316. If a father leaves minor children, the widow becomes their guardian in conjunction with a male co-guardian (*nang'hani*).

317 *a.* If a widow chooses to be inherited and to become the wife of a kinsman of her deceased husband (600), this relative becomes the co-guardian of her minor children.

NOTE. The mother is so obviously the natural guardian of her children, whether they are small or grown up, that she is never called guardian. If a man dies and leaves a widow and children there will then be a 'mother' and a guardian. In order to make the situation clear, the mother is considered in this chapter the 'guardian' and the appointed relative the 'co-guardian'.

*b.* If a widow refuses to be inherited but agrees to remain within her deceased husband's family, she is entitled to choose the co-guardian from among the close kinsmen.

NOTE. No case is known in which a mother of small children remained within her deceased husband's family and refused to choose a leviratic husband.

318. It depends entirely on the widow whether she remains in the holding of her deceased husband or moves into the house of her leviratic husband and the co-guardian of her children (574).

319. In a polygynous household each widow can choose her husband and therefore each 'house' can have its separate co-guardian.

320. In case of a *numba ya bugongo* the *nkima wa bugongo* must choose her husband and co-guardian from the nearest relatives of her deceased husband's maternal family, preferably one of the sons of the maternal uncle (Note to 38).

NOTE. The question arises why a maternal uncle is never the guardian of his minor great-nephews. Usually the maternal uncle (*mami*) leaves the office of guardianship and the inheritance of a *nkima wa bugongo* to one of his sons. In the Sukuma language no distinction is made between paternal and maternal cousins. The word in use is actually the same as that used for brother. This usage leads to a wrong conception of the relationship between the guardian and the deceased father of the wards.

321. If a widow and her leviratic husband decide to terminate their marriage and the widow chooses another member of the family as her husband (60B), no change is made in the guardianship of the children. The relative who was chosen by the widow as her husband and the co-guardian of her children after the *isabingula* remains co-guardian.

322. If a co-guardian dies, the mother may choose another leviratic husband and co-guardian from among the near relatives of the deceased or a co-guardian may be chosen by the family council.

323. If the mother dies, the co-guardian becomes the sole guardian of the children.

### B. *Appointment of co-guardian by the family*

324. If a widow refuses to be inherited or to remain with her deceased

husband's family, the guardian of her minor children is selected and appointed by the family council. Usually the relative who would have been the *nkuruwabo* of the deceased had there been no children is appointed.

325. If in a polygynous household all the widows refuse to be inherited one male guardian for all the houses is appointed.

## C. *Deprivation of guardianship*

326. If a widow thinks that her co-guardian is neglecting his duties, she has the right to bring her complaint before the family council.

327. The family council has the right to deprive a co-guardian of his office and appoint another member of the family instead.

NOTE. No court cases of this kind are known; such complaints are always settled in private.

328. If a widow neglects the house and her children the family council can decide to return her to her paternal family and to hand over the children to the co-guardian.

NOTE. Not a single case is known in which a widow neglected her children or squandered their property.

## D. *Authority and responsibility of guardians*

### *General rules*

329. Mother and co-guardian jointly take over the position of the deceased father within the family until the eldest son (*nkuruwabo*) is grown up and himself occupies the father's position.

NOTE. The functions of the guardian (mother) and the co-guardian are not clearly defined. The relationship of the two guardians must be one of friendship, otherwise a change would be considered necessary by all persons concerned. In practice the influence of the two guardians will depend on their respective characters and intelligence.

Generally speaking the authority of the mother is greater in the south than in the north, just as the property of wards in the south is more often considered their personal property than in the north. The difference between north and south may be illustrated by the following example. In Buduhe, if the sister of a ward is granted a divorce, and bridewealth has to be returned, it must be claimed from the full brother (minor or adult), and if there is no property it becomes his debt. In a similar situation in Nunghu, the guardian is responsible for repayment of bridewealth. Normally the relationship between mother and co-guardian is that of man and wife, and therefore both make their decisions as do parents about matters concerning their children. But it must be remembered that such a relationship is not obligatory and, if it does not exist, the co-guardian is supposed to interfere only as representative of the family interests in questions relating to property.

330. The mother runs the house and decides the number of fields to

be cultivated during the current year. She has the right to dispose of all crops except bulrush millet and sorghum and can use the proceeds of their sale as she likes; she also has rights of disposal of all cattle products (ghee, meat, and hides).

331. Any transactions in corn and in cattle must be undertaken after mutual consultation between mother and co-guardian.

NOTE. In all chiefdoms of the Sukuma Federation corn and cattle are treated alike in law. Corn is the true cash-crop of the Sukuma; cotton, ground-nuts, rice, beans, and all other minor crops may bring money to the cultivator which he uses for paying tax and for buying clothing and implements, but little of this constitutes permanent material gain. With corn the Sukuma peasant acquires cattle. It is the traditional currency with which he is thoroughly familiar. The demand for corn seldom falls owing to the fact that there is a semi-famine nearly every year somewhere in Sukumaland or in neighbouring areas. The peasant possessing a good quantity of corn does not sell it for money but barters it for cattle. But even if a man does not barter his corn in one season, he has no loss because he can keep it for two, or even three years. Native traders, not the cultivators themselves, buy the corn with cattle and bring it to the areas of scarcity where they barter it for cattle, obtaining more cattle for it than they paid originally. The corn sold on the markets comes from peasants who have only a small surplus or who need quick cash and have nothing else to sell at the moment.

The conventions of barter have no relation to the market prices of commodities, and there is a considerable difference between the market value of corn and cattle and that taken as a basis for barter. A heifer is obtainable for two bags of corn, a young bull for one bag. A bag of sorghum would fetch on the market Shs.6/- to Shs.7/- while the price for a heifer may go up to Shs.50/- and more. A family needing corn cannot buy it for money because peasants do not sell it for money. The Sukuma prefers the barter system; firstly, it is traditional; secondly, the handling of money, still a problem for many peasants, is avoided; and thirdly, the owner of corn sells his commodity on his own doorstep. An elder explained: If one sells a heifer at the auction, one is paid in money, but whatever may have been the price, one never contrives to buy two bags of corn for it. A part of the money disappears on the way home and the other part is lost while arrangements for buying corn are in progress.

It now becomes clear why corn is treated by law in the same manner as cattle. If a widow gave away too much corn—perhaps to her relatives—it would mean that stock would have to be bartered to replace it. On the other hand, if there is a surplus of corn, cattle can be acquired with it and cattle guarantee the prosperity of the whole family.

332. A mother has no right to betroth her daughter without the consent of her co-guardian who undertakes all duties regarding the arrangements for the marriage just as the bride's father would have done were he still alive.

333. The co-guardian has to handle all public business for the deceased's family which the widow, according to custom, cannot attend to (representation in court or at a cattle-market, &c.).

334. The authority of the co-guardian varies according to his relationship to the deceased father and according to the age of the wards.

*If the co-guardian is a close kinsman*

### 1. *If the wards are small children*

335. The co-guardian becomes in every respect the complete substitute for the deceased father. The wards become his children. The position of the mother as guardian is bound up with her position as the co-guardian's wife.

336. The children of the deceased occupy a special position in the sequence of heirs of the co-guardian, depending on their father's position in the sequence of heirs of his own father, i.e. the paternal grandfather of the wards. If the ward's father was the eldest among his brothers, the ward becomes the *nkuruwabo* of the co-guardian's family even if the latter has children of his own who are older. If the ward's father was the younger brother of the co-guardian, the eldest of the wards becomes *nzuna* in the co-guardian's house, irrespective of his age compared with that of the co-guardian's own children.

337. If a childless brother inherits the wife and children of his elder brother, the *nkuruwabo* of the deceased becomes *nkuruwabo* of the co-guardian and retains this position even if the co-guardian should afterwards marry another wife and have sons by her. But if an elder brother (childless) inherits the wife and children of his younger brother, the eldest of the wards remains *nkuruwabo* of the co-guardian only so long as the co-guardian has no male children of his own. The first-born child of the co-guardian would become *nkuruwabo* of his father and the eldest of the wards would follow him as *nzuna*.

338. The property of the deceased is taken over by the co-guardian and merged with his own. The wards cannot ask for an account when they come of age.

NOTE. No case is known in which a co-guardian has given an account of the estate to the wards when they came of age.

339. Whether the widow decides to remain with her children in the homestead of her first husband or to follow her leviratic husband into his house, the provisions of paras. 335, 337 remain unaltered (318).

### 2. *If the wards are grown children*

340. If the *nkuruwabo* at the time of his father's death has attained an age of approximately thirteen years, the co-guardian must keep the property of the wards separate from his own, because they then have no position within the sequence of his own heirs. The wards will inherit the property left them by their father in due course.

NOTE. Obviously, the rules contained in paras. 340–3 are very vague (Introduction to Chapter V). The underlying idea is probably either that a guardian can adopt the wards as his own children and merge their property with his, or

that the wards should remain wards, in which case the guardian should keep
their property separate from his own. But there is no rule permitting a guardian
to follow the first course, or binding him to follow the second. In any case the
guardian is the '*baba*' and as such can do no wrong (compare 344).

341. In this case the widow usually remains in the homestead of her
deceased husband and does not move into the house of the co-guardian;
she continues to live in the holding in order to keep it for the day when
the *nkuruwabo* will be able to take it over.

342. The mother as well as the *nkuruwabo* will exercise control over
the co-guardian and any transaction affecting the wards' property can
only be carried out with their full consent. They can always appeal for
help to the family council if the co-guardian should neglect their property or use it to his own advantage. The mother can also file a suit
against the co-guardian.

NOTE. There would be no objection to a mother filing a suit against a dishonest co-guardian if the relatives should fail to assist her. In such a case proof
of bad guardianship would probably not be difficult to produce. If the mother
does not take action in the interests of her children, and they themselves after
several years go to court, proof of misuse is almost impossible to obtain. Then
the usual solution is to award to the children the same number of cattle as the
co-guardian actually received when taking over the guardianship. This is not a
rule in itself. If exact numbers of losses in and additions to the herd can be given
by the wards, they are entitled to receive the exact number of beasts.

343. If such control has not been exercised a ward cannot, after many
years under guardianship, ask for an exact account including all details
about the death of beasts and the birth of calves. Equally, the co-
guardian cannot withhold cattle which are clearly the offspring of the
ward's herd.

NOTE. If the co-guardian voluntarily hands over the number of cattle which he
originally took over, the general opinion is that he is acting fairly and in accordance with tradition. He is not expected to keep a detailed account and is not
considered dishonest if he does not do so. A truculent attitude on the part of a
ward is deemed to be out of place.

344. A ward who thinks he has been wronged has the right to file a
suit against his guardian.

NOTE. This rule was decided upon by the chiefs of the Sukuma Federation
and their people in 1949. Formerly the relevant rules differed in the various
chiefdoms.

A. In UF, NF, BD, KF a ward could not file a suit in court against
his guardian; the courts refused to hear such cases and referred the complainant to the family council.

B. In SS, BS, KS, SBS, KM the court accepted such cases.

C. In BSN neither a full brother nor any other relative as guardian
could use property of the wards to his own advantage. A co-guardian
had to keep his own property and that of his wards strictly separated.

The mother of the wards, helped by the other relatives, exercised strict control. On the other hand the wards when they came of age could not file a suit in court if a co-guardian had misappropriated part of their property; they had to bring their case before the family council.

NOTE. Quarrels between guardians and wards are usually settled through arbitration by senior members of the family or by village elders. When such a quarrel reaches the court, two assumptions can be made with fair certainty: it will be almost impossible for anyone outside the family to determine the true facts of the case; the dispute has become so bitter that the parties and their witnesses will have a more than usual disregard for the truth. Reconciliation of accounts or interests will therefore be difficult to achieve. The provisions of para. 344 can only be taken at present as an attempt by the chiefs and their people to initiate more specific rules of guardianship and, ultimately, unification of these rules.

### If the co-guardian is a distant relative

345. The co-guardian has to keep the property of the wards separate from his own.

NOTE. Nearly every Sukuma cattle-owner has in his herd cattle which he has acquired in different ways or which belong to different people. He is required in law to keep them and their offspring separate, not physically, but in his mind. Frequently there are cattle inherited from his father or from paternal relatives, or received as bridewealth for daughters, or received in trusteeship, or acquired by his own efforts, or cattle of *kuyinza*, or cattle which he holds as guardian of minors.

346. The wards, when they come of age, have the right to ask the co-guardian for an account of the property, especially if their mother died while they were minors.

NOTE. As long as the mother is alive she is expected to exercise strict control over the actions of the co-guardian regarding her children's property. If the mother is found to be weak or too compliant with the wishes of the co-guardian, the rest of the maternal relatives have the right to intervene. They feel themselves to be the true blood relatives in a case where the guardian is a distant paternal relative; although they have no legal rights, they exercise great influence over the children and their up-bringing, because the children when they grow up will tend to look upon their maternal uncles as their next senior relatives, and follow their advice.

347. The co-guardian cannot be asked to give an account of the products of the herd which are his due. The guardian is also entitled to dispose of beasts of a ward's herd in the latter's interest.

NOTE. In practice, as in para. 343, the courts refuse to investigate deaths and births which have occurred in the ward's herd if the guardian asserts that disease, &c., has caused considerable loss. The court may ask for witnesses to such incidents. Generally and customarily the court considers the guardian only responsible for the original number of beasts which he received when he took over the estate. The cost of bringing up the children is roughly accounted for by this means.

348. While the authority of the co-guardian depends on factors mentioned in 334, the situation between the two guardians—mother and

co-guardian—is not legally altered by the degree of the co-guardian's relationship to the deceased husband.

NOTE. If the co-guardian is a near relative the question of whether the mother marries him or not does not affect his position as co-guardian; but if he is a distant relative his marriage to the mother does alter the situation to some extent. In these circumstances the authority of the co-guardian is obviously greater and control by outsiders is more difficult. Therefore, a mother may refuse to be inherited and to become the wife of a co-guardian who is a distant relative for fear that the property of her children may not be safe in his care and that, as wife, she will be less able to forbid transactions involving her children's property.

### E. *Distribution of property by the co-guardian between the heirs*

(The following rules refer only to cases where property has to be kept separate from that of the co-guardian.)

#### 1. *Children of the same mother who is still alive when they come of age*

349 A. It is Sukuma custom that the property is not distributed between the children so long as the mother is alive and living on her deceased husband's estate.

B. A different custom prevails in the chiefdoms of SS, KS, and BSN, where the property is nominally distributed after the father's death between his minor children, i.e. each child receives his share but the herd is kept together. No redistribution takes place if the cattle of a certain child's share should die.

NOTE. The distribution of the estate does not necessarily take place when the *nkuruwabo* has attained a certain age or when he wishes to marry or when a sister marries. The herd is kept together as long as all the heirs live in amity with each other and as long as an heir has no special reason for demanding his share. This was considered a custom and not a rule, and therefore no unification of rules A and B has been attempted.

350. Any one of the heirs when grown up is entitled to demand the distribution of the estate and the handing-over of his share.

351. When the *nkuruwabo* grows up, he takes over the guardianship of his minor siblings from the co-guardian, but the handing-over is not performed on any special day or with special ceremonies. The *nkuruwabo* grows into the guardianship. If ever he fails in his duties, the mother will check him, or if her efforts are unsuccessful she will call for the help of the former co-guardian or even of the family council.

352 A. The *nkuruwabo* is entitled to take cattle from his father's herd for paying bridewealth and, if the herd consists of no more than the number of beasts required for the bridewealth, he can take them all. Younger brothers have no claim against the elder brother for a share in the estate if the cattle have been used for payment of bridewealth.

B. If the father has left many cattle, one son after the other, as he comes of age and wishes to marry, receives cattle for payment of bride-wealth from the estate. The remaining cattle may be distributed only after the death of the mother.

C. Payment of *misango, njigu*, repayment of bridewealth in case of divorce of a sister, and payment of compensation for adultery committed by a brother can be met by using cattle of the estate. In the final distribution of the estate, no such payment would be regarded as a debt of the brother for whom it had been made.

D. If a brother needs one beast for paying a practitioner's fee for himself or a member of his family, he receives it from the estate if he has no property of his own.

E. If a brother wishes for a few beasts for trading, he must obtain the consent of the *nkuruwabo*, the mother, and a few senior members of the family, preferably the former co-guardian. In any case it would be understood that the profit of the transaction had to be put back into the estate.

NOTE. Generally it may be said that the estate is considered as capital which can be used for the purpose of perpetuating the family and for meeting necessary demands in connexion with this purpose.

353. If one of the brothers demands and receives his share, the other heirs can decide that the remainder of the estate, i.e. their shares, shall remain undivided.

### 2. *Children of the same mother who dies before they come of age*

354. If the mother dies, the co-guardian becomes sole guardian and is entitled to take the children and property into his house (323).

355. As soon as the *nkuruwabo* is grown up, he will take over the guardianship of his minor siblings, but he will not be able to do this before he gets married as he must give them a home.

356. If the *nkuruwabo* should fail in his guardianship of his younger siblings, the family council can decide that the property shall be distributed and the minors, together with their shares in the estate, be put once more under the guardianship of the original guardian, while the *nkuruwabo* is given his own share.

### 3. *Children of different mothers*

357. If the widows choose different co-guardians the property is usually distributed between the houses shortly after the father's death.

NOTE. If several widows choose the same co-guardian the estate need not be distributed.

358. The distribution of the estate within each house follows the rules contained in paras. 349–56.

## II. GUARDIAN OF ABSENT HEIR

### A. *If one heir is present but others are absent*

359. The heir who is present is entitled to take over the whole estate and to become the guardian of the shares of his absent coheirs until they return.

360. The heir and guardian of his coheirs is entitled to use property included in the shares of absent heirs so long as he makes a proper use of it, such as payment of bridewealth, *misango*, or *njigu*, compensation for adultery, payment to a practitioner or cost of rebuilding a house if the old one has been burned down, &c.

361. If the heir and guardian squanders the property of his absent coheirs, the family council has the right to distribute the property and to give the shares of the absent heirs into the guardianship of a near kinsman who is not an heir. But the family council cannot appoint a distant relative as guardian of the absent coheirs even if the heir squanders their shares.

362. When the absent heirs return they cannot make the family council responsible for having left the guardianship of their shares in the estate in the hands of the heir who was present.

363. When the absent heir or heirs return, he or they must take what is left of their shares if the guardian has not misused the property. They have the right to make the guardian responsible with his own property if he has squandered their shares in the estate.

NOTE. The rules of paras. 362 and 363 were decided upon by the chiefs of the Sukuma Federation and their people in 1949. Formerly different rules existed in different chiefdoms:

In BD, NF, UF, KF the returning heir had no right to ask the guardian for an account of the estate.

In BS, SS, KS, KM, SM the returning heir had the right to ask for an account.

364. If a son had sent money to his father for the purchase of cattle, or if the son himself had bought cattle and left them with his father, these cattle and their offspring are the private property of the absentee and are not counted in the estate. But if a brother who was coheir and appointed as guardian for the property of the absent heir should use the cattle, the absentee on his return could not file a suit against his brother, if the latter had used them for purposes acknowledged to be rightful in law (360).

365. A half-brother can only be appointed to look after the property of an absent half-brother and coheir if both brothers belong to houses in the same category, i.e. both houses must be *numba ya buta* or *numba ya bugongo*.

### B. *If all heirs are absent*

366. One co-guardian is appointed for the whole estate by the family council who must always be the nearest relative available, whatever may be his character and capabilities.

367. If he proves to be unable to look after the estate the family council can decide to replace him by another relative.

If the guardian is the next of kin, i.e. a paternal uncle or paternal cousin, the rules contained in paras. 360–3 may be applied.

NOTE. The idea is that the next of kin cannot be passed over but must be given an opportunity to prove whether or not he is fit to be a guardian. On the other hand, the mother of the absent heirs may still be alive and may be a capable woman; in this case it would not be necessary to replace an inadequate co-guardian. The family council is always reluctant to appoint distant relatives if there are close kinsmen available.

368. If no near kinsman is available, a distant relative, who is responsible for a strict separation of his own property from that of the absent heirs, is appointed as guardian.

369. If the mother of the absent heirs is still alive and is a capable woman, she becomes guardian and a relative is appointed as her co-guardian. The presence of the mother does not reduce the responsibility of the co-guardian (345, 346).

370. If the absent heir returns, he is entitled to ask for an account of the estate from the co-guardian. The co-guardian is responsible with his own property for losses for which he cannot give satisfactory reasons.

371. If the mother is alive there is no rule defining the way in which she and her co-guardian divide the produce of the herd between them. Usually the mother takes the produce of the herd and the co-guardian asks for what he wants. If there is no mother the sole guardian has the right to use the produce of the herd for himself (milk, ghee, meat of any beast which has died). The calves are the property of the heir.

372. If a beast dies, the guardian must call for witnesses and keep the hide as evidence that it has not been sold. In no circumstances is the guardian allowed to sell or slaughter a beast. If a beast is very sick, he has to wait until it dies.

373. The guardian cannot ask for any compensation for his work when the absentee returns.

374. The guardian is not allowed to spend the capital (cattle) itself for the maintenance of the herd.

NOTE. He cannot sell a beast in order to repair the cattle kraal from the proceeds of the sale or in order to pay a native practitioner for preparing medicine for the cattle of the heir. Such expenses are considered to be covered by the profits from the herd.

# PART III

# THE LAW OF PROPERTY

## CHAPTER VI

## LAND TENURE

### INTRODUCTION

SUKUMA land tenure rules are generally favourable to the well-being of the people, because 'they do not stand in the way of bringing all agricultural land to its most beneficial use'. (*Report of the Colonial Office Summer School on African Administration, First Session*, 1947, p. 62.) They are, in fact, a good example of the term 'usufructory right of occupancy'. The fundamental principle being that a man owns his land so long as he occupies it effectively (375) and he therefore cannot sell, pledge, or otherwise dispose of it. The system involves no insecurity of tenure because a holder cannot be dispossessed of his land for any reason except failure to occupy it and, since there is at present little or no land hunger, an owner is not pressed to dispose of land he is not actually cultivating. A son can inherit his father's holding because in the Sukuma conception a son is not only his father's heir, but his younger self (392C, 401A). The chiefs as well as their people—represented by the knowledgeable men who were my informants—were fully aware of the advantages of the existing system, and there was not the slightest doubt among them that any contravention of these rules or deviation from their principles should be avoided in any formulation of new rules. This opinion found expression in the unanimous approval of the formulation of the existing rules in 375, 377, 378, 400, 521, 522, and the unanimous acceptance of rules 408, 412, 467, 529, 530 which previously had been in force only in certain parts of Sukumaland.[1]

There is no indication that cultivators tend to neglect the improvement of their land because of the rules of land tenure. The reward for introducing better agricultural methods lies in the increasing yield and not in any increase in the intrinsic value of the land. That this fact is realized may be seen from the following remark made in council:

A cultivator who improves the fertility of his soil by superior methods of cultivation enjoys this advantage as long as he wants to. A man who has a cow in trusteeship and always leads the beast to good pasture cannot sell it because

[1] In view of the importance of these rules, the occasion of a general meeting of the Sukuma Federation in Malya was used to discuss every point of customary land tenure in the presence of an Agricultural Officer, Mr. J. T. Purvis, to whom I am indebted for his attendance as well as for many useful conversations.

the cow has become fatter than others; she remains a cow in trusteeship. The trustee has only the advantage of getting more milk.

It might be argued that a system of proprietary ownership would tend to result in improved agricultural methods. There is in fact a widely accepted school of thought which holds that individual proprietary rights must ultimately develop. Since, however, a holder of land can in no circumstances be dispossessed while he still occupies it, and since his rights to inherit are assured and the inheritance laws permit of no fragmentation, it is difficult to see how the present system can be bettered unless, by reason of land hunger or other economic change, the land itself acquires an intrinsic value.

The Sukuma rules of land tenure thus conserve individual rights in land to the highest possible degree without injury to the interests of the community. Therefore, taking the population as a whole, although it may sound a paradox, the 'usufructory right of occupancy' gives a greater measure of security to the holder than a 'proprietary right'.[1]

## 1. ACQUISITION OF LAND

### A. COMPLETE HOLDING

#### I. *General Rules*[2]

375. As long as a holder occupies his land effectively he cannot be deprived of it.

376. At present the authority for allocating land and for any other transaction in land is: the *basumba batale* in BSN, BD; the *banangwa* in all other chiefdoms.

NOTE. Formerly the *basumba batale* was the authority in BD, BSN, and BS; the *banangwa* in all other chiefdoms. *Basumba batale* exist in all chiefdoms and are the representatives of the inhabitants of a village; their influence is non-political and varies in the different local federations. In most chiefdoms they are concerned with the administration of land, and even where they do not act directly they are customarily informed by the village headman of any transactions in land which take place (see note to 385). The *basumba batale* are everywhere the leaders of the village organization for communal work. Their influence is weakest in the south, in the chiefdoms of the Mweli Federation (in ZM they do not exist), and strongest in the Binza Federation. The position of the *basumba batale* has been for many years in a state of flux with a tendency to diminish in importance.

[1] This introduction to the chapter 'Land Tenure' is written with reference to the Sukuma land-tenure system and is not necessarily of general application. The arguments are the outcome of many long conversations with Sukuma leading men.

[2] The ZM and SM rules of land tenure differ from those of Sukuma proper. These areas, formerly sparsely populated, are now being colonized, in rapidly increasing numbers, by Sukuma peasants emigrating from their homeland. For the time being two sets of rules of land tenure will have to be acknowledged side by side; one for the Zinza indigenous population, and one for the Sukuma immigrants who have taken up the land in accordance with Sukuma usage and who cannot be expected to hold it under rules other than their own.

Everywhere the village headman and the *basumba batale* work hand in hand. For instance, even in BSN, BS, BD the village headman is informed of the allocation of land by the *basumba batale*, and in UF a new-comer would first discuss his settlement with the *basumba batale* and seek their agreement before he approached the village headman for the actual allocation of the land. Everywhere they are the experts on boundaries in the *ilala* (unoccupied land).

It is emphatically stated by the chiefs that they never interfere in the allocation of land and that any applicant who approached them would be told to go to the village headman or to the *basumba batale* as the case may be.

There are two forums at which land questions may be discussed—the *ibanza lya milimo* and the *long'we*.

The *ibanza lya milimo* (also sometimes called *ng'wibilingo* or *lukiko*) is the meeting of all occupiers of holdings in the village. It is called together by a messenger of the village headman, and a representative of each *kaya* is bound to attend. If a husband should be absent, his wife has to go. The usual reason for calling together the *ibanza lya milimo* is to pass on Government orders, which the village headman has received through his chief and which usually refer to land or cultivation, and also to discuss any issue of common interest concerning the economic life of the community.

Although the *ibanza lya milimo* has no executive power, no inhabitants of the village, as long as they wish to remain in the village, can disregard its decisions. It is called together frequently and provides opportunities for a village headman to keep in contact with his villagers.

The *long'we* is a meeting of all inhabitants of a *gunguli* (parish) for the discussion of local affairs. This institution has lost its former importance and there are areas in which for years no meeting has taken place.

It is called together by the *basumba batale*, and the *ng'wanangwa* may be asked to attend, but he need not be invited. Questions of local interest are discussed and criticism is not avoided. Topics discussed may be: dissatisfaction with the village headman or his helpers; an unusual abundance of birds when the sorghum ripens, or of lions or hyenas arousing superstitious fears; lack of rain and epidemics among men or beasts. A very important function of the *long'we*, which might be called the plenary and representative assembly of the community, is the control of its members by the imposition of penalties for anti-social behaviour and the application of ostracism. (Sometimes penalties are imposed by a family council.)

### A. *Masumule (lwadida)*

This consists of a small fine, usually a few shillings and never more than a goat. It is imposed on a man for: disorderly behaviour such as insulting a girl; beating his wife severely (if a court case is avoided with the consent of both concerned); insulting his wife by using profane language about her mother; cursing or beating an old woman (if a court case is avoided); beating his mother; insulting elders; slander.

It is imposed on a woman for: cursing or beating her mother-in-law; disorderly behaviour, especially to old women.

The *masumule* is usually paid without delay and the transgressor rarely tries to defend himself. The community is judge, plaintiff, and witness all in one and if there is a doubt there is no case.

### B. *Bubisi* or *Bukindikwa (ostracism)*

To be ostracized means that nobody is allowed to visit, speak with, or help the man declared a *mbisi*. If the fire in his house goes out, nobody gives him fire; if his hut is in flames, nobody helps him to extinguish the fire; if his child dies, nobody helps him to bury it. A citizen who does not sever his connexion with a *mbisi* automatically becomes a *mbisi* himself.

This sanction is imposed if a man refuses to help bury a person; refuses first aid, i.e. to transport sick or wounded, or to help in emergencies such as fire; or to participate in ceremonies ordered for the purpose of dispelling evil influences directed against the community, or seriously and continuously disturbs the peace of the village by his dangerous or amorous temper.

The sanction is imposed without hearing the defendant, who is simply informed of the decision afterwards. A man cannot endure for long such exclusion from the community; he may get the interdict removed by paying a ransom fixed by the community. This payment need not be very high, a goat or few shillings are sufficient. The ransom is received by the elders and, if it consists of a goat, this is killed and eaten, the distribution of the meat following traditional rules; if it is paid in money, native beer or a goat is bought and consumed.

### C. *Kupeja*

This is a sanction, not imposed by the elders and the citizens alone but in consultation with the village headman and the *ntemi* himself. If repeated impositions of *bubisi* and payments of ransom do not change a man's anti-social behaviour, he is declared a *mbisi* once and for all; no ransom is accepted from him. This sanction in practice means expulsion.

*Masumule, bubisi,* and *kupeja* are still imposed and have not lost their wholesome influence on the behaviour of the individual as a member of the community. There is a tendency nowadays for differences to be taken to court for settlement, rather than to the elders and a gathering of the community. It is a general trend of the Sukuma to become court-minded.

377. If a holder does not effectively occupy his land or any part of it, and the need for it arises, the authority has the right to expropriate the holder from such parts of the unused land as it needs for allotment to another.

NOTE. A holder does not automatically forfeit a field because he has not cultivated it for a few years. The holder's title to his land or any part of it, and especially the title of a *nsesa* or heir, is seldom disputed; it is acknowledged *de facto* but not *de jure*.

*De facto*: Occupiers of large estates (*igobe*) often exclude other people from cultivating parts of their land while they use them as their private grazing reserves. They do not do this in contravention of the law; they are allowed to do so by permission of chiefs, village headmen, *basumba batale*, and by public opinion in general.

The owners of large *igobe* are all loyal citizens. Chiefs and *banangwa* can always rely on their assistance in the never ending struggle for power within a chiefdom. They represent the conservative African aristocracy. They are the old families of the chiefdom and everywhere chiefs, *banangwa, basweta, banang'oma*, court assessors, belong to these families. The common man cannot easily undertake to fight against this powerful class; in fact he has no desire to fight. In order to illustrate the situation it has been stated that if a village headman should deprive the holder of a large *igobe* of any part of it without good reason he would become very unpopular with his people. It is possible that the common man feels that the existence of large estates and their toleration protects him against being deprived of his own surplus land. This explains the fact that families requiring more land move into a new settlement area even though in the neighbourhood of their old homes a man owns land, the greater part of which he uses as his private pasture.

There is a widely observed usage, which is not formulated as a law, that plots of a *nsesa*, which are now in most cases owned by the second or third generation, are not appropriated on the grounds of their not being effectively occupied.

The same usage is observed if a husband is absent for any length of time and has left his wife living on his holding. The fields are left with her even if she cannot cultivate them all. Perhaps the authority may borrow fields if great scarcity of suitable land exists, but it would return them to the husband as soon as he returned.

*De jure*: Chiefs, *banangwa*, the owners of *igobe*, and the holders of land all know that a holder—if the necessity arises—must give up land which he does not use effectively. There can be no doubt that a *ng'wanangwa* could, for instance, open an *igobe* as pasture for common use, but it has never yet been done. On the other hand there are numerous instances of single fields being taken from the holder, if he has not cultivated them for several years, and given to another applicant. It is acknowledged that the authority should only act in this way if there are no other plots available to satisfy the reasonable demands of a new-comer or of an inhabitant of the village.

378. If such land or portions of it have to be expropriated because there is no other suitable land in the vicinity, it is the duty of the authority to try to obtain the holder's consent to the transaction.

379. The holder is not permitted to frustrate the order of the authority by:

(*a*) employing the method of fallowing fields to an unusual extent;

NOTE. The use of the term 'fallow' may give the impression that each cultivator has his rotation well organized and that one could see everywhere fields which are lying fallow. But this is not so. The Sukuma usually cultivates a field as long as possible, and only if it becomes exhausted does he leave it and choose a new field. Fallows are usually more or less unintentional. A man may find that he is unable to cultivate a certain field one year and therefore leaves it to lie fallow.

(*b*) cultivating small areas in each of his plots;

(*c*) allotting single fields to applicants (414);

NOTE. This rule is not a new one. If a village headman came to a man, who he knew had not been using certain parts of his land for a long time, with the intention of allocating those parts to an applicant for land, and was told that they had been given away by the holder to another person for temporary cultivation, he (or the *basumba batale*) would have the right to revoke this transaction and to dispose of the fields. If the borrower had already started cultivation, he would be allowed to harvest his crop, after which the fields would be disposed of by the authority.

(*d*) employing paid labourers in excess of the customary employment of villagers paid in kind. If, under certain circumstances, a man needs paid labourers for the cultivation of his holding, he must ask permission of the authority before he can employ them;

(*e*) cultivating with machinery. If a man wishes to cultivate fields outside his effectively occupied holding with machinery, he must first be allotted the land by the authority (411).

NOTE. Rules (*d*) and (*e*) were decided upon by the chiefs of the Sukuma Federation and their people in 1949. Formerly different rules existed.

The chiefs and their people realized that the Sukuma system of land tenure, originating in times of abundant land and of simple hand cultivation, could not protect the community against the occupation of vast areas of arable land by enterprising individuals, to the disadvantage of the community.

380. A holder cannot sell his holding or any part of it or enter into any transaction in which land is the subject (515).

NOTE. Formerly fields were bartered for goats or cattle in KF, BD, NF, and probably here and there in other chiefdoms. This is confirmed by Mr. D. W. Malcolm in his *Sukuma Land Utilization Report*, in which he gives an historical description of the Sukuma population. Although only one point is relevant to para. 380 a quotation seems to be justified on account of its general interest.[1]

'Besides considerations of soil, rainfall and water supply which influenced the location of the earlier settlements, it is easy to forget that as recently as 60 years ago the distribution of population was still controlled to a considerable extent by considerations of security. Most independent chiefdoms were isolated units and the people, however concentrated in certain areas, were unable to move into the neighbouring uninhabited lands on account of internecine warfare. The traditional Sukuma village was usually situated on high ground if not actually under the shadow of a granite tor. It was roughly circular in shape and protected by euphorbia hedges. Within these fortifications lived the whole village community with their stock, and the present organization of collective labour is a natural result of conditions in which it would have been dangerous to hoe alone. The arable and pasture lands of the village were in its immediate vicinity and often limited to the area in which the alarm could be heard. Under these circumstances the land in the immediate vicinity of the village attained an intrinsic value and the custom of paying in kind the occupier for the acquisition of a field developed.

'Then came the German Administration and with it the cessation of tribal warfare. It became safe to settle further from the centre of the village. The German authorities are said to have prohibited the system of land sales and individuals anxious to obtain good land began to move further afield and clear new areas. The spread appears to have been rapid and in a period of about 20 years the occupied area must have been very considerably extended. This process of expansion also removed the necessity for manuring which had been started in the south-west.'

## II. *Acquisition of holding by clearing a plot in the bush area (nhinde)*

381 A. A native or a stranger who wishes to clear a holding in the bush does not need to ask any authority so long as his plot is not near the plots of other cultivators. The boundaries of a *gunguli*, if they cut through areas of heavy bush, are sometimes vague and therefore the headmen of the *gunguli* which share the bush area will have to decide among themselves to which *gunguli* the new-comer belongs. His arrival may be the occasion for fixing the boundaries.

B. If it is obvious to which *gunguli* the *nhinde* belongs, the new-comer is expected in due course to inform the *ng'wanangwa* of his presence.

[1] I should like to express my appreciation of the valuable help I received from Mr. D. W. Malcolm when I first undertook researches in Sukumaland in 1936; and also to acknowledge the many instances, in the above-mentioned report, where points of law are illuminated and confirmed.

The *ng'wanangwa* himself or his deputy may then occasionally visit the settler. A holding of this kind is carved out of the bush without the help of the villagers and the hut is also built without their assistance.

NOTE. Motives for relinquishing a holding and seeking a new one are:

*Within the old country*

Fear of illness or misfortune; inheritance; invitation and offer of help from friends or relations in another area; quarrel with a member of the Native Authority.

*In a new country*

Ostracism; witch-weed and decreasing crop yields in general; increase in stock and insufficient grazing; possibility of acquiring a holding unrestricted in size.

This separation of causes is artificial to a degree. The reaction of a man to all these causes depends on his individual character and circumstances. But it may be said that men with a pioneer spirit will probably try a solution of their troubles in a remote area, while more timid sufferers will seek opportunities nearer to their old homes. In all cases the assistance of a near relative in a rehabilitation area will be an inducement if conditions there have proved favourable.

382 A. The new-comer (*nsesi*) can occupy as much land as he likes and no boundaries are demarcated by the authority.

NOTE. Areas in which a man can acquire a very large estate (*igobe* or *ikobe*) no longer exist in NF, except in a few small areas in Burima; UF, in Masanza I; KF, in Busmao, Nera, Magu, Sima; BD, in Ng'wagala, Nung'hu, Kigoku; BS, in Mondo, Buchunga, Mwadui; SBS; ZM, in Karumo.

Even in chiefdoms which still have *nhinde* available for new settlement, the areas are not extensive. Only in the rehabilitation areas west of Smith Sound does extensive settlement take place in the *nhinde*.

B. If there are already cultivators in the neighbourhood the new-comer must ask the authority for land to be allocated.

C. If the new-comer finds neighbours in the bush area boundaries are demarcated, usually by digging shallow pits at intervals of about five yards in light bush, or by marking the boundary with an axe in dense bush.

NOTE. The first settler in a large bush area has the chance of becoming later a *sweta* or *ng'wanangwa ndo* of the area if he is followed by other settlers; but he must be a member of the Sukuma tribe to attain such a position. The senior village headmen (*banangwa batale* or *banangwa baduma*) were originally relatives of the chief and their office was hereditary. Nowadays many of the village headmen are appointed by the chief and are seldom related to him.

383. When the settler has cut out his plot and created his holding, he holds the land under rules 375–80.

NOTE. Field-work is the joint task of man and wife. Normally all crops are cultivated by both husband and wife, including the field of sweet potatoes. The actual hours of work in the field are longer for the man than for his wife, as she often leaves the work to prepare food, fetch water, &c. Local variations exist; for instance, in the chiefdoms near the lake-shore potato fields are cultivated by women. The disposal of the crop is the right of the husband, but it is considered one of the requisites of a happy domestic life for him to consult with his wife before a transaction is undertaken. A wife is not allowed to dispose of any crop except for use as food for the household. In the exercise of this prerogative she is sovereign, and a husband who interferes and criticizes his wife's method of housekeeping is called a *manji*, and such criticism, if not justified, is considered a grave insult.

### III. *Acquisition of holding by allocation in an inhabited area (ilala)*

384 A. If a man wishes to obtain land for a holding he chooses in most cases a village where he has a relative living, or at least a very good friend. But even a stranger can ask for land and get it.

NOTE. A Sukuma tribesman considers himself related to eight families. This is not a rule, but eight is the number which a man, brought up in his father's house, should remember. The following clan names are taken as an example:

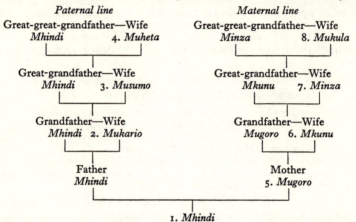

| Paternal line | Maternal line |
|---|---|
| Great-great-grandfather—Wife | Great-great-grandfather—Wife |
| *Mhindi*     4. *Muheta* | *Minza*     8. *Mukula* |
| Great-grandfather—Wife | Great-grandfather—Wife |
| *Mhindi*     3. *Musumo* | *Mkunu*     7. *Minza* |
| Grandfather—Wife | Grandfather—Wife |
| *Mhindi*     2. *Mukario* | *Mugoro*     6. *Mkunu* |
| Father | Mother |
| *Mhindi* | 5. *Mugoro* |

1. *Mhindi*

B. The new-comer settles down first in the house of his relative which he uses as a base while looking for suitable plots and a house site. When he has found what he wants he and his relative approach the authority and inform him of his intention to settle in the village and of the result of his search for suitable land.

NOTE. The Sukuma word for a holding is *migunda*, the plural of *ngunda*, a field. There is no specific word for a holding. This seems to indicate that the idea of a strictly defined and individually owned piece of land does not exist.

C. If the applicant is the son or brother of an inhabitant of the village he must still ask for an allocation of land if he wishes to found his own *kaya*.

385. Before the land is allocated the authority makes inquiries about the reasons for the emigration of the applicant, and about his character and popularity in his former domicile.

NOTE. If the applicant comes from so far away that it is not possible to obtain this information, he will have to wait for his land until the authority and the villagers decide by direct observation about his suitability as a settler and neighbour. Otherwise the usual custom is to dispatch two *basumba batale* or *banamhara* to the former domicile of the applicant.

It appears that this procedure involves two important aspects of social life:

1. It helps to maintain the authority of those men in the villages, be they village headmen or *basumba batale*, who need it for the execution of their other duties.
2. It permits the control of new-comers by the villagers.

These two important functions would cease to operate in all cases in which land became the subject of commercial transactions. The first does not need further explanation, the second perhaps does. The village is still organized on a communal basis—economically (common labour, mutual help, ostracism, village court of arbitration, water supply, grazing, &c.), and spiritually (a deep-rooted and general belief in magic). The well-being of the society is still protected, in many instances, by custom rather than by law. The power of the law can be invoked against anyone, but the strength of custom lies solely in the adherence of the whole community, and such adherence cannot be assumed in the case of a stranger. The stranger must prove to the community his readiness to accept its customs, and it must remain the privilege of the community to make the final decision as to his acceptance. For obvious reasons the former strict adherence to the original procedure is not always possible nowadays. But where the opportunity exists of ascertaining the applicant's antecedents, it is made use of.

386. If the applicant is accepted, the village headman and/or *basumba batale*, with a few neighbours as witnesses, go to show the new-comer the exact boundaries of his fields.

387. Boundaries (*lubimbi*) are demarcated by putting stones into the ground or by hoeing a line along the boundary and by using, wherever possible, natural features such as dry stream beds, paths, or trees and rocks.

388. If the boundary is a path, the actual path is considered tribal land, the two neighbours owning the land as far as the edge of the path.

Confirmed in D.C.'s Appeal 20/47. NF, Fulo. *Shelemba v. Paulo.*

389. No fees are payable to the authority or to the witnesses.

NOTE. It sometimes happens nowadays that an applicant gives the authority (village headman) a present in order to be allotted a big plot or a plot situated in another man's holding and not cultivated by him. But these cases are rare. It may be said that an applicant gets his land without fee or presents.

390. No rules exist with regard to the maximum size of an allotted holding; it varies according to the size of the applicant's family or the scarcity or abundance of land. A possible increase in the family or the necessity for fallow land is not allowed for. Claims to large pieces of land in the *ilala* are never entertained by the authority.

NOTE. Shifting cultivation is not and never was generally practised. In the south, where the people live in close settlements, a holder shifts his house, if he considers it advisable, to a plot in the immediate vicinity of the settlement. The abandoned house plot, *matongo*, is used for cultivation (431). A man may plant the same crop, such as bulrush millet, for ten or fifteen successive years in the same field. Mtama exhausts the soil more quickly but it can be planted in the same plot for many years, except in BSN.

It may happen that a cultivator gives up an exhausted field and looks for a substitute in the *ilala*, but if there is no suitable plot in the vicinity, he must try rotation or manure.

391. It is the custom for a new-comer to ask for the help of the community when he begins to build his house. The villagers contribute the poles and grass for thatching the roof, and they also help the new-comer to shift his belongings from his former domicile to the village.

NOTE. A characteristic Sukuma social institution is the great number of village organizations which serve various purposes but are principally institutions for mutual help in field-work. In various parts of the country the same names denote different types of organization. The following village organizations are common mainly in the north and are examples of this type of social activity.

*Elika* is the generic name for any group of people doing common work. (*Kisumba* in KF, UF.)

*Isalenge* is the village organization for mutual help. (KF, UF.)

*Buyobe* is a small working party of the *isalenge*.

(The *basumba batale* are the leaders of the *isalenge* and *buyobe*.)

*Ilima* is a small group of people invited personally by the owner of a field to help with cultivation.

*Bafunya* is a group of family members invited by one member to help in the cultivation of a field.

*Nyida* (in BSN called *Kumbu*) is the journey of the villagers to help a new-comer shift his belongings from the old to the new domicile.

*Igulilu* is the night cultivation society in SBS.

In addition to these organizations, members of secret societies can invite their fellow members to work in their fields for payment in kind. This mutual help of society members is now more common than that provided by the *elika*. Various secret societies exist in Sukumaland and a man, in order to become a member, has to undergo initiation rites.

The most widespread societies in which mutual help in field-work among members is very common are:

| | |
|---|---|
| *Buyeye* | society of snake-charmers |
| *Bugoyangi* | |
| *Bununguli* | society of porcupine hunters |
| *Bugumha* | dance societies |
| *Bugika* | dance societies |
| *Buyege* | originally a society for hunting elephants with bows and arrows. |

There are certain magic rites customarily performed in connexion with building a house.

After a man has chosen the place for his house he builds a *kigabiro* outside the building ground opposite to where the door will be. He invites the spirits to settle down there until the house is ready. Before he moves into the new house he prepares beer for the ceremony called *kushikirija numba* (to bless the house). Neighbours and elders of the village are invited. The pot containing beer is placed in the middle of the hut, and everyone draws some beer with a plaited cup, takes a mouthful and spits it against the wall. They say a short sentence such as: 'May the people live peacefully here' or 'May sickness and quarrels stay away from this house'.

A man of property will kill a goat for this occasion. Leaves of *nama* (combretum) and *ng'wale* (pterocarpus) are spread out near the door. The goat is first marked with flour and fat on the forehead, then killed, cooked, and served. The father throws the first bit of the meat on the leaves and says:

'My fathers, and all you twins born in my family in the past, this is your meat. May I live here happy and prosper.'

It is the custom in some places to extinguish the hearth fire the next morning and to kindle a new one by friction. From the first porridge cooked on the new fire the father takes a morsel and throws it against the wall, saying a sentence similar to the above.

IV. *Acquisition of holding by allocation of a relinquished holding (malale ga saka or malale ga fuluka)*

392 A. A man who relinquishes his holding has no right to hand it over to another man without the consent of the authority.

NOTE. It is perhaps necessary to state expressly that brothers, even if the estate in question is a *migunda ya ise*, must ask permission of the authority if one brother relinquishes the holding and another brother wishes to take it over. The family council may discuss the issue but the decision as to whether or not the brother of the outgoing holder is allotted the land lies with the authority.

B. Such holding reverts to the authority for re-allocation.

C. The only person to whom this rule does not apply is a son, who can take over a holding, if his father relinquishes it, just as he takes over the holding in the case of his father's death, without special permission of the authority.

393 A. A holder can allow a relative to occupy a portion of his holding so long as he himself lives on it, but he cannot do the same for a non-relative without permission of the authority (414B).

B. If such holder relinquishes his holding, he cannot hand it over to any person except a relative who has lived more than two years on the holding.

NOTE. This rule was decided upon by the chiefs of the Sukuma Federation and their people in 1949. Formerly the same rule existed but no time limit was fixed.

394. An abandoned holding need not remain an indivisible holding. The authority has the right to allot single fields from it or to allot the holding as a whole.

NOTE. The shift of population within a village in any year is still considerable. There is a saying: 'The subjects of the *Ntemi* are his monkeys (*Banhu bali nhumbili ya batemi*)', meaning that the people do not live for long in one place but are in constant movement from village to village or even from chiefdom to chiefdom. It must be added that the people who abandon their holdings because of superstitious fears may be acting wisely without knowing it. Often enough the house and yard have become unhealthy.

395. A *malàle ga sakà* is allotted by the authority; but everywhere, even where the authority is the *ng'wanangwa*, the *basumba batale*, as the representatives of the villagers, are customarily consulted.

396. The allocation is not restricted to an inhabitant of the village or chiefdom nor to a Sukuma; any suitable man is acceptable.

NOTE. The man who comes first gets the holding and no preference is shown to a member of the Sukuma tribe. General considerations only, such as the size of the holding and that of the family of the applicant, or his character or behaviour, decide the issue.

397 A. After the authority has allotted the plot the new occupier takes possession of it without further ceremony (except private rites of ancestor worship—*kitambo*).

B. The new-comer is shown the boundaries of the holding and fields by the village headman and *basumba batale*.

398. No fees are payable for the allocation of a *malale ga saka*.

NOTE. In BSN the occupier has to pay one head of cattle (*ng'ombe ya saka*) after one year to the *basumba batale* and *banamhara* of the village who kill the beast and distribute the meat.

399. Rules 375–80 are valid in the case of an allotted *malale ga saka*.

## V. *Acquisition of holding by inheritance*

400 A. A holding (*migunda ya ise*) is inherited undivided, i.e. one of the sons must take over the whole estate or leave it.

NOTE. The *nkuruwabo* has the first claim to the father's holding. If he already has his own home and refuses to leave it, one of his brothers may move into the father's holding. Very often the decision as to which of the sons shall enter into the father's holding is made long before his death. Probably one son after his marriage will remain with his wife in the parents' homestead. A son who has received a field from his father must return it to the estate after the father's death. If an elder brother after the father's death claims his right to inherit the father's house and estate, the decision as to whether the younger brother must give way to the demand of the elder lies with the family council.

B. He cannot choose certain plots and the house and leave the rest to another heir or to another applicant.

NOTE. This rule was agreed by the chiefs of the Sukuma Federation and their people in 1949. Formerly this rule was followed in NF, UF, KF, SS, BS.

A son who did not wish to take over the father's holding and who lived in the same *gunguli* as his father was allowed a first claim on single fields of his father's estate which were not situated in the vicinity of the house plot. (BSN, BD.)

NOTE. Sometimes a man returns to a field which was once occupied by his father or grandfather or by another near relative; there is in fact a certain tendency to return to such fields. This reoccupation by a relative may look sometimes as if a single field had been inherited. It very seldom happens that all the sons refuse to take over the father's holding. Intensive pressure would be exercised by the relatives, even if it should mean that one of the sons had to give up his own homestead.

401 A. Only a son is entitled to take over the father's holding without asking permission of the authority. Any other relative, even though the family council may have agreed that he should take over the estate, must be allotted the estate by the authority.

B. If there are no sons, but a daughter and her husband have been living on the holding of the father, or a sister and her family on the holding of her brother, these near female relatives are entitled to inherit the holding (393B).

402. The heir occupies the inherited holding under the same rules as his father did, i.e. under the provisions of 375–80.

NOTE. In practice the degree of equity applied by the authority and reinforced by public opinion is even greater in the case of inherited land than in the case of allocated land. For instance, if the heir has three small sons and the estate of the father consists of a large piece of land, the heir can be certain of keeping the land, as it is expected that in course of time his sons will help him to occupy the estate effectively (392C). No case is known in which an heir has lost part of his land in these circumstances; but it is also stated that there can be no doubt that an heir having no children, or perhaps only one child, would lose part of his land if it were needed; the authority would not take into account the number of possible grandchildren.

403. Trees and perennial crops, such as bananas, sisal, and sugar-cane, are divided among the heirs; except that trees planted in the immediate vicinity of the house are considered as belonging to the house and are therefore inherited by the heir to the house.

The small square rice plots (*majaruba*) are not divided between heirs, but are considered part of the indivisible holding. Customarily heirs are granted preferential rights to such plots when they apply for them to their headman or *basumba batale*.

404. Fields which have been improved by the owner by good cultivation and manuring belong to the indivisible holding. Heirs are not entitled to demand them separately if they do not wish to take over the complete holding.

NOTE. Such fields are not more fertile than a *litongo*, but a *litongo* plot cannot be demanded by an heir who does not take over the complete holding. There is no danger that a man would refuse to improve the fertility of a field because it could not be inherited separately when he died.

405. It is the general custom in a polygynous household that each wife after her wedding or after the birth of her first child is given her individual house and fields within her husband's *kaya* (homestead). If the husband dies no question of the distribution of land arises because each section of the family knows the fields belonging to it. The death of the father does not change the original division.

406. A field which is the personal property of the husband and is cultivated by all his wives together is called *kilaba*; the *kilaba* may be divided among the houses.

NOTE. The division of a *kilaba* between houses does not affect the question of fragmentation of land; a single share is seldom a big field and the shares generally become united again after a short time. No dispute with regard to the distribution of a *kilaba* is remembered. Some men like to have a *kilaba*, others consider it unnecessary.

## B. SINGLE FIELDS

407. Single fields are allotted by the same authority and in the same manner as a holding in the *ilala* or *ikera* (see 376, 377, 387, 389).

408. If a man wishes to cultivate a single field in the *ilala* he must ask permission of the authority. This rule refers to an inhabitant of the village as well as to an inhabitant of another village.

NOTE. This rule was decided upon by the chiefs of the Sukuma Federation and their people in 1949. Formerly, in UF, NF, KF, BSN, BD, SB, BS, a man could cultivate a single field within the boundaries of his own village without permission of the authority. In KS, SS, KM, SBS he could not cultivate without permission of the authority.

It has been generally realized that more control over the acquisition of single fields is necessary in modern circumstances and therefore the rules existing in the south were adopted. The delegates from BD, SS stated that in practice such control preserves the equilibrium between land under cultivation and land available for grazing in the *gunguli*. Without control there might be a shortage of pasture for the cattle of a *gunguli* because a few inhabitants, preferring agriculture to animal husbandry, could occupy and cultivate an unrestricted area in the *ilala*.

409. A bachelor cannot demand the allocation of a complete holding, but may apply for and receive single fields.

410. If a man has cultivated a field for one season, no other man can cultivate this field without the permission of the former cultivator or the authority, even if the field has remained fallow for a long time (*ilale*).

NOTE. If a man cultivates a field which has not been allotted to him by the authority, no other cultivator may deprive him of it, but his right to it is not recognized by the authority, which can, at any time, allot the field to an applicant, though in practice it is not likely to do so.

D.C.'s Appeal 51/45. U.F. *Zukuyo* v. *Nusome*.

In the judgement it was stated that no man can claim a *shamba* as his unless it is explicitly granted to him by a village headman; no one has a right to sub-let his *shamba* without the headman's permission; no man has a right to cultivate a *shamba* in a *gunguli* other than that in which he lives, except temporarily and with the permission of the headman.

411. If an inhabitant of one village wishes to cultivate a certain field in another village he must be allotted this field by the authority. The permission in such a case is only granted temporarily and can be withdrawn if an applicant arrives who wishes to settle in the village.

D.C.'s Appeal 51/45. UF. Nassa. *Masome* v. *Zakayo*.

Zakayo cleared the bush and cultivated a field of cotton for five years in a neighbouring village, while himself living three or four miles away. He never sought or received permission from the headman to cultivate this field. The headman Masome, on receiving an application from a new-comer wishing to settle in the village, ordered Zakayo to vacate the field. Zakayo refused to leave but the court decided against him.

NOTE. This situation is frequently met with in the *isanga*, the sandy belt round the lake-shore, which is very suitable for the growing of sweet potatoes. The village headmen allot single fields to applicants who come from other villages. The occupiers, who remain living in their distant holdings, are allowed to keep the fields in the *isanga* and have their regular potato harvest as long as they are not required by the same village headman to give them up. They must always be allowed to collect the harvest before relinquishing the field.

### Transfer of single field

412. A holder cannot give away a field to another man, whether relative or stranger, without permission of the authority.

NOTE. Rule 412 was decided upon by the chiefs of the Sukuma Federation and their people in 1949. Formerly this rule was followed in: BS, SBS, SS, KS, KM. In NF, UF, KF, BSN, BD a man could give a single field to a relative, but not to a non-relative, without asking permission of the authority.

413 A. If a holder relinquishes his holding, the occupier of a single field within the holding cannot retain the field without permission of the authority.

B. If a holder has allowed a person to cultivate a field, or has given a field to anyone as a present, such action, whatever may have been the clauses of the contract, is not recognized as valid after the death of the holder. Even if the occupier of the field in question can prove that he paid for permission to cultivate it, he has to return the land immediately on the death of the original occupier and has no right to claim compensation.

414 A. A holder can lend a field to a relative but not to a non-relative without permission of the authority.

NOTE. A man may borrow fields, not because he has not sufficient land and cannot obtain land in his village, but because he is short of a certain type of land necessary for the cultivation of a certain crop. For instance in SBS (Busiha) or BD (Sengerema), adequate soil for the cultivation of groundnuts is scarce and people try to borrow plots from relatives or friends living in more fortunate areas.

B. A holder can only lend fields to relatives so long as he himself is occupying his holding (393A).

D.C.'s Appeal 2/47 NF. Fulo. *Kilumba* v. *Ngereza*.

Kilumba claimed from Ngereza a cassava field, which his brother Masolwa had given to him when he himself moved to another village. The field had been allotted by the *ng'wanangwa* to Ngereza and the court held that it therefore belonged to Ngereza.

NOTE. The application of these rules is the same as that of rules 375–80. A holder often allows a neighbour or a stranger to cultivate one of his fields without asking permission from the authority.

415. It is unknown for anyone to pay rent for a borrowed field.

## 2. LAND HELD BY VIRTUE OF OFFICE

### (568 et seq.)

### A. *By a Ntemi (chief)*

*The Ikuru* (Residence of a chief)

416 A. The *ikuru* of the chief is considered *Butemi* property.

B. If a chief wishes to build a better house than the one he occupies in his *ikuru*, he must build it outside the *ikuru*. If he builds it inside, neither he nor his heirs can later claim reimbursement of expenses.

NOTE. Rule 416 (B) is one of the new rules accepted unanimously by the full meeting of chiefs and their people in Malya in 1949. The rule was proposed by *Ntemi* Masali of Samuye.

C. If there are houses in the *ikuru* which had been built or greatly improved before the enforcement of rules A and B, it is acknowledged that a chief who is deposed, or the heir of a chief who is not chosen as successor to his father, is entitled to compensation for expenses incurred in improving the house but not for sums spent on its maintenance.

NOTE. Rules 416A–C were decided upon by the chiefs of the Sukuma Federation and their people in 1949. Formerly no rules existed but the immovable property of a chief was always considered to be *Butemi*.

*Njingo gwi Ikuru*

417. The *ikuru* of a chief is surrounded by many fields comprising the *njingo gwi ikuru* or *itongo li ikuru*. Most of the settlers round the *ikuru* are *banikuru*, i.e. distant relatives of the chief or selected retainers; their fields are intermingled with those of the chief himself.

418 A. The *njingo gwi ikuru* is administered directly by the chief and neither village headman nor *basumba batale* have any influence in the allocation of plots in it.

B. The chief's fields are cultivated by his wives, female relatives, servants, and by the *banikuru* living in the *ikuru*. The acreage of the *njingo gwi ikuru* varies and is often considerable. Its boundaries are commonly known although they are not specifically demarcated. In some places, for instance in the chiefdoms of KS, SM, and BS, the villagers round the *njingo* are called upon to help in its cultivation.

419. The *njingo gwi ikuru* is *Butemi* property.

*Traditional fields (Migunda ya ikuru)*

420. In nearly all the villages of his chiefdom huge fields are cultivated for the chief. The sites of these fields have not changed for many years. The chief gives orders as to the crop which is to be planted in each field. In the big chiefdoms the *ng'wambilija*, in smaller chiefdoms the

*ng'wanangwa*, is responsible for organizing the work. Recently the chiefs have begun to engage reliable men as salaried estate managers.

421. At any time a chief can open a new *migunda ya ikuru* in a *gunguli* in which there was none before. A new field is very seldom laid out in an old *gunguli*, as it would be difficult to find a sufficiently large portion of good land unoccupied. New *migunda ya ikuru* are frequently opened in *gunguli* which have recently become densely populated.

422. The *migunda ya ikuru* is *Butemi* property.

423 A. Each able-bodied man of a village must cultivate a certain area, usually 45 square feet, of the plot for the chief. If he is sick his wife must do the work for him.

B. The cultivators receive for the work compensation in kind (a beast or beer) or in money, generally 30 cents for 45 square feet. Money is usually paid for the cultivation of cotton.

C. It is the custom to give the compensation when the work has been done, except in the case of sorghum fields, where compensation is paid after the harvest.

424. Corn is either stored near the fields under the care of a reliable man or transported to the *ikuru* by lorries.

NOTE. Mr. D. W. Malcolm writes in his report (158): 'First the subjects paid *sekule* to the chief, consisting of the payment of one basket of grain by each household of the chiefdom. When Europeans arrived, tribute was stopped and the tax was introduced. The chiefs arranged that each village should plant one field and send the whole of the produce to the chief. This was discovered by Government and stopped. In 1934 the District Commissioner sent round tax collectors to investigate. When the chiefs heard of this, they paid out cents and meat. Some of the people refused to accept payment whereupon the chiefs paid them by force, puttings cents in their houses. Then the chiefs started the present system of having large fields of their own scattered all over their countries, for the labour of which they pay by contract.'

*Temporary fields*

425. After discussion with his village headmen, the chief may decide where he wishes to have fields cultivated for him in the current year. He then calls the leaders of the village *elika*, or the leaders of a dance society, and arranges a works contract with them. The compensation is usually in kind (in ZM, SM money is paid), and the work is supervised by the chief's messengers, or *banikuru*, or by the village headmen themselves. It is possible that in the course of time such a temporary field may become a *ngunda gwi ikuru*.

426. These fields are held under the usual tenure of single fields (407–11).

D.C.'s Appeal 12/43. NF. Fulo (Bukumbi). *Paulo* v. *Ntemi Antonio*.

Paulo was chosen by the village headman to work in the chief's field on several occasions: eight days in November 1940, eight days in 1941, and three days in 1942; for which he claimed wages of 20 cents per day. The chief (defendant) explained: 'It is the custom for me to call upon the inhabitants of a village when I want my field in that village cultivated and to agree with them that I shall pay so much for the cultivation and harvesting of a particular field. When the work is done, I pay out what I have agreed in cash or kind and it is shared out equally among those who worked. There is no individual wage-earning. If the plaintiff did not get his share it is his own fault.'

The court accepted the chief's statement regarding the practice of the country and held that the plaintiff had produced no evidence whatever that he had agreed with the chief to work for certain wages, or that the chief had not paid for the work at the time. The plaintiff should bring an action against the people who worked with him and did not give him his share.

### B. By Ng'wambilija and Ng'wanangwa Ntale (572) (sub-chief and senior village headman)

427. In many chiefdoms (for instance, BD, KF, BSN) the chief may choose one village or another to cultivate a common field for the ng'wambilija or ng'wanangwa ntale. This gunguli would have no work to do for the chief in the same year. In other chiefdoms the ng'wambilija or ng'wanangwa look after themselves and make their own arrangements with the villagers.

428. Customarily, one person from each house works (nhembe or lubili) for one day in the year in the fields of the village headman; they are not necessarily given any specific task, and they receive compensation in kind for the days worked. The basumba batale organize the work and call for a certain number of villagers for every phase of field-work, including the tilling and the harvesting of the crop.

NOTE. A village headman is also given customary gifts in kind by his villagers.

D.C.'s Appeal 21/45. Fulo (Burima). Masanyiwa v. Ng'wanangwa Maneneo.

Masanyiwa acted as soi-disant representative of the interests of the community and claimed payment for work done for the headman and for food delivered to him. The witnesses agreed that it is customary for the local women to bring presents of small quantities of food to a newly appointed headman.

429. If a village headman has inherited office and holding from his father or brother, he cannot be deprived of the holding if he loses his office.

430. If a man on becoming village headman takes over a holding with his appointment, he loses the holding when he loses the office.

NOTE. In this case he must either return to his private holding, if he has retained it, or he must apply for land.

431. In KS, SS, BD (Sengerema) the village headman is entitled to take over the matongo (Note to 390). He cannot keep it if he loses his office but must hand the plot or plots over to his successor.

D.C.'s Appeal 60/45. Fulo (Mwanza). Keya v. Galiyela.

Galiyela was discharged from the headmanship of a village about May and

Keya was put in his place. The new headman claimed one field from Galiyela (allegedly held by the latter *ex officio*) as this was his right as headman and he himself had no fields. The court held that Galiyela must hand over the field to Keya after he had harvested the crop.

NOTE. In all other parts of Sukumaland the *litongo* belongs to the holding and cannot be separated from it.

## 3. GRAZING LAND

### I. *Public rights*

432. All uncultivated land and all fields during the period between crops are subject to common rights of pasture. The grazing is free to any man, Sukuma or non-Sukuma, to an inhabitant of the village or to a man living in another village or chiefdom, irrespective of the number of his cattle or other stock. A cattle-owner is free to send his cattle anywhere for grazing except into reserved grazing land.

NOTE. Customarily a certain rotation in grazing land is followed during the different seasons of the year. As soon as the long rains start, the cattle are driven to the fallows nearest to the house, and during the following months to more distant fallows in a steadily expanding circle. After the long rains the cattle are driven into the *ikungu*. After the grain harvest they are driven into the grain fields. In many areas regulations with regard to the preservation of stalks have been issued, and in these areas cattle must remain in the *ikungu*. September/ October marks the beginning of the worst season for grazing and grazing reserves may be opened at this time, but in bad years these will not see the stock through the whole dry season; after the first rains, November/December, the man with only a few cattle will graze them in the *idimilo*, but men owning much stock will send their herds into the *mbuga* where the grass grows quicker.

### II. *Private rights*

A. *Njingo* (area surrounding a dwelling)

433. Usually, but not invariably, the *njingo* is fenced in by a euphorbia hedge or by sisal; its size varies but never exceeds about 2 acres. Sometimes it is planted with crops, sometimes it is left for grass fallow where calves and sick or old stock may graze when the herd is sent further away. The use of the *njingo* is reserved for the holder.

B. *Igobe* (large estates) (Note to 154)

434 A. The *igobe* includes the *kaya*, the *migunda*, and private pasture; its boundaries are demarcated with sisal or euphorbia planted at fairly close intervals.

B. If the occupier of an *igobe* does not use all the pasture for his cattle, he can cut the grass and sell it.

C. *Igobe* exist in NF, BD (Ng'wagala), BSN, BS, KM, SM, ZM, SS, KS; very few *igobe* exist in BD (Ng'unghu); there are no *igobe* in SBS.

C. *Ilale* (fallow land)

435 A. No one is allowed to send his cattle into corn-fields after

harvest before the owner himself has started to herd his cattle there; only then is the field free for public grazing.

B. Men without cattle have to be asked for their permission before a man is allowed to drive his cattle into their corn-fields. It is unknown for a man to sell the right of grazing in harvested fields, but a man can cut the straw (*mabelele*), collect, and sell it.

## D  Private Ngitiri (grazing reserve) (*Ngitiri ya buli kaya*)

436. If space is available a new-comer may be allocated a small *ngitiri* with his other fields even if he has no stock. Private *ngitiri* exist in varying frequency in KF, BD, BS, but not in NF, UF, KS, SS, SBS.

NOTE. The idea of creating a *ngitiri* possibly derives from the ancient custom that the disposal of the straw in the fields after harvest is reserved for the owner. Another possible explanation is that a cattle-owner found it very useful to ear-mark a piece of land near his house as a reserve for calves and old or sick animals. The institution of *ngitiri* was not introduced by the Sukuma on account of scarcity of pastures due to increasing population and cattle wealth. It started while land was abundant. When land begins to be scarce, private *ngitiri* cannot be maintained, and collective *ngitiri* are created.

The *ngitiri* is never measured and allotted to the cattle-owner according to the number of cattle. Its size varies according to the available space. It represents only a small proportion of the land available for grazing. The greater part is free land (*ibara*).

437. The boundaries of a private grazing plot are marked by hoeing a line or by planting euphorbia or sisal at intervals along the boundary.

NOTE. A private *ngitiri* is distinguished from an *igobe* by the fact that the boundaries of an *igobe* are well demarcated by a closely planted line of euphorbia or sisal.

438 A. A man with a private *ngitiri* for which he has no use can give other people the right to graze their cattle there. It is not usual to ask for payment, except in KF where payment consists of a goat or sheep.

B. A man can lend a portion of his *ngitiri* for cultivation subject to rules 412 to 415. The corn-stalks are usually considered to be the property of the owner of the *ngitiri*.

439. The occupier of a private *ngitiri* must give it up, retaining only about three acres, if the authority requires it for allocation to an applicant for arable land or for the organization of a collective *ngitiri*.

NOTE. This rule was decided upon by the chiefs of the Sukuma Federation and their people in 1949. Formerly the same rule existed and was applied in accordance with usage described in note to 377.

NOTE. The fact that a man is allowed to have three acres as his private grazing land entitles him to retain three acres which cannot be re-allocated even if he does not cultivate them (377).

## III. *Collective rights*

### Collective ngitiri (*ngitiri ya gunguli*)

440. Collective *ngitiri*, inaugurated either by the village authority itself or by the Veterinary Department, exist nearly everywhere. The *ngitiri* of the Veterinary Department are opened by the chief, the *ngitiri* of village authorities are opened by the authority.

NOTE. Rules have been enacted under the Native Authority Ordinance to protect *ngitiri* and to punish cattle-owners who send cattle into them before they are opened.
The institution of collective *ngitiri* was inaugurated by the Germans in BD, BSN, but private grazing reserves have existed, especially in KF, as an ancient institution.

441. The size of a *ngitiri* varies. Sometimes a few sub-areas (*kibanda*) or a *gunguli* have a collective *ngitiri* of considerable size.

442. The boundaries of a collective *ngitiri* are demarcated by stones, sisal, &c., or by natural boundaries such as trees, hills, rocks, &c.

443. In BSN all *ngitiri* are reserved for the use of the inhabitants of the area to which the *ngitiri* belong. In KS, SS the *ngitiri* of the village authority are reserved for the use of the village; the *ngitiri* of the Veterinary Department are open for general use. In all other chiefdoms, after a *ngitiri* is opened, any cattle-owner, whether a member of the community or not, is allowed to send cattle into it.

444. After years of use the authority may decide to open the *ngitiri* for cultivation and demarcate another area as *ngitiri*.

NOTE. This is done when cultivated areas become exhausted, or more often when the *ngitiri* becomes unhealthy for stock on account of ticks and unsuitable grass.

445. One community may have several separate *ngitiri* because inhabited areas must be excluded when selecting reserves.

446. The authority may permit the cultivation of fields within the *ngitiri* with such crops as ripen quickly, i.e. which can be harvested before the *ngitiri* is required for grazing.

447. In all chiefdoms a new-comer to the area is entitled to the use of the collective *ngitiri*.

### 4. WATER RIGHTS

#### A. *Human consumption*

448. Any source of water, such as a stream, spring, well, pond, &c., is free for everyone.

449. Any source of water situated in private ground, whether natural

or dug or constructed by the holder, is free for everyone. No holder can monopolize the use of a water source in his holding.

450. If a number of men dig a water-hole in a river bed or on any piece of land, the water is free for everyone. If a man has dug a water-hole for a certain purpose, for instance, for making bricks or building a house, the water is still free for everyone.

451. If a village or a sub-area of a village decides under the leadership of the village headman and/or the *basumba batale* to construct a common water-hole, one man from each house must help with the digging. If a man does not participate in the common work he cannot be deprived of the use of the water, but he may be punished by the village organization. The villagers cannot claim exclusive rights to the use of such water.

NOTE. Although Sukumaland is not blessed with abundant water the distance between any *kaya* and the nearest drinking-water supply is never so great as to make the fetching of water a full time job at any time of the year.

## B. *Cattle consumption*

452. Any source of natural water customarily open for the watering of cattle, or any source declared to be open by the authority, is free for everyone.

NOTE. Natural sources of water are those mentioned in 448. Sources of water to be declared open by the authority are mainly the recently constructed *lambo* (artificial ponds).

453. Water-holes may be used only by those who constructed them, whether it be the water-hole of an individual cattle-owner or a water-hole constructed by the inhabitants of a *kibanda* or *gunguli*. To water cattle at another man's water-hole without permission is punishable. Often the transgressor is required, as a penalty, to enlarge and clean the source of water.

454. These privately constructed water-holes can only be used by strangers after having obtained permission from the authority. It is permissible to charge rent for the use of the water. The permission is given only for short periods, usually until the cattle-owner has finished the construction of his own water-hole, or has found free water for his cattle. The rent is high.

455. If a man opens up a source of water within the boundaries of his holding, no other man is allowed to send his cattle there for watering without permission of the holder.

456. A new-comer cannot close any source of water (*bukumbiji*) on his land which he found already in public use on his arrival. This applies to water-holes which may have been constructed by the former occupant or by the community and the *basumba batale*. The new holder cannot close

a path leading to a water source and keep it only for the use of his own cattle. His own cattle must have a path to it and therefore no excuse is accepted for closing the path on the grounds of crop damage.

457. The right to dig water-holes is not restricted. Inhabitants of one chiefdom who run short of water for their cattle can dig water-holes in another chiefdom.

## 5. RIGHTS OF WAY

### *Nzira ya Maguru* (Foot-path)

458 A. A man has the right to re-aline a path leading through his land unless by so doing he causes hardship to the users of the old path.

B. In KS a man requires the permission of the village to change a path.

C. If a man closes an old path and opens a new one, he must make the new path passable for pedestrians.

### *Ipanda* (Cattle path)

459. Such a path cannot be closed or its course changed by an individual, even if he is the occupier of the land through which the path leads. Any change must be decided upon by the village headman together with the villagers.

## 6. RIGHTS REGARDING MISCELLANEOUS PRODUCE[1]

### *Crops*

460. A husband is the sole owner of all crops grown on his holding and has the right to dispose of them. If there is no husband the cultivator of the field is the owner of the crop.

461 A. If a man marries a woman who is living on her own land it is necessary to hold a ceremony to make the husband the master of the house; otherwise the woman remains the owner of all crops, even if the husband has helped in the cultivation.

B. If the woman agrees to hand over her holding to her new husband (and this is the usual procedure) the elders of the village (*banamhara*) and the kinsmen of the wife are called together. The husband must pay his wife in kind for all food in store, then all the hoes in the house are tied together and handed over to a relative of the wife. The husband has to provide new hoes and from then on he has the right to dispose of the crops.

NOTE. Quite a number of women have their own holdings. A woman may have continued to live with her mother on her father's holding after his death, or a divorced woman may refuse to live with relatives. There is no prohibition of her acquiring land from the authority by allocation.

[1] For rights regarding houses, trees, and plots planted with other than annual crops see paras. 515–30.

*Manure*

462 A. In SS, KF, UF, NF, ZM cattle manure is free for everyone, even if it is in the cattle kraal.

B. In BD, BSN cattle manure is reserved for the cattle-owner during the month of September when manure is transported to the fields. During this month permission must be obtained from the cattle-owner by anyone wishing to take manure from his cattle kraal.

NOTE. The reason why manure is not privately owned is that the cattle graze on the common and it is therefore felt that the cattle-owner has no right to reserve manure for himself.

## Produce of the bush

*Fruit, honey, beeswax, gum*

463 A. Wild fruits in the bush are free to everyone.

B. Honey and wax of wild bees may be collected by any inhabitant of the area. A stranger is not allowed to collect honey and wax without the permission of the headman.

C. The maker of a beehive is the owner of the honey and wax of the bees which have settled in the hive.

D. The collection of gum is free to everyone, Sukuma or non-Sukuma.

NOTE. To reach a wild bees' nest, pegs are driven into the trunk of the tree to serve as a ladder. Any man who does this has a right to collect the honey and wax.

*Grass, building-poles, fuel*

464. The collection of these commodities is free to everyone, except in areas which are expressly closed, such as *ngitiri* or forest reserves.

465. The collection of fuel is free to everyone, even in another man's holding, except in NF where dry branches of a tree are the property of the holder.

*Trees*

466 A. Trees which a man has planted or trees growing on the land allotted to him are his property.

B. If a man wishes to make a tree plantation he can only do so on the three acres of his *ngitiri* which he is always allowed to retain (see 439).

467. If a man has acquired an *igobe* on which are trees (*mihushi* area), he cannot keep more than two acres as his private forest reserve (*ngitiri ya miti*) if the community decides to claim the rest of the *mihushi* area from him.

NOTE. Rules 466B and 467 were decided upon by the chiefs of the Sukuma Federation and their people in 1949. Formerly no rules existed.

# CHAPTER VII

# CATTLE[1]

## INTRODUCTION

ALTHOUGH stock (*shitugo*) and especially cattle play an important part in the life of the average Sukuma, he is primarily a cultivator of the soil and not a cattle-breeder.[2]

Corn and vegetable relishes are the staple foods of the Sukuma, not meat or milk, although meat has always been very much appreciated and is eaten on all ceremonial occasions. With an improved standard of living the consumption of meat is steadily increasing. It is the constant desire of a Sukuma peasant to increase the number of his cattle, but first in his thoughts are the products of his fields because they normally guarantee his own and his family's subsistence. Stock was the currency for large payments before money was known and it was the only investment which brought interest and security (*shillingi jitobialaga*—shillings do not breed). The possession of stock still enables the Sukuma to marry and to meet emergencies such as famine, payments in case of adultery, *misango*, *njigu*, &c. But the wealth of a Sukuma consists not only of a big herd; a well-filled grain store and a large family are at least equally important to him. In fact they are all interdependent; a large family produces much corn with which many cattle can be acquired, and with many cattle many wives can be obtained who in turn guarantee a large family (Note to 331).

Wealth (cattle) is not acquired by the Sukuma in order to live better than others or to gain respect and influence in the community. It is a striking feature of Sukuma social life that no trace of a caste or class system is apparent. It is impossible for an observer to distinguish rich and poor men by their clothes, or their importance in discussion or their general demeanour. The growth of snobbishness has been prevented by intense superstitious fear. A man was afraid not only of the envy of his neighbours, if he tried to be ostentatious, but even more so of the envy of the gods. The difference in standards of living between rich and

[1] For other laws and customs regarding cattle see: Bridewealth paid in cattle, paras. 1–18, 33, 110, 111. Payment of ceremonial cattle, paras. 19–24, 26, 27. Cattle paid as compensation, paras. 176, 177, 188, 231, 300, 313. Cattle under guardianship, paras. 352, 364, 371–4. Sale of cattle, paras. 531–50. Inheritance of cattle, paras. 573–86.
The Sukumaland Federation, Livestock Restriction Rules, Appendix III.

[2] Prof. Schapera writes in his *Native Land Tenure in the Bechuanaland Protectorate*: 'Wherever people combine agriculture with animal husbandry, the problem arises of partitioning out land for the pursuit of the two activities.' The Sukuma attitude to the problem is best illustrated by the remark of a *nsumba ntale* repeated in Mr. D. W. Malcolm's Report: 'If 10 or 50 strangers came to this village and said that they wanted to settle here, they would be given land, and as a result some of our cattle might have to be sent elsewhere.'

poor is very slight. Improved houses are still rare, and the staple food and daily menu are the same everywhere. Possibly the rich man eats a little more meat and drinks a little more milk than the poor one, although it is more likely that he leaves the milk for his wives and children and prefers beer for himself.

Both sentimental and material considerations underlie the reluctance of a Sukuma cattle-owner to sell a useless beast. On the sentimental side he feels a certain obligation towards an old cow which has calved many times, or an old beast descended from the ancestral herd. On the material side the obstacles are:

1. the peasant's scant appreciation of money;
2. the possibility of exchanging an old beast for a young animal, should some member of the community need a slaughter animal;
3. the possibility of using an old beast as payment for field-work done with communal help;
4. the possibility of bartering dried meat, if the old beast should die, for corn which it would be difficult to buy with money in times of food scarcity.

## I. TRUSTEESHIP

### (Bubilisi)

468. The usual procedure for giving cattle into trusteeship is as follows:

A. After preliminary arrangements have been made the owner sends his son accompanied by a close relative or a friend with the cattle to the trustee.

B. The cattle are marked with the owner's brand.

C. No special witnesses are called for the handing over of the beasts. Very likely all the neighbours of the trustee are witnesses. If he had no cattle before, the building of a kraal (lugutu or lubigiri) is proof of the transaction. He may even have to ask a neighbour to keep the cattle for him until he has finished the kraal. If the trustee has cattle of his own, the number of these is well known and an addition to his herd cannot be kept secret.

D. If owner and trustee live far apart, probably a permit from the Veterinary Department for the movement of cattle will be necessary, and this document may be useful as evidence of the transaction.

NOTE. The custom of giving cattle into trusteeship is very common. Usually the owner starts the connexion by giving a few cattle into trusteeship and increases the number only after he has seen that the cattle thrive under the care of the trustee. It is seldom that an owner leaves more than about fifteen beasts with a trustee. Owners prefer as trustees men without cattle of their own who live near good pastures and water and who have children to do the herding. In many areas it is quite usual to give cattle into the trusteeship of a brother-in-law, partly in order to supply milk for the nephews, partly because a sister can be trusted to look after her brother's interests.

The usual reasons for giving cattle into trusteeship are:

1. Fear of diseases and epidemics. If the herd is divided into several small herds each one of which is kept apart from the others, the danger of a total loss is slight.
2. Scarcity of pasture and water. In years of insufficient or badly distributed rainfall the chance of saving some of a divided herd is considerable. In such emergencies the owner, having the advantage of a long-standing connexion, may be able to find a temporary home for the rest of the herd with his trustee.
3. Lack of herd-boys. If a man has not many children, or if they are all attending school, the herding of a big herd becomes a serious problem.
4. To conceal riches. Superstitious fear, as well as real fear based on the experience that wealth arouses the envy of the powers that be, causes the owner to find a means of concealing the true extent of his possessions.
5. To help friends or relatives. This motive is seldom met with.

It is well known that trusteeship means a loss for the owner, but as long as the losses remain within reasonable limits, he seldom takes a serious view of them; he knows that if he were to exercise strict control over his *milisilwa* the trusteeship would not last long. On the other hand the owner would dislike the idea of having all his cattle in his own kraal because it would be contrary to tradition and inimical to the prosperity and security of his herd. Strangers are preferred to relatives as trustees, because with the former trusteeship remains a business affair, while with the latter the owner cannot easily maintain authority and if cattle have been misappropriated he can probably do no more than give his consent. Sometimes a man without cattle offers his services as trustee to a cattle-owner, but more often the owner looks for a trustee and begins the negotiations.

469. Cattle given into trusteeship remain the property of the owner together with their offspring.

NOTE. No contract is drawn up between owner and trustee when the cattle are handed over. The rules of trusteeship are generally known and need no confirmation.

470. The trustee is entitled to the unrestricted use of the produce of the herd.

471. If a beast dies the trustee must inform the owner at once. The birth of calves need not be reported immediately.

472 A. In SBS the meat of a dead beast is the property of the trustee.
B. In all other chiefdoms the meat is the property of the owner, with the exception of one front leg and the intestines. If the trustee lives far away from the owner he must barter the meat for sorghum and keep it for the owner or sell it for cash and pay the money to the owner.

473. The hide of a beast which has died is the property of the owner, and it is the duty of the trustee in all circumstances to keep it and hand it over to the owner at the first opportunity. The hide is regarded as a necessary proof of the death of the beast.

474. If an animal disappears the owner cannot make the trustee responsible for the loss unless he can prove that the trustee has stolen or slaughtered the beast.

475. If a trustee uses cattle for payment of bridewealth, the owner has the right to enforce the return of the cattle regardless of the legal consequences for the married couple (104).

476. If the trustee dies, the owner usually comes to the house of mourning and explains after the *isabingula* (614) his claim to ownership of certain cattle. If the owner fails to appear at the *isabingula*, he has not thereby forfeited his right to claim the cattle.

477. If the owner dies, his heirs have the right to terminate the trusteeship if they wish to do so, regardless of whether it has been mentioned by the owner before his death or not.

478 A. In BSN a trustee can give a bull into the trusteeship of another man if there are too many bulls in the herd. He can also give a cow which has not enough milk for her calf into the trusteeship of a man who has cows in calf and agrees to help.

B. In all other chiefdoms a trustee is not allowed to give trustee cattle into the trusteeship of another man without the consent of the owner.

479. A trustee is not allowed to castrate a bull without permission of the owner.

480. It is the general custom for an owner to visit his trustee once a year in order to mark with his own brand the calves born during the year.

481. The owner is entitled to take away some or all of the trustee cattle at any time without explanation or previous notice.

482 A. The owner is not allowed to take his cattle away from their pasture in the absence of the trustee. If he does so, he cannot make the trustee responsible later for any deficiency in numbers. The owner must take over the cattle direct from the trustee.

B. When the owner takes over the cattle from the trustee, no witnesses need be called. If the owner does not come himself, he must send his son or a man known to the trustee and accredited by the production of a stick, a snuff-box, or any other object which the trustee can recognize as the owner's property.

NOTE. The owner and trustee are friends when the connexion is begun and they must remain so the whole time, otherwise the connexion is severed at once. The foundation of trusteeship is a certain degree of honesty. The traditional honesty prevalent in the 'good old times' did not spring from a higher conception of moral obligations but from beliefs which have now decreased considerably in strength. A belief which played an important part in this connexion was '*msholo*'—

belief in a magical connexion between two otherwise independent events. Thus a trustee who could have misappropriated a calf or a head of cattle with impunity, abstained from doing so because he expected eventually to be punished by a loss exceeding his original profit. It is obvious that such a belief is easily confirmed, because any misfortune subsequently befalling the evil-doer is ascribed by him to his previous fault. Another example of *msholo* is the following: A man goes to the coast to work and comes back with property. He fails to distribute it in the customary manner among his relations or friends. Some years later he again looks for work at the coast, but everything goes wrong. He will say, '*nasanja nalimsholo* (I have met my fate)'.

The unlucky person does not think that he is intentionally hindered by anyone else, for the other people concerned do not know that they are connected with his ill-luck. The victim believes that he himself has caused the trouble. This may sometimes explain the seemingly inexplicable attitude of a Sukuma in court. Even if he thinks the accusation made against him unjust, he quietens down after having first shown fight. This is not due to fatalism in our sense of the word, but rather to his conviction that his present situation has nothing to do with the case in question but is the result of some transgression in the past.

483. With regard to the use of pasture and water the trustee and not the owner is responsible to his community.

## Trusteeship in absence of owner

484. If a cattle-owner intends to leave the district for any length of time, he usually places his cattle in the trusteeship of a relative. No form of contract is concluded and the absentee cannot ask for an account when he returns.

485. If the owner thinks that he has been cheated he can file a suit in court.

Note. Formerly courts refused to hear such cases between relatives. The affair was considered a matter to be decided by the family council.

486. If a cattle-owner gives his stock into the trusteeship of a non-relative the kinsmen of the absentee have the right to insist that the cattle be handed over to them if the trustee fails to look after the herd properly, or if he uses the cattle for his own ends. The trustee cannot refuse to surrender the cattle.

Note. Cases in which an absentee owner of cattle gives them into the trusteeship of a non-relative are very rare.

487. No contract is concluded between the owner and his trustee. It is understood by both that the trustee is entitled to the produce of the herd (470).

## Temporary trusteeship (Lugundiga)

488. When in any area grass or water becomes scarce, individual owners or village herd clubs may send their cattle into areas where conditions are more favourable. They negotiate with a resident in the area and conclude an agreement with him.

NOTE. There are now certain areas the use of which for grazing, &c., is controlled by the Veterinary Department.

489. The usual questions to be agreed upon are:

1. Whether herdsmen are supplied by the owner or the trustee.
2. Whether the *lugundiga* shall last until the next rainy season or for a shorter period.
3. Whether the produce of the herd is the property of the trustee or not.
4. If a beast dies, to whom the meat and the hide belong.
5. To whom calves born during the trusteeship belong.
6. Whether the owner has the right to interfere with the management of the herd.
7. Whether any fees are payable to the trustee.

## II. *KUKONHELEƷA* OR *KUMISHA*

490. This is the name given to the procedure by which a calf, whose mother has died or has no milk, is sent by its owner to another man who has a cow in milk.

A. In BSN the owner of the calf pays the owner of the foster mother Shs.5/-, for which sum the calf remains with the foster mother for about one year. Often the cow lives in the kraal of the owner of the calf because the rearing of a calf means work.

B. In all other chiefdoms the custom is practised only among neighbours and for friendship's sake, without the conclusion of any contract or the promise of any payment.

## III. GIFT OF CATTLE

*(Nang'inha ya ng'ombe)*

491. A gift of cattle must be made before witnesses. The witnesses are usually the donor's children, his wife or wives, a few near kinsmen, and neighbours. The presentation is celebrated by a beer drink and all the participants are *ipso facto* witnesses.

NOTE. Chiefs make presents of cattle if a man kills a lion. The chief takes the fat and the hide. Gifts of cattle are otherwise very rare.

492. If a man who has received cattle in trusteeship should later declare that he received them as a gift, he must produce witnesses to the presentation (468c).

NOTE. In many cases of this kind the marking of cattle and their offspring may help to determine ownership. Two kinds of markings are recognized: the tribal marking (*lumeng'ho lwa kutu*) which is always performed on the ears; for instance, the Bakwimba use a saw-like cut on the right ear, the Bagoro clan cut the top of the right ear. The second marking is the owner's private mark, usually a brand, called *lumeng'ho lwa moto*. If an owner has not previously marked his cattle he will do so before giving them into trusteeship. Private markings often have to be changed; for instance in case of bridewealth cattle, or in case of customary payments. Sometimes the new owner puts his brand over the old one, but often he just brands the newly acquired beasts anywhere. Thus it may happen that a cow has several private markings, which may be confusing and not helpful in determining ownership. But the markings of calves are of much greater value and help to fix the ownership of the mother cow. For instance, in case of trusteeship the brand will be that of the owner; in case of a present it will be that of the recipient. If the owner, in case of trusteeship, has neglected to brand his calves it is his own fault and he can hold no one responsible for any loss except himself.

493. Whether a gift of cattle is acknowledged after the death of the donor depends on the reason for which the gift was made. The maximum number of cattle acknowledged as a gift is two beasts. The heirs are entitled to claim the return of cattle in excess of this number.

494. Gifts of more than two head of cattle may be acknowledged if they have been given to a relative to enable him to perform a sacrifice, or as help in the payment of *njigu*, or for the payment of bridewealth.

495. Gifts not acknowledged are those made by a man to one of his wives or to a relative of his wife.

496. If the heirs claim the return of a gift, the recipient must return it together with the offspring; but if any of the cattle have died while they were in the recipient's care, he does not have to replace them.

497. Gifts made by family members to assist one of the family in the payment of bridewealth never become a debt.

D.C.'s Appeal 65/44. KM. *Gabriel* v. *Mafulinga*.

Mafulinga had received from his maternal uncle six head of cattle to pay bridewealth. The donor's son claimed return of the cattle stating that they were only a loan made by his father to his nephew. The court held that these cattle should be regarded as a gift as they were given for the payment of bridewealth.

498. The cattle which a father gives to his son for the payment of bridewealth are not deducted from the son's share in the estate after the father's death, even if the recipient is a younger son.

## IV. RULES OF HERDING

499. Usually a man who possesses more than about thirty beasts has to herd his own cattle. The owners of small herds join in herding their cattle together and the joint herd of several owners is called *ludima*. The number of cattle in a *ludima* is usually not more than sixty beasts; the number of owners combined in one *ludima* varies.

NOTE. Certain practical rules with regard to the management of a herd are observed.

1. Usually the cattle-owner counts one adult bull and one bull calf to ten cows. In a herd of about thirty cattle three bulls and three bull calves are considered the right number.

2. The rest of the bulls are either exchanged for heifers, a biggish bull for a small heifer, or they may be castrated and used for ploughing. Opportunity for barter is not always forthcoming and there may be periods during which the number of bulls exceeds the norm.

3. Useless beasts, like supernumerary bulls, are not eliminated automatically, because the owner always prefers to wait for an occasion for barter. Thus it may happen that useful stock have to share the meagre pasture with many useless beasts.

4. In all major herds there is a bull which is never sold, if it can be avoided, but is kept until its death. This bull is dedicated by the owner to ancestral spirits, and it is recognizable by the bell round its neck. The owner always keeps one or two young bulls, descendants of the one with the bell, to replace it on its death. The bull is called by the name of the owner's ancestor.

500 A. No man is obliged to join a *ludima* and even a small cattle-owner can herd his few cattle independently if he likes to do so.

B. A cattle-owner can join or leave the *ludima* at any time.

501. The members of a *ludima* herd the cattle in turns, for periods of equal length, irrespective of the number of cattle in the possession of any individual member. A spell of herding lasts from three to five days.

502. The *ludima* has no official leader. The leader is the member whose turn it is to herd.

503. The herding of cattle does not follow strict rules in the matter of pasture or division of the common, and with regard to the seasons only a general plan is followed (Note to 432).

NOTE. The cattle of individual owners or those of a *ludima* are driven by the herdsman to an area which he considers suitable for the day (*chilugala*). The herdsmen of a village do not arrange beforehand a division of pasture between them for the following day. If by chance several herds meet in a pasture they all herd together. A certain competition among cattle-owners may arise, but the rivalry is slight since each cattle-owner desires to keep his herd as near his house as possible.

504. The cattle of a *ludima* are driven by the owners to a meeting-place (*chilula*) and handed over to the herdsman of the day. In the evening the owners have to fetch their beasts from the same meeting-place; if an owner is late the herdsman cannot leave the cattle or just let them find their own way home; either he must bring them to the house of the owner after the other members have collected their cattle or he can take them to his own house.

NOTE. It is a widespread custom, especially in southern Sukuma, for the herdsman to return home with his cattle for the midday meal.

### Responsibilities of herdsman

505. The herdsman is responsible for any damage to property done by cattle under his care, except in the event of a heavy storm or a stampede of the herd, when the herdsman may lose control over the cattle which may then do damage to crops.

NOTE. In some areas compensation for damage done by cattle is paid by the family of the herdsman.

506 A. An owner is not responsible for damage caused by his cattle at night if they break out of the kraal. The owner is merely told to reinforce his kraal.

B. In BS the owner is responsible for the damage.

507. The herdsman is responsible if he harms a beast by throwing a stick, stone, or spear at it.

508. The herdsman is not responsible if a beast dies or is lost because he neglected his duty as herdsman; for instance, if a beast strays into an area where *marwa*, a plant poisonous to stock, is known to grow.

509. In no circumstances may the herdsman hand over a beast to any man other than the owner during the time of herding. The herdsman is responsible for the loss of the beast, if he hands it over to anyone else, even if the man should show as his authorization articles belonging to the owner, such as those mentioned in para. 482B.

510. If the member of a *ludima* whose turn it is to herd changes his day with another member, the responsibility lies with the one who actually does the herding.

511. If a member of a *ludima* delegates his duty of herding to a non-member, he remains responsible for the safety of the cattle for the day.

512. If a beast injures a man no compensation is payable by the owner to the injured person. If the beast injures people repeatedly the owner may be warned and asked to slaughter the animal.

513. If a beast kills a person no *njigu* is payable, unless the owner has already been warned. The owner must always kill such a beast.

514. The herdsman is entitled to refuse to herd a sick animal or a cow which is expected to calve during the day.

# CHAPTER VIII

# SALE

## IMMOVABLE PROPERTY

### A. *Land*

### I. *Plots planted with annual crops*

515. While no sale of land is admissible (380), sale of standing crops is known but seldom practised. If the occupier sells a crop because he is leaving his holding it is understood that he is selling the crop and not the land.

NOTE. Even if a man should say that he has sold his plot (and actually in colloquial usage the parties to the transaction talk about buying or selling a plot) it is understood that only the plants above the ground are sold, and not the earth itself. In addition to the transactions in corn mentioned in the note to 331, and in 584, a man frequently borrows corn from a neighbour, if he has miscalculated the needs of his household. Such a debt is repaid in kind without interest, measure for measure, after the next harvest. In UF and KF (and in many other chiefdoms for debts of *misango* and *njigu*) the corn harvest of a debtor can be distrained. After the corn is threshed, the village headman and some elders decide the quantity which they consider necessary for the subsistence of the cultivator and his family, and the rest is given to the creditor in payment of the debt. Ten *ngele* or *migelo* count as the equivalent of one cow. If there still remains a debt the procedure is repeated the following year.

516. If a standing crop is sold on account of pressing debts, the buyer is responsible for all field-work and the vendor is not responsible for the size of the yield.

### II. *Plots planted with other than annual crops*

517. A man can sell the crop but he cannot sell the plot.

518. The buyer is entitled to harvest as long as the crop which he has bought bears fruit.

NOTE. For instance, a man may buy a banana plantation and the plot is bigger than the planted area. The buyer would not be allowed to plant bananas in the uncultivated part of the plot unless he has been allotted the plot by the authority. The buyer can cut bananas as long as the plants produce them without replanting. Another example is that of a man who has bought a plot of sugar-cane. He can cut the canes as long as the original plants exist, but he cannot stick shoots into the ground unless the plot has been allotted to him.

519. The buyer cannot:

1. replant the plot with the same sort of plants unless the plot has been allotted to him by the authority;

2. cut down the plants which he has bought and plant other crops on the same plot unless the plot has been allotted to him by the authority.

## B. Trees

520. The same rules are applied with regard to trees which the occupier has planted himself and trees which he found on the land when it was allotted to him.

NOTE. There are no individual trees of ritual importance in Sukuma. There is, however, a superstition that if a man cuts a tree which has been left standing for some purpose by his predecessor he may suffer a loss. Certain species of tree play a part in the rites of some dance societies, and a member may be reluctant to cut down such trees.

521. If a man relinquishes his holding the trees thereon revert, together with the holding, to the community.

### I. Trees in the homestead

522. Trees planted in the immediate vicinity of the house are considered to be part of the homestead and therefore cannot be sold separately. If the house is sold in accordance with the rules of paras. 529, 530, such trees may be considered improvements to the house. The occupier, if he relinquishes his holding, can ask for compensation from the new occupier for the value of the trees. If the new occupier cannot or will not pay for the trees, the outgoing holder can cut and sell them.

### II. Fruit-trees in the Migunda

523. A man can sell a plot of fruit-trees within his holding unless the trees are planted in the immediate vicinity of his house (522). If he sells the plot, it is understood that he has sold only the trees and not the land. If the buyer does not ask the authority that the land between the trees may be allotted to him, such land can be allotted for cultivation to any applicant.

NOTE. It often happens that one man owns the mango-trees which are planted at wide intervals and another man cultivates the ground between them.

524. If a man sells trees, either while he is still occupying his holding or when he intends to relinquish it, he must inform the authority about the transaction and name the buyer.

NOTE. If the buyer of trees should be considered by the community to be undesirable as a settler, he is not allotted the land between the trees, or any other land.

### III. Sisal and trees other than fruit-trees in the Migunda

525. The occupier can cut such trees and sell them and remain in occupation of the plot. He can also sell the standing trees to be cut within a short time, if he relinquishes the plot.

526. The plot from which trees have been sold for immediate cutting reverts after the cutting to the community. The buyer of the trees has no right to any trees which may afterwards grow on the plot.

527. An occupier cannot sell trees for any purpose other than immediate cutting, whether he is retaining occupation of the land or intending to relinquish his holding.

528. If a man sells sisal poles the buyer has no right to the sisal plants after he has cut the poles.

## C. Houses

529 A. The following rules refer to houses which have been erected not with the help of the inhabitants of the village, but at the expense of the owner. Such houses cannot be sold unless the village headman and/or the *basumba batale* agree that the purchaser is a suitable person to settle in the village.

B. The village headman and/or the *basumba batale* may not allot the holding, which includes the house, without helping the owner to obtain from the would-be settler a reasonable price for his house.

530. If the price asked by the owner is disproportionate to the value of the house, the village headman and/or the *basumba batale* can ask the owner to pull down the house and remove the usable parts of it, such as the roof, doors, and windows and, if he likes, even the bricks.

NOTE. These rules were decided upon by the chiefs of the Sukuma Federation and their people in 1949. Formerly these rules were applied in UF (Masanza II).

In BS, GS, SBS, KS a man who had relinquished his holding had to relinquish his house without any right to claim compensation for improvements.

In other chiefdoms, no rules existed and no instances of transactions in house property are known.

NOTE. The compromise contained in paras. 529, 530 represents a progressive step, as in most areas no question of compensation for improved houses has hitherto been admitted. Although it has been realized that the owner of a house should be compensated for improvements, it has also been agreed that he cannot sell it without the permission of the authority; the plot on which the building has been erected belongs to the community and not to any individual. In accordance with Sukuma conceptions there cannot be a freehold owner of a house because there are no freehold plots. The builder of the house has used stones, earth, water, and poles for its erection, but these commodities are public property; thus the public has a share in each house; this is the justification for the rules applying to the matter of improvements, whereby control of new-comers by the village is assured and the unity of house and holding is maintained.

Recently applications have been received from persons requiring a plot on which to build a house for the purpose of carrying on a trade or profession but not requiring farm-land. The applications have not been only for plots in trading centres, but for plots on tribal land also. No provision for such situations exists in customary law since, until recently, there was no question of a house existing without its *migunda*, and there was no precedent for the sale of a house apart from the land on which it stood. Control of ownership of houses is customarily exercised by the community by virtue of its rights over the land. Thus, an outgoing holder cannot prevent the reallocation of his plot of unused land for cultivation.

## MOVABLE PROPERTY

### A. *Cattle*

I. *General rules*

531. The beast to be sold must be produced when the contract of sale is concluded. The procedure of showing a similar beast to that which it is proposed to sell is admissible, but is very seldom employed.

NOTE. The Sukuma avoids if possible the sale or purchase of cattle, and cattle auctions are seldom used for the purchase of cattle. Firstly, the beasts sold at auction are mostly bulls, oxen, or old and useless beasts, good only for slaughter. Secondly, the purchase of a beast at an auction is unsatisfactory from the point of view of the breeder, who will wish to know the pedigree of an animal before buying it. The Sukuma prefers to barter his cattle. The average Sukuma cattle-owner, i.e. the owner of from ten to twenty beasts, is nearly always in process of carrying out a stock transaction.

For example, on the occasion of a wedding, the father needs a good beast for slaughter. He will look round until he finds someone who can give him one ox (*nzeku*) for two young heifers. (Formerly oxen were cheaper—only one heifer was exchanged for an ox.)

As payment for common work a man may need a young bull, while he has only more valuable beasts in his herd. He exchanges an ox for two heifers, and exchanges one of these for two young bulls, one of which he gives to the *elika*.

For breeding purposes a man wishes to introduce a bull from another man's herd; he may get the bull in exchange for a very good heifer.

For festivities, doctor's fees, or sacrifices, a man wishes to use a few goats, but he has none. He exchanges a bull for 5 goats, a heifer or a cow for 10 goats approximately. The rates of exchange are not now so rigidly fixed as they used to be.

532. Not less than two persons are required as witnesses to a sale.

533. Once the beast has been transferred from the vendor to the purchaser it cannot be returned, nor can the sale be declared void, unless the vendor has given undertakings regarding the quality of the beast before witnesses which afterwards prove to be false.

NOTE. For instance, a man buys a cow in calf and the vendor asserts that the cow always has plenty of milk. When the calf is born the cow has no milk and the calf dies. The buyer hears that the same thing happened when the cow had her first calf in the house of the vendor. The buyer can return the cow and demand .the purchase money.

534. If a beast awaiting transfer after sale dies or becomes sick, the loss falls on the buyer.

NOTE. This rule was decided upon by the chiefs of the Sukuma Federation and their people in 1949. Formerly no fixed rule existed. In some courts the vendor was held to be responsible for the money and the buyer for the beast; in others the vendor was held to be responsible as long as the beast remained in his homestead, even if he had already received the purchase money.

NOTE. Usually the beast cannot be taken home by the buyer at once as a stock removal permit from the Veterinary Department is necessary.

## II. *Payment by instalments*

535. If no special arrangement has been made, the beast automatically becomes the property of the buyer on the payment of a first instalment of the price, even though it remains with the vendor.

536. A time limit is always fixed for the payment of instalments of purchase money.

537. If the buyer fails to pay the instalments according to arrangement, the vendor has two alternative courses open to him:

1. He can repay the instalments already received and declare the transaction void.
2. He can claim payment of the remaining instalments in court as a debt.

538. If the beast remains in the house of the vendor until all instalments have been paid, the milk is the vendor's property; but if the cow calves, the calf is the property of the buyer.

539. If the beast has been transferred to the buyer, the milk is the property of the buyer.

540. If the beast dies, the buyer must complete payment of the remaining instalments on the appointed days. Meat and hide of the beast are property of the buyer.

541. A buyer can pay the instalments earlier than was arranged and take the beast with him. The vendor cannot refuse to accept payment.

542. The vendor cannot dissolve the contract, pay back the instalments, and keep the beast if the buyer elects to pay sooner than was arranged.

543. The vendor is not allowed to sell the beast to another buyer while the contract remains valid.

544. If the vendor's property is seized for debt, the buyer's beast cannot be attached; it has the status of a beast in trusteeship.

## III. *Sale of an unborn calf (Kudima Nkila)*
(Custom known in BSN and ZM)

545. A man buys, in the presence of the usual number of witnesses, a female calf not yet born of a certain cow. If the cow has a male calf

instead, the next birth is awaited. If this is a heifer, the contract is fulfilled; if it is a second male calf, the buyer has the right to take the cow while the two bull calves remain with the vendor.

546. If the cow dies before the calf is born, the money has to be returned or becomes a debt.

547. The vendor must inform the buyer as soon as the calf is born.

548. The calf becomes the property of the buyer at its birth, but remains with the cow for about one year. The milk is the property of the owner of the cow, i.e. the vendor.

549. Should the calf die during its first year, the buyer is entitled to the next heifer calf of the same cow.

550. If the cow becomes barren before it has borne a female calf, the buyer takes the cow.

### B. *Building material*

551. Material which has been used for house building can only be sold if the occupier has built the house without help of the village community. The occupier can then sell the house for demolition (529, 530).

552. The buyer is not allowed to use the building for any purpose except that of demolition, which must start within a reasonable time.

NOTE. Rules referring to transactions in movable property are of recent date. Formerly only barter existed, the usual commodities being cattle and corn (Note to 331). Sukuma cattle traders (*bagaragara* or *batundanya*) exchange their stock for corn which they carry on donkeys into areas of scarcity, where they exchange the corn again for cattle at a profit of about 100 per cent. The average price which they obtain for their cattle in areas where there has been a good harvest is:

1 heifer = 12 petrol-tins of corn = 10 *ngele*
1 bull  = 6     ,,     ,,  = 5  ,,
1 goat             = 1  ,,

They resell the corn at the following rates:

6 petrol-tins of corn = 5  *ngele* = 1 heifer
3    ,,     ,,  = 2½  ,,  = 1 bull

Commodities such as building materials and grass were not bought, because houses were built with the help of the community. Clothing was not bought by individuals from traders. Chiefs, who were the sole possessors of the ivory which was the main commodity acceptable to traders, acquired cloth which they gave away as tokens of favour. The original dress of the Sukuma consisted of skins, but cotton cloth was woven locally and made into blankets. This cloth (*kagonho*) was always very expensive. There are still a few craftsmen in KF (Busmao and Nera), BSN (Ntusu), KS (Msalala) who make these blankets. The price of a big blanket is now Shs.40/-.

Another medium for barter was the hoe. The most skilful blacksmiths were the Longo in SM (Note to 165). Hoes were acquired in exchange for salt, goats, or cloth, and were often exported to neighbouring countries; for instance, a regular trade existed with Iramba, where hoes were bartered for cattle and also for rhino horns, which could profitably be exchanged by chiefs for cloth imported by traders. The Longo gave 6 hoes for one goat; in Iramba one could get a cow for 10 hoes. The price of a rhino horn in Iramba was 15 to 20 hoes, an elephant tusk was exchanged for 100 to 200 hoes according to size. The native trade caravans were joined by many people, who followed famous leaders such as Makunya and Mtelegeza whose fame still lives in Sukuma.

# PART IV

# THE LAW OF SUCCESSION

## CHAPTER IX

## INHERITANCE

### INTRODUCTION

THE eldest son of a family, who is the main heir, represents the living link between his generation and the previous ones, i.e. between the living siblings and the long line of ancestors who have become spirits. The *nkuruwabo* is heir to the family paraphernalia used in the rites of the ancestor cult (*ku-gabila*); in some areas the birth of the first son is the occasion for rites in which the father's procreative power is transferred to his first-born son. Therefore, the inheritance laws take cognizance of the special position of the *nkuruwabo*. In primitive Sukuma Customary Law he could not be disinherited or deprived of his position because such action would have severed the connexion between the family and the spirits of its ancestors.

Consideration of the Sukuma social structure shows that the position of the eldest son and heir requires moral qualities not commonly met with, and that he readily acknowledges his obligations although this may demand material sacrifices. The position is characterized by a well-balanced equilibrium of rights and duties. For instance, there are very few rules regulating the obligations between father and children, while those concerned with relations between the eldest brother and his younger siblings are numerous and frequently applied. Awe and fear—traditionally important factors in the relationship between father and sons—depend fundamentally on the characters of the persons concerned, but tradition is so strong that they are displayed even if they are not felt. The roots from which spring affection and trust between siblings are apparently not rational. Family life itself does not emphasize brotherly or sisterly love and sentiments between siblings are not the subject of teaching. Experience may have taught the members of an unsophisticated society that for safety and security the bond between siblings is more important than that between parents and children, the main function of which is to protect the baby and the young child against the various dangers of nature until it is strong enough to fend for itself. From the time when he becomes an adult until death, a man needs protection against society itself; only a strong bond uniting close kinsmen can guarantee security for the individual.

553. When a man dies, a member of the household or a neighbour at once goes to inform the nearest relatives of the deceased, whose duty it is to come to the house. A few hours after death the body is buried.

The existence of a grave in a field, cattle-kraal or any other place conveys no special right to the land.

NOTE. Owners of cattle are buried in the middle of the cattle-kraal; other persons are buried in the *njingo*. The grave is marked with a stone. From time to time a son may perform rites of ancestor worship on the spot, even after the cattle-kraal has been moved. If the son emigrates to another district, he may take with him the stone which then becomes a part of the paraphernalia used in the rites of the ancestor cult.

The grave of a *ng'wanangwa*, if he is the descendant of an old family, is also dug in the cattle-kraal; it is well kept and the name of the dead man is not forgotten. The domicile of an old family is not so readily or so frequently changed as that of a commoner. Where misfortune falls on the whole village, such a grave may be the site of sacrifices performed in the public interest.

Graves of chiefs are known and visited at least once a year in connexion with rites intended to ensure a good harvest.

554. The mourning lasts three to five days according to the importance of ·the deceased and is prolonged if some of the kinsmen have to be awaited. On the last day of mourning the *isabingula* (ritual cleansing) is performed.

NOTE. The following are examples of rites which have always varied in different areas. Nowadays they are not always performed even where they used to be customary.

1. All those taking part in a funeral are supposed to be ritually unclean until water, in which the leaves of the *irumba* plant (*Ocimum* sp.) have been soaked, has been sprinkled over them, and they have been shaved. Sometimes the mourners wash hands and face in this water. This procedure is called *isabingula*.
2. If a man dies in a strange village he is buried by the inhabitants, but the village is considered to be ritually unclean. The morning after the burial a root of the *mtandazi* plant (*Dolichos* sp.) is dug up and a piece of it is thrown on the ground before every door in the village.
3. If a wife dies the husband has to undergo a ritual cleansing and is led to a cross-roads where his hair is shaved (Note to 95).
4. A man with two wives, one of whom has died, is not allowed to have intercourse with the second wife until he has given a bull to her brothers. This beast is called *ng'ombe ya ntwe*. Cleansing ceremonies similar to those described in para. 132 have to be performed.
5. If a husband dies the widow is shaved and her brothers have to provide a goat which is killed; some of its *kipu* is smeared on the widow's head and some is used as described in para. 132.

555. The *ntale wa ndugu* is responsible for the correct observance of the mourning procedure. His functions are purely procedural and of no legal significance.

NOTE. For instance, he has to order that a beast shall be slaughtered and it is his task to organize the cooking for the relatives arriving for the mourning. If any invitation has been overlooked, it is for him to repair the omission. Questions with regard to property are not settled by him.

The *ntale wa ndugu* not only performs functions in connexion with death and mourning; he is also the permanent chairman of the family council. This is the managing board of the family and consists of a group of near relatives attending a family meeting. Though this inner circle can meet by itself and its decision would hardly be disputed by the rest of the family, it is usual to call a general family meeting. Every member of the family is allowed to attend a family council and has a right to speak in it; but if he is a stupid man, no one will listen to his words and, after a few such experiences, he will leave the talking to those relatives who have proved themselves,clever councillors. The prominent members of a family are easily recognizable by the fact that the others wait for them and do not start any discussion until they have arrived.

Members of the inner circle are not chosen, they just belong to it. Similarly the *ntale wa ndugu*, sometimes called also *munamugi*, is not chosen but is simply acknowledged as leader.

The participants in a family council meeting are not always the same. For instance, if a widow wishes to complain against the guardian of her children (326), only the relatives immediately concerned would come together and discuss the issue. A very wide circle of relatives would come together if a relative died leaving no next-of-kin as heir; the council would then have to find an heir among the more distant relatives.

556. The only definite decision made immediately after the *isabingula* and before the mourners depart concerns the future of the widows and the guardianship of minors. If necessary, a discussion also takes place about the assets and liabilities of minors.

NOTE. The winding up of an estate does not entail the making of an inventory or the appointment of an administrator or executor, offices which are unknown.

## THE HEIRS (*Bali*)

557. Inheritance is patrilineal.

NOTE. A few cases are known in which a sister's son inherited property when a man died leaving no other male relatives. Should a distant paternal relative of the deceased appear later, he would have the right to claim the inheritance. Such cases should not happen in future in view of the newly introduced rule that daughters may inherit, which extends the circle of rightful heirs.

558. Three grades of heirs are recognized:

A. *Nkuruwabo*, main heir.
B. *Nzuna kwandya*, second heir.
C. *Nzuna kabili, kadatu*, &c., minor heirs.

### A. *Nkuruwabo*

559. 1. If there are sons the main heir is:

I. *in a monogamous household*:
the eldest son.

II. *in a polygynous household*: the eldest son of the first wife (*nkima ntale*) irrespective of his age;

the eldest son of the second wife, if the first wife has no sons; if the first wife gives birth to a son after the death of her husband, this son is recognized as the *nkuruwabo* of the deceased father.

2. If there are daughters but no sons the first heir is:

I. *in a monogamous household*: the eldest daughter;

II. *in a polygynous household*: the eldest daughter of the first wife irrespective of her age; the eldest daughter of the second wife if the first wife has no children.

NOTE. Rule 559. 2. was decided upon by the chiefs of the Sukuma Federation and their people in 1949. Formerly the right of inheritance by women was acknowledged in BD, KF, BS, SS, SBS, KS. Women had no right of inheritance in NF, UF, BSN, KM, ZM, SM.

NOTE. Sukuma customary law, as it was applied before the advent of Europeans, did not recognize the right of women to inherit property. Subsequently, for unknown reasons, this right was recognized by the courts of several chiefdoms, first in special cases and later generally. It is said that Nung'hu and Ng'wagala applied it earlier than other chiefdoms. During the last few years, in all chiefdoms, including those which had never accepted a reform of the inheritance law regarding women, daughters have been given a few beasts voluntarily by the heirs; single cases are also known in which a court gave to daughters a share of the father's property. (Zinza Appeal case 42/44.) It may be said that family councils and even courts showed a tendency to award shares of the estate to daughters, even in those areas where they could not inherit by a generally acknowledged rule.

3. If there are no children, or if the children are minors, the first heir is the father of the deceased.

NOTE. It lies in the discretion of the father whether he takes over the inheritance or leaves it to the brothers of his deceased son. Widows are always left to the brothers of the deceased (levirate).

4. If there are neither children nor father the first heir is:

I. *in a monogamous household*: the eldest full brother;

II. *in a polygynous household*: the eldest full brother or, if there are no full brothers, the eldest half-brother.

NOTE. In a polygynous household the estate of one house is distributed between the full brothers to the exclusion of half-brothers, even if one of the half-brothers is the *nkuruwabo* of the whole family. Often in such a case the half-brother receives a token gift from the heirs.

5. If there are no near male relatives the first heir is the eldest sister.

D.C.'s Appeal No. 4/48. Ibadakuli. *Guga v. Bt. Mwandu*.

Bt. Mwandu's brother died and she was appointed his heir. Guga was the maternal uncle of the deceased and claimed the inheritance because he had paid bridewealth for Mwandu. The sister's right of inheritance was confirmed by the court.

6. If there are no close kinsmen the first heir is the eldest paternal uncle.

7. If there are no near relatives the first heir is the next paternal relative, however distant.

NOTE. The more distant the relationship between the deceased and the relative who may inherit the property, the more important becomes the function of the family council in appointing the heir. The number of heirs having equal rights increases in direct proportion to the remoteness of relationship. In choosing an heir among distant relatives of the same degree the family council will take into account the character and ability of the claimant as well as the nature of his personal contact with the deceased.

In every generation the descendants of senior brothers have the first right to inherit, but if it is necessary to go back a few generations it obviously becomes difficult to decide who is the rightful heir. Data referring to previous generations become unreliable in course of time. Thus the human element is taken into consideration. All those relatives who remain in contact with each other consider themselves the 'family'. The connexion is chiefly maintained at such important family events as births, deaths, marriage, payment of *njigu*, and rites of the ancestor cult. This explains the importance which an African attaches to his presence in the family circle on such occasions. It is not always sentiment or love of adventure which induces him to undertake long journeys; it is the knowledge that contact with his family gives him rights and also entails duties.

8. If there are no relatives the first heir is the Native Treasury.

## B. *Nzuna kwandya*

560. 1. If there are sons the second heir is:

I. *in a monogamous household*: the second son;

II. *in a polygynous household*: the second son of the first wife; if the first wife has only one son, the first son of the second wife.

NOTE. The order of seniority of heirs is: firstly all sons of the first wife; secondly all sons of the second wife.

2. If there are daughters but only one son the second heir is:

I. *in a monogamous household*: the eldest daughter;

NOTE. Neither in a monogamous nor in a polygynous household can the eldest daughter receive a larger share of the inheritance than her youngest full or half-brother.

II. *in a polygynous household*: the eldest daughter of the first wife; or the eldest daughter of the second wife, if the first wife has no daughter.

3. If there are no children the second heir is:

I. *in a monogamous household*: the younger brother;

II. *in a polygynous household*: the younger full brother or the eldest half-brother if there is no full brother.

4. If there are no close kinsmen the second heir is the younger paternal uncle.

### C. *Nzuna kabili, kadatu, &c.*

561. With regard to the rights of minor heirs to a share in the estate the foregoing rules are similarly applied.

NOTE. In a case where the father or a remote relative is the heir, no minor heirs are recognized and the property is not divided.

## *Special rules determining the sequence of heirs*

### I. *Monogamous household*

562. If a son, who himself has children, dies before his father, these children do not receive that share of their grandfather's estate which would have been their father's. They receive shares as minor heirs after all their paternal uncles and aunts.

563. These children have to accept the position of minor heirs whether they are minors or adults when their grandfather dies.

564. The eldest son of the original heir, when he grows up, retains the title and exercises the privileges of his position in relation to his paternal cousins.

NOTE. The *nkuruwabo* would call his paternal uncles 'father', but their sons would call him 'father'.

565. The right of inheritance appertains to one collateral group of relatives. The estate is never distributed among family members of different degrees of relationship.

NOTE. For instance, if a man has no sons and only one brother, the brother becomes his sole heir and none of the paternal uncles has a right to a share.

### II. *Polygynous household*

566. The status of *nkuruwabo* remains with the members of the house of the first wife so long as there is a younger brother alive who can take over. If there are no younger brothers the status of *nkuruwabo* is assumed by the eldest son of the second wife.

### HEIRS OF WOMEN

### 567 A. *Unmarried girls and wives without children*

The heir is the father; failing him, full brothers and sisters; failing them, half-brothers and half-sisters;

     ,,     ,,     a paternal uncle;
     ,,   him, the nearest paternal relative.

### B. *Wives with children*

The heirs of property acquired by the wife are the children in sequence according to age and their shares are in descending scale of value. Inherited property passes to relatives as in 567A. The husband is excluded from the inheritance of his wife's property in all circumstances.

## HEIRS OF CHIEFS

568. Chiefs own two kinds of property:

A. Private property (*sabo ya ntemi*).

This comprises all objects which a chief has bought with his own money as well as presents which he has received as chief. In this category are included his cattle, his houses other than official residences (*ikuru*), and his personal belongings.

B. Property which chiefs own *ex officio* (*sabo ya butemi*).

This comprises the royal insignia and the traditional cult objects of the chiefdom; the special cattle, identified by the bells they wear, and their offspring; the residence and the lands appertaining to it (416–20).

569. The son who succeeds to the chiefdom becomes the *nkuruwabo* of the family; as *nkuruwabo* he inherits a larger share of the father's estate than his brothers. He exercises the rights and duties attaching to this position in accordance with the customary law. It rests with him to distribute the estate of his father with the assistance of older members of the family.

570. The private property of a deceased chief is distributed between his children in accordance with the rules of inheritance (Note to 578).

571. There are no special rules with regard to succession, which nowadays is generally patrilineal.

If the successor to a chief is not his son, the sons of the successor, and not the sons of the former chief, are in the first line of succession to their father, but neither branch of the family can claim a legal right to succession.

NOTE. The chiefs of the Sukuma Federation agreed upon these rules in 1949 (though in fact rules 568 to 571 have always been followed).

### HEIRS OF VILLAGE HEADMEN

572. The property of village headmen is their private property except for fields which they have allotted to themselves during their term of office or which have accrued to them by virtue of their office (430). If a deposed village headman, or the heir of a village headman who is not taking over the office of his father, wishes to keep such land, he must ask the authority which administers the land for the reallocation of it.

NOTE. The situation with regard to village headmen varies greatly in the different chiefdoms and is at the moment in a state of flux. Originally the position of headman (*ng'wanangwa*) was inheritable by one of his sons. If all the sons were still minors a brother of the deceased took over. When the latter died, the office was not inherited by one of his sons, but by a direct descendant of the original *ng'wanangwa*.

Usually when the father became old, he chose one of his sons as helper and this son became *ng'wanangwa* when the old man died. If this was not done the family of the deceased *ng'wanangwa* chose his successor. Commoners had no right to choose the *ng'wanangwa*. Daughters could inherit the office, if no sons were available. The new *ng'wanangwa* had to be confirmed by the chief. In course of time a custom has been established in many areas whereby the chief appoints the village headman.

## DIVISION OF PROPERTY

### LIVESTOCK

### A. *In a monogamous household*

1. *If the heirs are minors*

573. The cattle are not distributed.

NOTE. For the sake of clarity and continuity the following chapter duplicates paragraphs already contained in previous chapters, mainly that concerned with guardianship.

574. If the mother remains in the house of her deceased husband the cattle are left with her. If she moves into the house of her leviratic husband and the co-guardian of her children, she takes the cattle with her (318).

2. *If the heirs are adults*

575. The livestock is distributed among the heirs in unequal shares according to their positions in the sequence of heirs.

NOTE. A herd is considered small if it consists of less than ten beasts. If such a herd has to be divided between several sons, the youngest son would receive not more than one or two beasts. If the small herd remains together, it is probable that after a few years each son will receive a number of cattle sufficient to become the parent stock of a future herd. Very often, therefore, adult heirs do not distribute the estate, but leave the herd in the father's homestead. If the mother is still alive she remains in the house and looks after the cattle in the interest of all the heirs.

576. The herd is given into the trusteeship of the *nkuruwabo*. If a younger brother has taken over the father's holding (Note to 400A) the cattle in the house come under his care, but the *nkuruwabo* retains the right of disposal (352A).

577. When the cattle are distributed, not only is the number of beasts in each share fixed, but the individual beasts are specified. There is no exact rule about the proportion which each share bears to the total number of cattle left by the deceased.

578. The principle of distribution is that the shares, beginning with that of the *nkuruwabo* and ending with that of the youngest son or daughter, are graduated in a descending scale.

Note. Examples of distribution:

If there are three heirs and the estate consists of

|  |  | 30 cattle | 20 cattle |
|---|---|---|---|
| the *nkuruwabo* | receives | 12 beasts | 9 beasts |
| „ *nzuna* I | „ | 10 „ | 6 „ |
| „ *nzuna* II | „ | 8 „ | 5 „ |

If there are four heirs and the estate consists of

|  |  | 30 cattle | 20 cattle |
|---|---|---|---|
| the *nkuruwabo* | receives | 10 beasts | 8 beasts |
| „ *nzuna* I | „ | 9 „ | 6 „ |
| „ *nzuna* II | „ | 7 „ | 4 „ |
| „ *nzuna* III | „ | 4 „ | 2 „ |

These empiric figures show that the difference between the shares received by the heirs is small and that the smaller the estate the larger proportionately is the share of the *nkuruwabo*.

579. If one of the heirs thinks that he has not received the share due to him, he can file a suit in court. He must accuse his coheirs, not the elders of the family and the *nkuruwabo* who divided the estate.

Note. This rule was decided upon by the chiefs of the Sukuma Federation and their people in 1949. Formerly, in NF, UF, KM, ZM, KF, BSN, BD, the courts refused to hear such cases and referred the complainant to the family council. In BS, SS, SBS, KS the courts agreed to deal with such cases.

Note. Before an heir files a suit he should bring his complaint before a family council, the members of which will probably be called as witnesses by the court.

### B. *In a polygynous household*

#### 1. *If the heirs are minors*

580. The cattle are usually distributed among the houses immediately after the death of the father.

581. The principle of distribution is that the shares, beginning with that of the house of the first wife (*nkima ntale*) and ending with that of the last wife, are in a descending scale.

582. The distribution of the estate is performed by the family council under the chairmanship of the *ntale wa ndugu*. There is no rule determining the size of the share of a certain house in proportion to the whole estate. The council takes many relevant points into consideration, for instance, the number of children in each house.

#### 2. *If the heirs are adults*

583 A. It lies in the discretion of the heirs to leave the herd together or to distribute it.

B. If the half-brothers decide that the estate of the deceased should be distributed, the individual shares of each heir are in a descending scale, beginning with the share of the *nkuruwabo* and ending with the share of the youngest son or daughter.

NOTE. Example of distribution:

A man leaves two wives, each with two children, and the estate amounts to fifteen head of cattle:

The *nkuruwabo* receives 6 beasts
  „ *nzuna* I   „ 4 „
  „ *nzuna* II   „ 3 „
  „ *nzuna* III   „ 2 „

## 3. *Ng'ombe ya kuyinza*

584. The cattle acquired by any one house of the polygynous household are called *ng'ombe ya kuyinza*. The usual way of acquiring these cattle is by bartering for cattle corn which has been grown by one of the wives on her fields. As long as the husband is alive, he is the owner of the *ng'ombe ya kuyinza* and can dispose of his property as he likes. It is not customary for the husband to use a beast from one house to help another house without first asking the wife of the house, but the wife has no right to forbid her husband to do what he thinks best.

NOTE. Cattle belonging to the common estate, which the husband may have given into the care of particular houses, must after his death be distinguished from *ng'ombe ya kuyinza*.

585. After the father's death the *ng'ombe ya kuyinza* are considered part of the common estate and are distributed among all the children in the customary way.

NOTE. This rule was decided upon by the chiefs of the Sukuma Federation and their people in 1949. Formerly this rule was followed in SS, KS. In SBS, NF, UF, KM, KF, BSN, BD, BS the *ng'ombe ya kuyinza* became the property of the house which had acquired them and were inherited by the children of that house.

NOTE. The chiefs and their people had first agreed to accept the rule of the majority (north) but decided finally to accept the rules of SS and KS (south). Arguments for and against were proffered by the protagonists of both opinions. The main argument of the south was that a wife, after ten years of married life, during which she had given birth to several children, would normally have less *ng'ombe ya kuyinza* than a wife with only one child who was considerably less impeded in field-work. But at the distribution of property after the father's death, the many children will have between them a small number of cattle as far as *ng'ombe ya kuyinza* are concerned, while the single child of the other house will have all the cattle belonging to that house for itself. Thus the *nkuruwabo* of the whole family, being one of many children of the *nkima ntale*, might inherit less cattle than a minor heir of another house of his father. Such a situation would not be in accordance with Sukuma ideas of inheritance. The argument of the north was that the rule accepted in the south would make the wives of a polygynous household lazy in field-work, to which the south answered that this did not happen in practice with their womenfolk and that husbands in the south are equally interested in big harvests as elsewhere. The rule of the south, which was finally accepted, tallies with rule 586.

586. The cattle of bridewealth which a father received for his daughters are counted as common property of the father and are distributed after his death among the sons of all houses.

NOTE. This rule was decided upon by the chiefs of the Sukuma Federation and their people in 1949. Formerly this rule was followed in BS, SBS, BD, SS, KS. In NF, UF, KF, BSN the bridewealth received for a sister was not counted as common family property and was inherited by her full brother.

## MONEY AND PARAPHERNALIA

587. Money left by the father is distributed between his children in a descending scale from the *nkuruwabo* to the youngest son or daughter.

NOTE. It was formerly the custom to give larger shares to daughters than to sons in all chiefdoms where daughters were excluded from inheritance.

588. If the children are minors the mother is given the money and with the help of the co-guardian will usually buy stock with it.

589. Money (like *ng'ombe ya kuyinza*) earned by one house in a polygynous household becomes the common property of the estate and is inherited by all the children.

NOTE. Rules regarding the inheritance of money are considered unimportant. It is explained that in most cases the money left by the deceased is spent on the entertainment of the mourners.

590. The paraphernalia of the ancestor cult are inherited by the *nkuruwabo*.

## LAND

For division of land in connexion with inheritance see paras. 400 et seq.

## PATRILINEAL AND MATRILINEAL SUCCESSION

### A. *In a monogamous household*

#### 1. *Property inherited by the parents*

591. The children of a *numba ya buta* (38) can inherit only property accruing to their father from his paternal relatives. The children of a *numba ya bugongo* can inherit only property derived from their father's maternal relatives; the property inherited by the father from his paternal relatives is taken by his brothers.

592. It is the custom everywhere to give to the children who have lost the right of inheritance a share of the estate as a present; usually it is not very big. Only in BS is this present obligatory.

NOTE. The sons of the second wife in a polygynous household, i.e. the minor heirs, might inherit many cattle while the *nkuruwabo* himself and the other sons of the first wife inherited none. This would be the case when the *nkima ntale* had been married with property received from a maternal uncle of the husband and when the husband left only property which he had inherited from his paternal family, i.e. *buta* property. The *bugongo* children of the *nkima ntale*, i.e. the *nkuruwabo* and his brothers, could not inherit this *buta* property, but the children of the second wife could inherit it, if their mother had been married with property derived from the paternal relatives of the husband.

593. Children of a *numba ya buta* may inherit property of their father's maternal relatives if they have first paid back to the paternal relatives the amount of the bridewealth paid for their mother. In this way the house becomes a *numba ya bugongo*.

594. Children of a *numba ya bugongo*, if they wish to inherit property of their father, must first pay back to their father's maternal relatives the bridewealth paid for their mother. The maternal relatives cannot refuse to accept the payment.

NOTE. The rules contained in paras. 593 and 594 were decided upon by the chiefs of the Sukuma Federation and their people in 1949. Formerly no rules existed.

NOTE. Undoubtedly the exclusion of legitimate children from the inheritance of their father's property which they had helped to herd and with which they grew up through all the years at home is nowadays felt by the people themselves to be an injustice. This explains the introduction of the provisions of 593–4. The existence of equity in this case and the readiness to introduce laws which take full account of it show clearly how the rigorous conception of 'family' is giving way, under external cultural influences, to considerations of the importance of property in human society—a notion which is rapidly developing in Africa.

The practicability of these new rules will have to be proved by experience. Changes effected in the membership of a family by the payment of bridewealth are not rare (246, 269, 628).

## 2. *Property acquired by the parents*

595. Property acquired by father or mother is inherited by their children without regard to the origin of the bridewealth paid for their mother.

NOTE. This rule was decided upon by the chiefs of the Sukuma Federation and their people in 1949. Formerly this rule was followed in BS, SBS, KS, SS. In UF, NF, BD, KF property acquired by the father became paternal property and that acquired by the mother maternal property exclusively.

Some areas differentiated between property acquired within a short time, such as the spoils of war and hunting (ivory), which was considered property of *buta*; and property acquired by labour over many years (fees of practitioners, transactions in cattle trade) which were considered property that could be inherited by the children without regard to the origin of the bridewealth paid for the mother of the heirs.

### B. *In a polygynous household*

596. Children can only inherit property corresponding to the origin of their house, i.e. children of a *nkima wa bugongo* cannot inherit any share of the property which the father inherited from his family, and vice versa.

597. Property acquired by the parents is inherited by all children.

598. Property acquired by the wife of a house follows the category of the house.

NOTE. If the father dies the *ng'ombe ya kuyinza* of a *numba ya bugongo* are inherited by the children of that house. In this case the provisions of 585 are not valid because in no circumstances can the *buta* and *bugongo* rules be superseded.

599. The husband is fully entitled to use the property of all houses, acquired by the wives of these houses, without regard to the origin of the bridewealth paid for the wives.

## INHERITANCE OF WIDOWS (Levirate)

600. A widow (*nchilwa*) must choose the man who is to inherit her from among the brothers of her deceased husband if there are any; if there are none, from among the nearest kinsmen. These and the family council may sometimes agree to a widow choosing another of the deceased's relatives, but they will never agree to her choosing an outsider.

NOTE. After the *isabingula* the *ntale wa ndugu* sends one or two of the relatives to the widow of the deceased to ask her if she has decided to be inherited and, if so, by whom; if she refuses to be inherited and wishes to go home; or if she wishes to stay with her children on the estate of her deceased husband without being inherited.

It is still the usual practice for widows with or without children to remain with the family of the deceased husband and to agree to be inherited by one of the near relatives.

After a widow has decided to be inherited, at least a month must elapse before she becomes united to the man of her choice. Usually the time is much longer, sometimes as much as a year.

In the chiefdoms of BSN the eligible relatives who wish to inherit the widow compete for her favours. They bring presents, help in field-work and, in short, try to appear in a good light. Finally the widow chooses her husband from one of these relatives.

601 A. A widow can choose to be inherited by her stepson.

B. If a widow does not get on with the relative she has chosen as husband, she can break with him and refer the matter to a family council (321). She can then either choose another relative of the same collateral group without the performance of any special ceremony, or she can declare that she wishes to stay with her children within the family of her deceased husband but to give up all intimate relations with any of his near kin (610).

NOTE. Such cases have up to the present been decided only before a family council and never in court. A Sukuma saying is: '*Nchilwa ni nkima wa matongo ati wa munhu umo*—The widow is the woman of a deserted plot, she is not for one man only.'

602 A. The position of a widow is determined by whether she has given birth to children or not.

B. Account is taken of children who have died, without regard to the age at which they died; even still-births, abortions, and miscarriages may be counted if evidence of the existence of a foetus is forthcoming.

NOTE. Possibilities of proving the existence of a foetus are shown in the following case:

D.C.'s Appeal 27/48. Fulo. *Kabesa* v. *Milembe*.

Kabesa filed a suit against his father-in-law Milembe because the latter had deducted two cattle for a child when bridewealth had to be returned. Kabesa first denied the birth of the child, but it was proved that he had gone to Milembe's house where an abortion occurred and had buried the foetus and further that he had shaved his head after the burial. As Kabesa could not persist in his denial, the court held that Milembe was right in deducting cattle for the child.

## A. *Childless widow*

603. A childless widow is inherited by one of the heirs but only by mutual consent. If she refuses to be inherited, she is allowed to return to her family (85A).

604. If the relatives of the deceased husband refuse to inherit the widow or neglect to provide for her (556), she must leave her husband's family and can return to her own family (85B) or go elsewhere.

Case quoted in 194 refers.

605. The option exercised by relatives of returning a widow to her family is not affected by the length of time she was married to the deceased.

606. If a man leaves two childless widows they can both choose the same heir. If the chosen heir is the younger brother of the deceased, the elder brother cannot object.

607. If a widow living within the husband's family gives birth to a child after the death of her husband, the child is taken to be that of the deceased whether or not there is a possibility of another man being the father.

NOTE. A posthumous child is entitled to a share of the deceased's estate. This rule has no significance if the leviratic husband is a near relative (335).

608. A widow who was a *nkima wa bugongo* must choose her leviratic husband from among the maternal relatives of her deceased husband, such as the sons of the maternal uncle who paid the bridewealth; otherwise the rules are the same as those referring to a *nkima wa buta* (603–7).

## B. *Widow with children*

609. Such a widow can either agree or refuse to be inherited. In the latter case she can choose to remain with her children living within her deceased husband's family (318).

NOTE. Widows with daughters now (since the acceptance of rule 559. 2) hold the same position as widows with sons; formerly they came under the category of childless widows.

610. If she remains with her husband's family, she is not free to choose lovers. If she has lovers the family has the right to object and,

if the widow does not obey, the family council can return her to her family while the children remain with the paternal family (194).

NOTE. It is not easy for a widow with children to live in peace with her deceased husband's family if she refuses to be inherited. She is not allowed (although the law is not always strictly enforced) to have intimate relations with other men on pain of being returned to her paternal family, which means repayment of a part of the bridewealth and relinquishing the children. This control by the deceased husband's family is justified in the Sukuma mind by the conception that a marriage is contracted by two families, rather than two persons. The institution of the levirate is in itself a proof of this; other provisions in the customary law proving the existence of this conception are found in 285, 336, 608.

## C. *Status of inherited widow*

611. A widow who has agreed to be inherited retains the status of a legal wife (132).

NOTE. For instance, the leviratic husband is entitled to claim compensation in case of adultery.

## D. *Maintenance of widow*

612. The maintenance of a widow who refuses to be inherited, or who has been refused by the deceased husband's relatives, falls on her paternal family, and in the first instance on those members of it who received her bridewealth.

NOTE. Most widows, even when past an attractive age, are inherited willingly because a woman, as long as she is fairly healthy, is not a liability but a highly valued asset to any family in which she lives. She produces more food than she eats and the proceeds of the surplus harvest are more than she needs for the purchase of clothing. The motive for returning a widow to her family is nearly always the fear that she may be a witch. An old woman, for no other reasons than her age and appearance and disposition, is often suspected of possessing a knowledge of black magic, and therefore everyone is afraid to take her into the house. Even if the old woman lives with one of her children, she does not occupy an honoured place in the house. She is never badly treated but she herself knows her place and, as they say, she will never eat fat pieces of meat but will gnaw the bones. It may be imagined that the maintenance of such an old woman becomes a problem if everyone, including her own relatives, is afraid to live with her.

613. If the widow's home is very far away and she refuses to be returned to her family, the court may consider ways to safeguard her maintenance.

## CLAIMS AND DEBTS OF THE ESTATE

### A. *General rules*

614. After the *isabingula*, the heirs discuss claims outstanding for assets due to the estate and debts for which the estate is liable.

615. If the heirs are minors, the guardian, with the help of the near relatives, is responsible for the settlement.

NOTE. For most business transactions a man calls his wife and children as witnesses. Therefore, the widow and children, even if they are still minors, are consulted about the liabilities and assets of the deceased. Very often a man also calls a neighbour as witness to business transactions.

616. There is no time limit for the presentation of claims by creditors. Both claims and debts are inherited.

617. After the relatives gathered for the mourning have returned home, claims on the estate by creditors must be presented to the *nkuruwabo* of the deceased.

### B. *Collection of assets outstanding*

618. Only the *nkuruwabo* or, if he is a minor, his guardian has the right to demand payment from a debtor. He acts as the representative of all the heirs.

619. When payments are made by a debtor after the property of the deceased has been distributed among the heirs the *nkuruwabo* must distribute these payments as they are received between the coheirs in the appropriate proportions.

### C. *Payment of debts*

620. The *nkuruwabo* (or his guardian) is responsible for the payment of the father's debts. If they are claimed before distribution of the property, they are paid from the estate. After the distribution of the estate the creditor can deal only with the *nkuruwabo*, and can sue him for payment of debts.

621. It is the duty of all heirs to help the *nkuruwabo* in the payment of the deceased's debts, even with their own property if the father died without leaving any property (78).

NOTE. This rule was agreed by the chiefs of the Sukuma Federation and their people in 1949. Formerly a strict custom but no rule existed.

NOTE. No case is remembered in which the coheirs refused to help the *nkuruwabo* pay the debts of their father, even if the father had left nothing but debts. But the chiefs and their people were afraid that the authority of the family council, which has been sufficient until now to enforce this custom, might diminish in future. Therefore they considered it necessary to introduce a rule.

622. Relatives other than children of the deceased are not responsible for the payment of debts unless they have inherited property of the deceased.

NOTE. For instance, a man cannot be sued by a creditor for a debt incurred by his deceased brother if he inherited no property from the deceased.

623. Before other debts are paid from the estate, wages due must be paid to labourers and artisans.

NOTE. This rule was decided upon by the chiefs of the Sukuma Federation and their people in 1949. Formerly no rule existed.

## WILL

### A. *Oral*

624. The institution of making verbal wills is an old one although not often practised. If a man wishes to make a verbal will, he must call at least six relatives as witnesses. If there are no relatives available, elders of the village are admissible as witnesses.

625. A man cannot transgress the rules of customary law by his will (exception 626) and he cannot appoint an heir outside the circle of those who are entitled to inherit.

NOTE. If a man in making his will does not follow the rules of customary law, it is not the duty of the witnesses to contradict him. But provisions of the testament which are contrary to the rules of customary law are not executed after the testator's death. For instance, if a testator stipulates that his brothers and heirs shall not claim return of bridewealth if the widow refuses to be inherited, the heirs could nevertheless claim it after his death.

Although everyone knows that the rules of customary law cannot be altered by a man's last will, many men express wishes regarding the disposal of their property. They use the institution of the will to express their displeasure with an heir. Thus, for instance, a father may disinherit a son even though he knows that after his death the estate will be distributed among all his sons. The father simply makes the solemn declaration of disinheritance in order to effect an improvement in the relations between father and son. The most common reasons are adultery of a son with his stepmother, lavishness of a son at his father's expense, repeated theft in the house of the parents, refusal of a daughter to marry and to give up her various love affairs. The formulae used are of the following kind (said by the father before witnesses):

'Since you have always been only a loss to me, today I will pay for you, but remember it is for the last time. Do not come into my house again until I die. When I die I want other people to bury me.'

. . . . .

'I have borne you, I tell you, but I hope you will wander without rest. If you marry may your wife be barren. I have had a child whom now I have no more.'

. . . . .

'My fathers, look down upon your grandchild who insulted me! I pray that he shall have no home, that he shall remain without peace and shall suffer, comfortless, until he dies.'

. . . . .

No son will disregard a ceremonial curse of this kind, which implies disinheritance. He will do his best to appease his father and to persuade him, with the help of relatives and elders, to revoke his words.

626. The testator has the right to change the sequence of heirs.

NOTE. This rule was decided upon by the chiefs of the Sukuma Federation and their people in 1949. Formerly various rules existed.

NOTE. Great importance is attached to the introduction of this rule, in the hope that it will restore their lost authority to fathers. Formerly sons were afraid to fall out with their fathers because they depended exclusively on them for payment of bridewealth as there were few ways in which a young man could obtain for himself the necessary amount of cattle. It is now not so difficult for a young man to acquire property, and therefore young people feel independent and have lost respect for the older generation. It is hoped that the fear of losing position within the family and some of the property in case of inheritance will have a wholesome effect. The provision of 626 represents also a compromise between north and south when read in connexion with 627.

627. A man cannot completely disinherit by will a person entitled to inherit.

NOTE. This rule was decided upon by the chiefs of the Sukuma Federation and their people in 1949. Formerly a testator could disinherit an heir in SS, KS, BS, SBS.

628. A father can disinherit a son by the procedure of *kujimula*. In this case the father returns his son to his wife's family and receives five head of cattle, thus giving his son the status of an illegitimate child.

NOTE. The procedure of *kujimula* is necessary for disinheritance; the fact that a son has left his father's house after a quarrel and is living with the maternal family is not considered in itself a proof of disinheritance.

Ibadakuli (Tinde) Appeal No. 15/45. *Guga v. Bt. Mwandu.*

Guga claimed from Bt. Mwandu the property of her brother which she had inherited. He stated that the deceased, who was his maternal nephew, had been expelled by his father and had lived in Guga's family for many years. Guga had even paid *misango* for him. The court held that Guga could not claim inheritance on these grounds, as it was not proved that the deceased had been disinherited by his father.

629. The maternal family of the child cannot refuse to accept him and must return the cattle.

NOTE. The custom of *kujimula* is known in BS, BD, SBS, but is not practised in other chiefdoms.

630. The heirs of a disinherited son are not his natural brothers but his maternal relatives, if he dies childless.

D.C.'s Appeal 1/46. Bukwimba. *Filippo v. Nanayi.*

Filippo was a maternal relative of Kaliyaya, deceased. Kaliyaya had been disowned by his father and went to Filippo who received him well. Kaliyaya looked upon Filippo as a father. When Kaliyaya died, Filippo inherited his property. Then one day Nanayi, a half-brother of Kaliyaya, appeared and claimed the inheritance. The court held that Nanayi had no claim to it, as their father had disowned Kaliyaya. When the father died, Kaliyaya had received no share of the estate because he no longer belonged to his paternal family; therefore, his maternal relative Filippo was his rightful heir.

631. Wishes and legacies of the testator are executed if they are not contrary to custom (493–8).

## B. *In writing*

632. The institution of making a written will is not yet widespread and no rules for the correct procedure have been issued.

## DISTRIBUTION OF ESTATE BY THE FATHER
## DURING HIS LIFETIME

633. If a father distributes the estate during his lifetime, this distribution is valid, even if he does not follow the laws relating to inheritance. His decision cannot be impugned after his death by a disinherited son.

634. An heir who has been disinherited or who thinks that his share is not adequate can file a suit against the coheirs.

NOTE. This right is granted to the heir because he had no opportunity of trying to propitiate the father; but he has little chance of securing a redistribution of the estate if it can be proved that it was the express will of the father to disinherit his son, or to reduce his share.

# APPENDIX I

# THE FEDERAL COUNCIL OF SUKUMALAND[1]

THE administration of the Sukumaland Federation is domiciled at Malya situated on the Tabora–Mwanza railway line. Malya is also the headquarters of the Sukumaland Development organization which aims at the rehabilitation and development of the natural resources of the whole area.

The Sukumaland Federal Council in Malya consists of the forty-six chiefs as well as one *mugunani* (councillor) from each sub-chiefdom. No exact rules were issued as to how these councillors were to be elected. Very soon after the inauguration of the Council it became obvious that it was an unwieldy body for carrying on business, and it was therefore decided to form an Advisory Committee consisting of fourteen chiefs, four of whom retire annually. This committee has to prepare agenda for the meetings of the Federal Council, and to scrutinize in detail all financial matters, estimates, and supplementary expenditure of the Native Treasuries. The Federal Council normally meets twice a year and the Advisory Committee three times, each under a permanent chairman.

The legislative functions of the Federal Council are of great importance and full use is made of them. Legislation on all matters of general importance to the whole of Sukumaland is enacted here.

### The Local Federations and Chiefdoms of the Sukuma Federation

| Local Federations | Groups | Abbreviations | Chiefdoms |
|---|---|---|---|
| MWANZA DISTRICT | | | |
| Mwanza Federation | Nyanza | NF | Mwanza |
| | | | Bujashi |
| | | | Busukuma |
| | | | Bukumbi |
| | | | Burima |
| | | | Bunegeji |
| | Usega | UF | Nassa |
| | | | Masanza I |
| | | | Masanza II |
| GEITA DISTRICT | | | |
| Mweli Federation | Zinza Mweli | ZM | Karumo |
| | | | Buchosa |
| | Sumbwa Mweli | SM | Bukoli |
| | | | Buyombe |
| | | | Busambiro |
| | Kamba Mweli | KM | Msalala |
| | | | Mwingiro |

[1] The following is an extract from a manuscript written by B. J. Dudbridge and J. E. S. Griffiths entitled 'The Development of Local Government in Sukumaland, Tanganyika'.

| *Local Federations* | *Groups* | *Abbreviations* | *Chiefdoms* |
|---|---|---|---|
| KWIMBA DISTRICT | | | |
| Kwimba Federation | | KF | Nera |
| | | | Busmao |
| | | | Buhungukira |
| | | | Magu |
| | | | Sima |
| | | | Ndagalu |
| MASWA DISTRICT | | | |
| Binza Federation | Binza Sukuma (Ntusu) | BSN | Ntusu |
| | | | Itilima |
| | | | Dutwa |
| | | | Kanadi |
| | Binza Dakama | BD | Ng'wagala |
| | | | Sanga Meatu |
| | | | Kimali Meatu |
| | | | Nung'hu |
| | | | Kigoku |
| | | | Badi |
| | | | Sengerema |
| SHINYANGA DISTRICT | | | |
| Shinyanga Federation | Binza Shinyanga | BS | Seke |
| | | | Mondo |
| | | | Mwadui |
| | | | Buchunga |
| | | | Buduhe |
| | Siha Busiha Shin-yanga | SBS | Busiha |
| | Siha Shinyanga | SS | Shinyanga |
| | | | Samuye |
| | | | Tinde |
| | | | Busanda |
| | | | Busule |
| | Kamba Shinyanga | KS | Luhumbo |
| | | | Nindo |
| | | | Msalawe |

## APPENDIX II

The following draft rules under Section 16 of the Native Authority Ordinance were drawn up by the Native Authority of the Sukuma Federation and await approval by the Governor.

## BRIDEWEALTH, MARRIAGE, AND DIVORCE (SUKUMALAND) RULES

In exercise of the powers conferred upon Native Authorities by Section 16 of the Native Authority Ordinance and with the approval of the Governor, the following rules are hereby made:

SUKUMA LAW AND CUSTOM

1. These rules may be cited as the Bridewealth, Marriage, and Divorce (Sukumaland) Rules and shall have effect in the administrative districts of Kwimba, Maswa, Shinyanga, Mwanza, and Geita, and shall come into force on the . . . . . . day of . . . .

2. The amount of bridewealth payable shall be limited to the maximum amounts shown in the schedule hereto.

All courts shall take cognizance of bridewealth only up to the maximum limits. Any payment made in excess of these limits shall be deemed to have been a free and voluntary gift on the part of the husband, and to be irrecoverable at law.

3. Particulars of all customary unions shall be reported to the Native Court in the area in which the bride is domiciled. The following persons shall be required to appear before the Court as witnesses for this purpose:

(a) the husband and the wife;
(b) the father of the wife or his deputy;
(c) one independent witness for each party.

4. All relevant particulars shall be recorded in a register kept by the Court and on certificates which are issued by the Court to the parties.

5. Such particulars shall include full details of the total bridewealth agreed upon by the two parties and shall show all payments made and outstanding in this respect. All further payments made shall be reported to the Court and entered both in the Court register and on the certificates.

6. The fee for registration shall be Shs.2/-.

7. Application for registration, as described in rule 3 above, shall be made within one month following the ceremony legalizing the customary union according to tribal law. Failure to do so will render the responsible party liable to a fine not exceeding Shs.6/-.

8. Particulars of all decrees of divorce shall be entered in a separate register kept by the Court and divorce certificates shall be issued to either party on application.

9. The particulars mentioned in rule 8 above shall include full details of the amount of bridewealth, if any, which is refundable. Any payments made in execution of the decree shall be reported to the Court and entered in the register and on the divorce certificate.

10. The fee for registration of a divorce shall be Shs.4/- payable by the plaintiff in each case.

If the divorce case has been decided by arbitration before village elders, the case must be registered at a Native Court and divorce certificates must be issued.

11. Nothing in these rules shall have effect on or be applicable to marriage contracts made or bridewealth paid prior to the day on which these rules come into force.

SCHEDULE

*Maximum remissible*

For all chiefdoms *except* the Mweli Federation.

1. If the bridewealth is payable in cattle of which
   not less than three shall be bulls   .  .  15

2. If the bridewealth is payable in goats or sheep   *Maximum remissible*
(on the basis that one cow equals ten goats or
sheep and one bull equals five goats or sheep)          135

3. If the bridewealth is payable in cash (on the
basis that one cow equals Shs.40/-, and one
one bull equals Shs.20/-)  .   .   .   .            540/-

For the Mweli Federation *only*.

4. If bridewealth is payable in cash.   .   .      300/-
   in addition one castrated goat   .   .   .         1/-
   in addition cash   .   .   .   .   .               4/-

5. If bridewealth is paid in hoes   .   .   .       300
   in addition one castrated goat   .   .   .         1/-
   in addition cash   .   .   .   .   .               4/-

Provided that:

(*a*) in every case ceremonial beasts or gifts which are paid in connexion
with the conclusion of a customary union and which *can* be claimed
in the event of divorce, shall be included in the limits set out under
items 1 to 5 above.

(*b*) The above limits do not refer to the bridewealth payable or
received by chiefs in respect of their wives or female relatives.

(*c*) The maximum limit of bridewealth to be paid or received by a
*ng'wanangwa*, *munang'oma*, a direct descendant of a chief, a regent,
or a deposed chief shall be increased by one-third in each case shown
under 1–5 above.


# APPENDIX II.

The following rules under Section 16 of the Native Authority Ordinance have recently been approved:

## THE SUKUMALAND FEDERATION LAND
## SETTLEMENT RULES

In accordance with the powers conferred upon Native Authorities by
Section 16 of the Native Authority Ordinance, the following Rules are
made by the Native Authority of the Sukumaland Federation.

1. These Rules shall be called the 'Sukumaland Federation Land
Settlement Rules', and shall only apply to such areas as may be prescribed
by resolution of the Federal Council of the Chiefs of Sukumaland.

2. In these Rules the term 'Subordinate Native Authority' shall mean
any Native Authority designated as subordinate to the Native Authority
of the Sukumaland Federation in the order of establishing the latter.

3. In these Rules the term 'Parish Land Council' shall mean a Council
comprising the Parish Headman and five delegates chosen by the people
of the Parish.

4. In these Rules the term 'Advisory Land Council' shall mean a
Council comprising the District Commissioners of the Districts concerned,

the Subordinate Native Authorities concerned, the Sub-chiefs of the Sub-chiefdoms concerned, the Parish Headmen concerned, two delegates elected by each of the Parish Land Councils concerned, and two other officers to be nominated by the Provincial Commissioner.

5. In these Rules the term 'Land Usage Area' shall mean a Parish or group of Parishes designated by the Advisory Land Council.

6. In these Rules the term 'Land Usage Area Council' shall mean a Council comprising the Subordinate Native Authorities concerned, the Sub-chiefs of the Sub-chiefdoms concerned, the Parish Headmen concerned, and two delegates elected by each Parish Land Council concerned.

7. In these Rules the term 'Stock Unit' shall mean one bovine or donkey, or five small stock, viz. goats and sheep.

8. The Advisory Land Council shall determine the maximum number of residents for each Parish, and having compared it with the actual number shall accordingly place the Parishes in the various classes in Schedule I to these Rules.

9. The Advisory Land Council shall prescribe the maximum number of Stock Units to be kept in any Land Usage Area.

10. The Land Usage Area Council may prescribe areas of reserve grazing in addition to the usual Parish grazing reserve. It may also declare areas open or closed for grazing by stock from other Land Usage Areas.

11. (i) No person shall occupy an existing vacant habitation, or shall erect or occupy a new habitation without first obtaining a permit from the Subordinate Native Authority concerned.

(ii) The applicant shall apply to the Parish Land Council concerned who may, if it is prepared to recommend the application, provide him with an application form in accordance with Schedule II to these Rules.

(iii) The completed application form shall be submitted by the Parish Land Council to the Land Usage Area Council, which shall advise the Subordinate Native Authority whether a permit should be granted or refused.

(iv) If any person is entitled by rules of Customary Law dealing with inheritance or guardianship to enter into an existing habitation, he may apply for and shall be granted a permit to do so.

(v) Any person contravening the provisions of this Rule shall be liable on conviction to a fine not exceeding 200/-, or to imprisonment with or without hard labour for a period not exceeding two months, or to both fine and imprisonment.

12. (i) It shall be an offence for any person to move stock from one Land Usage Area to another without first obtaining a permit in writing to be issued by the Land Usage Area Council of the area into which it is proposed to move the stock.

(ii) The Land Usage Area Council shall not issue a permit for stock to enter its area unless the number of stock in the area is below the maximum prescribed under Rule 9.

(iii) If any person is entitled by the rules of Customary Law dealing with 'Winga', 'Njigu', or 'Misango' to move cattle, an application shall be made to the Land Usage Area Council and a permit shall be issued. Also any person entitled by the rules of Customary Law dealing with

'Kuyinza', may apply for and shall be issued with a permit to move in sufficient cattle to make his herd up to ten head.

(iv) The Land Usage Area Council may issue a permit for permanent entry or for entry for seasonal grazing only.

(v) Any person contravening the provisions of this Rule shall be liable on conviction to a fine not exceeding 500/-, or to imprisonment with or without hard labour for a period not exceeding two months, or to both fine and imprisonment.

## SCHEDULE I

*Class 'A'*

'Open Parishes', namely, Parishes in which the actual human population is substantially less than the number prescribed under Rule 8. Permits to enter these Parishes may be issued until such time as the prescribed maximum density is reached.

*Class 'B'*

'Restricted Parishes', namely, Parishes in which the actual human population approximates to the number prescribed under Rule 8. Per-permits may only be issued to compensate for emigration and death.

*Class 'C'*

'Reserved Parishes', namely, Parishes which are closed to settlement. No permits to enter may be issued, until such time as they may be opened for settlement.

*Class 'D'*

'Closed Parishes', namely, Parishes where the actual human population substantially exceeds the number prescribed by Rule 8. No permits to enter may be issued.

*Class 'E'*

'Bush-Edge Parishes', namely, Parishes which abut on tsetse fly infested bush which are open for settlement subject to the applicant contracting to remain in the Parish for a minimum period of three years. Permits may be issued until such time as the population has reached the number prescribed by these Rules. The form of contract shall be in accordance with Schedule III of these Rules. These contracts shall be terminable by the Court concerned for good cause shown.

## THE SUKUMALAND FEDERATION LIVESTOCK
## RESTRICTION RULES

In accordance with the powers conferred upon Native Authorities by Section 16 of the Native Authority Ordinance the following Rules are made by the Native Authority of the Sukumaland Federation.

1. These Rules shall be called the 'Sukumaland Livestock Restriction Rules'. They shall only apply to such areas as may be prescribed by resolution of the Federal Council of the Chiefs of Sukumaland.

2. In these Rules the term 'Subordinate Native Authority' shall mean

any Native Authority designated as subordinate to the Native Authority of the Sukumaland Federation in the order establishing the latter.

3. In these Rules the term 'Parish Land Council' shall mean the Council set up under Rule 3 of the Sukumaland Federation Land Settlement Rules.

4. In these Rules the term 'Advisory Land Council' shall mean a Council comprising the District Commissioners of the Districts concerned, the Subordinate Native Authorities concerned, the Sub-chiefs of the Sub-chiefdoms concerned, the Parish Headmen concerned, and two other officers to be nominated by the Provincial Commissioner.

5. In these Rules the term 'Land Usage Area' shall mean a Parish or number of Parishes as designated by the Advisory Land Council.

6. In these Rules the term 'Stock Unit' shall mean one bovine of the age of one year and over or donkey, or five small stock, viz. goats and sheep.

7. The Advisory Land Council shall prescribe in each year the maximum number of stock units for each Land Usage Area, and may order that all or part of the livestock surplus to that number in the Land Usage Area shall be sold or removed from the area in a prescribed period. On such an order being given each stock owner shall be required to remove or sell a number of stock units kept by such stock owner inside the Area in the same proportion as the number of stock units ordered to be sold by the Council shall bear to the total number of stock units in the Area. Such an order shall not apply to any person who holds less than ten stock units in the Land Usage Area.

8. Any person who shall fail to move or sell his stock in accordance with any order made under the above Rule shall be guilty of an offence and shall be liable on conviction to a fine not exceeding 500/-, or to imprisonment with or without hard labour for a period not exceeding two months, or to both fine and imprisonment.

9. Any stock keeper who shall refuse to allow the stock in his keeping to be counted in such manner as may be prescribed by the Subordinate Native Authority shall be guilty of an offence and on conviction shall be liable to a fine not exceeding 500/-, or to imprisonment with or without hard labour for a period not exceeding two months, or to both fine and imprisonment.

# GLOSSARY

Nouns are not entered under stems, but as they appear in the text—in their singular or plural form, as the case may be. Verbs are entered in their stem form, i.e. the prefix *ku* is omitted. The numbers in the right-hand column indicate the paragraphs in which the vernacular word is used. I am indebted to Mr. H. S. Senior, of the Tanganyika Administration, whose Sukuma Vocabulary (MS.) I used on many occasions. The use of the consonants *l* and *r* varies in different areas.

## A

|  |  | Law para. |
|---|---|---|
| Angalucha (*v.*) | 1. to say 'good morning'. |  |
|  | 2. first visit of son-in-law to the house of his bride. | 113 |
| Atigwaga buthiku | 1. he does not hear at night. | 234 |
|  | 2. impotence. |  |

## B

|  |  |  |
|---|---|---|
| Baba (*n.*) | father. | Note to 340 |
| Baba buko (*n.*) | father-in-law (of wife or husband). | Note to 3 |
| Babuja ba shikalile | delegates for the investigation of family circumstances. | 109 |
| Babuja ba winga | delegates for the negotiation of a betrothal, match-makers. | 109 |
| Babuta (*n.*) | paternal relatives. | 38, 41, 595 |
| Bafunya (*n.*) | family members cultivating together. | Note to 391 |
| Bagaragara (*n.*) | men who sleep without house and bed, traders. | Note to 552 |
| Bakombe (*n.*) | the relatives of the bride who are delegated to take over the bridewealth cattle after negotiations. | 110, Note to 151 |
| Bakwilima (*n.*) | friends of bridegroom. | 114 |
| Bali | heirs. | 557 |
| Balunja (*n.*) | delegates of bridegroom. | 109, 122 |
| Bamigongo (*n.*) | maternal relatives. | 38 |
| Banamhara (*n.*) | village elder | Introduction to Chapter II, 127c. Note to 398, 461b |
| Banang'oma | *see* Munang'oma. |  |
| Banangwa (*n.*) | village headmen, *see* Ng'wanangwa. |  |
| Banikuru (*n.*) | relatives of chief or retainers living in the residence. | Note to 129, 417, 425 |
| Bashindekeji (*n.*) | companions of a wooer when he goes to meet the girl of his choice. | 131 |
| Basumba batale (*n.*) | *see* Nsumba ntale. |  |

| | F | Law para. |
|---|---|---|
| FUNDA FUNDA (v.) | to have an abortion. | 217 |

| | G | |
|---|---|---|
| GABILA (v.) | to sacrifice to the spirits. | Introduction to Chapter IX |
| GUMIRA (v.) | to throw something over a person. | 129 |
| GUNGULI (n.) | elevated place, parish. | Note to 376, 381, Note to 400, Note to 408, 421, 453 |

| | H | |
|---|---|---|
| HAHA (v.) | to pledge a daughter. | 145 |
| HANIRA (v.) | to betroth a minor daughter. | 144 |
| HARUSI KABUNGA (Swahili) | form of marriage. | 127 |

| | I | |
|---|---|---|
| IBANZA (n.) | 1. council and court house. | 66, 139, Note to 167 |
| | 2. sleeping-house of unmarried men. | Introduction to Chapter II |
| IBANZA LYA MILIMO | assembly of cultivators of a village. | Note to 376 |
| IBARA (n.) | land not individually occupied. | Note to 436 |
| IBENGWE (n.) | compensation in case of adultery among relatives. | Note to 173 |
| IBINDO (n.) | circular veranda round the house. | Introduction to Chapter II |
| IDIMILO (n.) | grazing area. | Note to 432 |
| IGOBE (n.) | big estate. | Note to 377, Note to 382A, 434, Note to 437, 467 |
| IGULILU (n.) | society cultivating at night. | Note to 391 |
| IGWEGWE (n.) | compensation for injuries. | 230 |
| IHANE (n.) | village organization of the senior age grade. | Introduction to Chapter II |
| IKERA (n.) | fallow land. | 407 |
| IKUNGU (n.) | bush. | Note to 432 |
| IKURU (n.) | residence of chief. | Note to 129, Note to 177, 416, 424, 568 |
| ILALA (n.) | unoccupied land in an inhabited area. | Note to 376, 384, 390 and Note, 407, 408 and Note |
| ILALE (n.) | fallow land. | 410, 435 |
| ILIMA (n.) | small group of people cultivating together. | Note to 391 |
| INGILA (v.) | to enter. | 132 |
| IPANDA (n.) | cattle track. | 459 |

*Law para.*

| | | |
|---|---|---|
| ISABINGULA (*n.*) | ritual cleansing after death. | 305, 321, 476, 554 and Note, 614 |
| ISALENGE (*n.*) | village organization of cultivators. | Note to 391 |
| ISANGA (*n.*) | sandy soil. | Note to 411 |
| ISANGA LIDOTO | wet bracelet (fig. expression). | Note to 97 |
| ISANGA LYUMU | dry bracelet (fig. expression). | Note to 97 |
| ITONGO (*n.*) | 1. field in the vicinity of homestead. | Note to 404, 431 and Note |
| | 2. site of abandoned house and cattle kraal. | Note to 390 |

## J

| | | |
|---|---|---|
| JIMULA (*v.*) | to receive back cattle of bridewealth. | 66, 628 |

## K

| | | |
|---|---|---|
| KAGONHO (*n.*) | cloth locally fabricated from cotton (*Buluba*). | Note to 552 |
| KANDIKIJA (*v.*) NG'WANA | to press heavily a child. | 217B |
| KASHWENDE (*n.*) (Swahili) | syphilis. | Note to 185 |
| KASOGONE (*n.*) | gonorrhoea. | Note to 185 |
| KAYA (*n.*) | homestead. | 115, Note to 148A, Note to 376, 384C, 405, 434, Note to 451 |
| KENGEREZI (*n.*) | small ventilation hole in wall of house. | Introduction to Chapter IV |
| KIBANDA (*n.*) | subdivision of a parish. | Introduction to Chapter II, 441, 453, |
| KIGABIRO (*n.*) | a small hut, about 3 feet high, dedicated to rites of ancestor worship. | Note to 391 |
| KIGEMBE (*n.*) | hump-back. | Introduction to Chapter IV |
| KIKINDIKAMATA (*v.*) | to legalize | 269 |
| KILABA (*n.*) | field, the harvest of which belongs exclusively to a certain member of the family. | 406 |
| KINDIKILA (*v.*) | to betroth minors. | 140 |
| KISEMBO (*n.*) | crippled child. | Introduction to Chapter IV |
| KISUMBA (*n.*) | group of people doing common work. | Note to 391 |
| KITAMBO (*n.*) | rite of ancestor worship. | 397 |
| KITINDE (*n.*) | beast to be slaughtered for the delegates of bridegroom. | 111 |
| KIZUMO (*n.*) | curse. | 164 |
| KONHELEJA (*n.*) | feeding of calf by foster cow. | 490 |
| KUMBU (*n.*) | = NYIDA. | Note to 391 |

*Law para.*

| | | |
|---|---|---|
| KUMPA MGENI (Swahili) | sororate (to give him a stranger). | 135 |
| KWANG'WANA (*v.*) | to legitimize a child. | 269 |

## L

| | | |
|---|---|---|
| LAMBO (*n.*) | artificial pond. | 452 |
| LEHYA (*v.*) | to elope with a girl. | 117, 121, 151 |
| LEKANA (*v.*) | to separate, to divorce. | Introduction to Chapter II, 166 |
| LELA (*v.*) NDA | (of a lover), to look after the pregnant woman, to go and live with her. | Note to 281 |
| LITONGO (*n.*) | *see* ITONGO. | |
| LONG'WE (*n.*) | assembly of villagers. | Note to 376 |
| LUBIGIRI (*n.*) | hedge of trees, cattle kraal. | 468 |
| LUBILI (*n.*) | work for village headman. | 428 |
| LUBIMBI (*n.*) | boundary of field. | 387 |
| LUDIMA (*n.*) | watch, turn, association of cattle-owners for common herding. | 499 |
| LUGUNDIGA (*n.*) | temporary pasture. | 488 |
| LUGUTU (*n.*) | cattle kraal. | 468 |
| LUKIKO (*n.*) (Ganda) | assembly of villagers. | Note to 376 |
| LUMENG'HO LWA KUTU | cattle mark on the ear. | Note to 492 |
| LUMENG'HO LWA MOTO | cattle brand. | Note to 492 |
| LUSALAGO (*n.*) | blood-brotherhood. | 163 |
| LUSHIKU LWA KUTOLA | wedding night. | 114 |
| LYA (*v.*) BUKOMBE | to participate in wedding feast. | 110 |

## M

| | | |
|---|---|---|
| MABELELE (*n.*) | stalks of grain crops. | 435B |
| MAGASA (*n.*) | remaining instalments of payment, especially of bride-wealth. | 55, 62, 137 |
| MAJI (*n.*) | common sleeping-place of boys as well as of girls. | Introduction to Chapter II, Note to 177 |
| MALALE GA SAKA or MALALE GA FULUKA | a relinquished holding. | 392, 395 |
| MAMBULIA (*n.*) | sexual play of children. | Introduction to Chapter IV |
| MAMI (*n.*) | maternal uncle. | Note to 3, Note to 320 |
| MANJI (*n.*) | a man who is measuring everything, a man of grasping nature. | Note to 383 |
| MASUMULE (*n.*) | fine to be paid for transgression of custom. | Note to 232, Note to 376 |

Law para.

| | | |
|---|---|---|
| Matongo | see Itongo. | |
| Mayu buko | mother-in-law of wife or husband. | Note to 3 |
| Mbale (n.) | ironstone. | Note to 165 |
| Mbiji (n.) | leprosy. | 93 |
| Mbina (n.) | see Bina. | |
| Mbisi (n.) | a man who has been ostracized. | Note to 376 |
| Mbuga (n.) | low land of usually dark, heavy, clay soil. | Note to 432 |
| Mbuli ya kilezu | customary gift to relative of bride. | 25, 80b |
| Mbuli ya kweja kaya | beast slaughtered for cleansing the bridal bed. | 132 |
| Mbuli ya kwingilila | ceremonial goat slaughtered for the guests attending levirate marriage. | 132 |
| Mbuli ya kwinja bana hagati | ceremonial gift of a goat offered by a levirate husband to a widow who has children from first marriage. | 132 |
| Mbuli ya lushu | goat, part of bridewealth. | Note to 11 |
| Mbuli ya luswagilo | goat given to the delegates of bride's father. | 28, 80e,  111, 127(c) |
| Mbuli ya maji | ceremonial goat, part of bridewealth. | 22(c), 80a |
| Mbuli ya mumagulu ga ng'ombe | = Luswagilo. | 28 |
| Mbuli ya ng'wambi | goat paid for preparing the bridal bed. | 114 |
| Mbuli ya nkima ntale | gift to first wife in case of second marriage | 148b |
| Mbuli ya ntwe | customary payment in case of death of spouse. | Note to 62 |
| Mhela (n.) | practitioner's fee. | Note to 254a |
| Mhembe (n.) | whistle. | 428 |
| Migelo (n.) | see Ngele. | |
| Migilo (n.) | see Ngilo. | |
| Migunda (n.) | see Ngunda. | |
| Migunda ya ikuru | fields appertaining to the chief's residence. | 420 |
| Migunda ya ise | inherited holding. | Note to 392a, 400 |
| Mihushi (n.) | trees (Acacia fisheri). | 467 |
| Milisilwa (n.) | trustee. | Note to 468 |
| Misango (n.) | see Nsango. | |
| Misha (v.) | to send a calf to a foster-mother. | 490 |
| Mpango (n.) | bridewealth. | Introduction to Chapter I |
| Msholo (n.) | spell. | Note to 482b |
| Munamugi (n.) | clan leader, head of family. | Note to 555 |

*Law para.*

| | | |
|---|---|---|
| MUNANG'OMA (*n.*) | hereditary councillor. | 10, 83D, Note to 129, 156, 177 and Note, 300, 313, Note to 377 |
| MUNYAMPARA (*n.*) | member of the *Ihane*. | Introduction to Chapter II |
| MWANGU GITI NG'OKO | quick as a cock, *ejaculatio praecox*. | 236 |

### N

| | | |
|---|---|---|
| NABALABYA (*n.*) | flirtation. | Introduction to Chapter II |
| NALICHA (*n.*) | fine for sheltering eloping couple. | 211 |
| NANG'HANI (*n.*) | guardian. | 316 |
| NANG'INHA (*n.*) | gift. | 491 |
| NASANJA NALIMSHOLO | I am bewitched, I have met my fate. | Note to 482B |
| NCHILWA (*n.*) | widow. | 600 |
| NEJI (*n.*) | regent. | 177 |
| NELENELE (*n.*) | idiot child. | Introduction to Chapter IV |
| NFUMU (*n.*) | diviner. | Note to 202, Note to 221 |
| NGELE (*n.*) | basket for measuring food. | Note to 515 |
| NGILO (*n.*) | taboo. | Note to 160 |
| NGITIRI (*n.*) | grazing reserve. | 436, 464 |
| NGITIRI YA BULI KAYA | grazing reserve appertaining to a house. | 436 |
| NGITIRI YA GUNGULI | grazing reserve appertaining to a village. | 440 |
| NGITIRI YA MITI | grazing reserve, private forest reserve. | 467 |
| NG'OMBE YA BUCHAMINALA | customary payment in case of junior levirate. | 132 |
| NG'OMBE YA BUDUGU | payment in case of marriage between relatives. | 161 and Note |
| NG'OMBE YA BUGABU or NG'OMBE YA BUTIGU | payment of one head of cattle, if wife follows husband though bridewealth is not fully paid. | 26 and Note, 57, 80, 115 |
| NG'OMBE YA·ITONO | = NG'OMBE YA MAJI. | 20 |
| NG'OMBE YA KIPYA MOTO or NG'OMBE YA LINA | nominal bridewealth. | Note to 63 |
| NG'OMBE YA KUFUMIRA | *see* NGWEKWE. | |
| NG'OMBE YA KUGIJA | head of cattle, part of bride-wealth in *kulehya*. | 121, 127 |
| NG'OMBE YA KUGILA | ceremonial gift of father-in-law to his daughter-in-law. | 27, 80 |
| NG'OMBE YA KUPELEJA | *see* NGWEKWE. | |

| | | Law para. |
|---|---|---|
| Njingo | area surrounding a dwelling. | 433, Note to 553 |
| Nkima ntale | senior wife of a polygynous household. | 559, 581 |
| Nkima wa bugongo | wife for whom bridewealth is paid by maternal relative of bridegroom. | 38, 91, 320 and Note, 596, 608 |
| Nkima wa buta | wife for whom bridewealth is paid by paternal relative of bridegroom. | 38, 608 |
| Nkuleji (n.) | spinster. | 128 |
| Nkuruwabo (n.) | first-born son. | 48, 77, Note to 246, 266B, 286c and Note, 324, 329, 336, 340, 351, Note to 400A, Introduction to Chapter IX, 558, Note to 559/4, 566, 569, 576, 617 et seq. |
| Nkwilima (n.) | son-in-law. | 1 et seq. |
| Nkwilima wa bakima | the name given to a lover by the relatives of his concubine. | Note to 36 |
| Nsango (n.) | compensation payable for illegitimate pregnancy. | 120, 125, Note to 177, Note to 191, 288, 352C, 360 |
| Nsesi (or Nsesa) (n.) | the first settler in bush land. | Note to 377, 382 |
| Nshoto (n.) | plant (Plumbago zeylanica). | Introduction to Chapter II, footnote |
| Nsugwa (n.) | bondman. | 43 et seq. |
| Nsumba ntale | leader of the elika in a kibanda. | Note to 31, Introduction to Chapter II, 376 and Note, Note to 379 (c), Note to 385, 386, 395, Note to 398, 403, 428, 451, 456, 529 |
| Nsungi (n.) | bride for whom a high bridewealth is paid. | 10, Note c. |
| Ntale wa ndugu | clan leader, head of family. | 555 and Note, 582, Note to 600 |
| Ntemi (n.) | chief. | 156, Note to 177 |
| Ntoji (n.) | bridegroom. | 113 |
| Numba ya bugongo | family with matrilineal succession. | 38, 320, 365, 591 |

| | | Law para. |
|---|---|---|
| NUMBA YA BUTA | family with patrilineal succession. | 38, 365, 591 |
| NYALOHA (n.) | wedding dance. | 114 |
| NYALUBA YA BUSHIMBE | divorce certificate. | 90 |
| NYIDA (n.) | village organization. | Note to 391 |
| NZEKU (n.) | ox, bullock. | Note to 531 |
| NZIRA YA MAGURU | foot-path. | 458 |
| NZUNA (n.) | younger brother. | Note to 246, 336, 337, 558 |
| NZUNA WA KABILI | the second of the younger brothers. | 558, 561 |
| NZUNA WA KWANDYA | the first of the younger brothers. | 558, 560 |

### P

| | | |
|---|---|---|
| PALIKA (v.) | to marry two wives. | 148 |
| PEJA (v.) | to expel. | Note to 376 |
| PULA (v.) | to run away with a woman. | 151 |
| PUMULA (v.) | (of a woman) to follow her lover into his house. | 128 |

### R

| | | |
|---|---|---|
| RUGARUGA (n.) (Swahili) | bodyguard of chief before arrival of Europeans. | Note to 129 |

### S

| | | |
|---|---|---|
| SABO YA BUTEMI | property appertaining to the office of chief. | 568 |
| SABO YA NTEMI | private property of chief. | 568 |
| SHIKA NKWILIMA | arrival of son-in-law. | 114 |
| SHIKIRIJA (v.) NUMBA | to bless the house. | Note to 391 |
| SHILANDI (n.) | wife's share in harvest. | 157, Note to 255 |
| SHILATU (n.) | sandals, practitioner's fee. | Note to 254A |
| SHITUGO (n.) | livestock. | Introduction to Chapter VII |
| SHWENDA (v.) | to rub in, to infect. | Note to 185 |
| SIMBA NTI | to dig plants (for medical use). | Note to 254A |
| SUNGAMATA (n.) | name given to head of cattle which is a part of the blood-money. | 313 |
| SWESULA (v.) | to elope with a girl. | 151 |
| SWETA (n.) | helper of village headman. | Note to 377 |

### T

| | | |
|---|---|---|
| TUMBATI (n.) | tobacco. | 29, 80F, 111 |
| TWALILWA (v.) NDA (n.) | to be informed about the pregnancy. | 281, 306 |

### W

| | | |
|---|---|---|
| WIKOLOGOSHA (n.) | flirtation. | Introduction to Chapter II |

### Y

| | | |
|---|---|---|
| YINZA (v.) | to barter. | Note to 345, 584 |

# INDEX

*Reference figures indicate law paragraphs*